DREAMERS REFUSE TO BE VICTIMS

PER ARDUA AD ASTRA

(Through Adversity to the Stars)

MILAN "LOU" VOTICKY

 FriesenPress

Suite 300 - 990 Fort St
Victoria, BC, V8V 3K2
Canada

www.friesenpress.com

ISBN
978-1-5255-3104-0 (Hardcover)
978-1-5255-3105-7 (Paperback)
978-1-5255-3106-4 (eBook)

1. BIOGRAPHY & AUTOBIOGRAPHY, PERSONAL MEMOIRS

Distributed to the trade by The Ingram Book Company

TABLE OF CONTENTS

My cousin Harry Knopfelmacher, who was born on the same day in the same hospital as I was. On December 18, 1943, at the age of nine, he was brutally murdered in the gas chambers of Auschwitz-Birkenau. But for the courage and foresight of my parents, Arnold and Annamarie (Anka) Voticky, that would have been my fate as well.

My parents, who fought for the survival of their family against the brutal repression of both Nazi Germany and the communist Soviet Union. They saved our lives and the lives of at least ten others who, in turn, produced a further two dozen Canadian and US citizens. It was thanks to my intelligent and brave parents that I survived the Holocaust.

My wife, partner, and most trusted advisor of sixty years, Catherine May Voticky. Her love, wisdom, advice, guidance, questions, friendship, and encouragement have allowed me to reach an unimaginable level of success in my life. I met this wonderful woman in Montreal on May 21, 1956 (Victoria Day), fell in love with her at first sight, and married her after getting my Navigator Wings a year and a half later. She has advised and supported me and provided us with two bright and beautiful daughters—Linda and Liza.

The Chinese people for their kindness, hospitality, and generosity in welcoming us to their land when the rest of the world turned its back on Jewish refugees. If not for the Chinese people, there would have been 18,000 more Holocaust victims and I would not be here to write this book.

The courageous Jewish resistance to the Nazi butchers in the Warsaw Ghetto. They proved that Jews can and will fight to protect their families, and they set a good example for the people of Israel to live up to their motto: Never Again!

German industrialist Oskar Schindler; Swedish ambassador Raoul Wallenberg, and Swiss vice-consul Carl Lutz in Budapest; the Japanese vice-consul in Lithuania, Chiune Sugihara, whose humanity and decency saved thousands more people from the Holocaust, including members of my own family; and Britain's Sir Nicholas Winton, who single-handedly saved 669 Czech Jewish children. Together these men saved tens of thousands of innocents.

Donna Niemy, our lifelong friend, who, with great love and devotion, took care of her disabled husband, Walt, my oldest and best friend, for almost eighteen years before she passed away after a tragic accident in Canmore, Alberta in July 2014.

Onil (Lach) Lacharité, my CF-100 All Weather Fighter Pilot for three years (1958–1960). His skill and our teamwork kept us both alive through bad weather, mechanical failures, and some very close calls when we flew in the North American Air Defense Command during the Cold War. We grew up together, learned to work as a team, and matured together to become an Air Defense Command Top Gun All-Weather Fighter Crew in defense of our country. We were one of the top nine Fighter Crews in Canadian Air Defense Command in 1960.

Mona Chong, my faithful associate for the past twenty-nine years, an irreplaceable jewel in my business career; and our entire team at Admax International Investments. All forty-two of them gave their hearts, souls, and skills to the success of our company and its great achievements, including two straight years of producing the No. 1 mutual fund in Canada (Regent Korea Fund 1994 and Admax Global Health Sciences Fund 1995).

Our RCAF Station Moisie soccer team (1961–1963), the greatest sports team that I have ever been honoured to be a part of and associated with. Hard work, perseverance, and courage made up for a lack of experience and technical soccer skills. This team won the Quebec Armed Forces Championship two years in a row.

To the 1.8 million "Dreamers" in the United States who are facing deportation to native lands they left as very young children. Most of the Dreamers who were brought to the US by their parents do not speak the language of their country of birth, and they face unemployment, discrimination, and violence if they are forced to return. It is my hope that the US government will stop using the lives of these innocent young people as a political football, and that the US courts and Congress will resolve the shameful situation by permitting the Dreamers to gain US residency as soon as possible and offering them a pathway to citizenship in the great country where they grew up.

Last, but certainly not least, to Canada for providing refuge and opportunity to our family in our second exile. I am proud to be a Canadian and honoured to have been able to serve in the Royal Canadian Air Force and North American Air Defense Command for nine and a half years, and with the Victoria Rifles (Reserve) of the Canadian Army for a year and a half. I believe that I have thus repaid part of my debt to my great and wonderful adopted home.

THANKS AND ACKNOWLEDGMENTS

There have been many great people in my life who have had a positive influence on me and contributed to my success. I will try to acknowledge them all, but if I have missed anyone here, it will be because of memory not intent.

My brother, Michael, an excellent businessman with a razor-sharp mind, whose big heart, love of family, and good ideas were invaluable to us in caring for our late mother. He has proven to be a terrific father and grandfather.

Air Canada retired Captains Gordie Jones, a real World War II hero and a man who saved 105 lives after a terrible midair collision over Havana, Cuba, and Gordon McCready, who guided and trusted me while flying. They both encouraged me in my post-flying career as my first and third clients.

Lorie Haber and Gary Litwack, good friends, good men, and excellent lawyers who guided Admax for many years, and Paul Schroeder, whose business and auditing advice played a large part in the success of Admax.

Tony Dewerth, a great leader in the investment industry, as well as partner and friend, who almost always beats me at golf—except at Turnberry, Scotland, where I cleaned his clock playing my best golf game ever.

Brigadier General Walter Niemy, my oldest friend, a buddy on 432 All-Weather Fighter Squadron at Bagotville, Quebec and at RCAF Station Moisie, Quebec—a man with a brilliant mind and more courage than any person I've ever met, a lifelong skiing and golfing friend, who always challenged my intellect and broadened my horizons. I never did beat him at golf or downhill skiing. Our brotherly love for each other and mutual trust were unforgettable. He survived a horrendous skiing accident on Vail Mountain, which, after seven hours of surgery, left him a quadriplegic for twenty years. Throughout those years he lived a full life watching his grandchildren grow up, his greatest joy. When he passed away in July 2017, the pain of his passing was relieved by the knowledge that twenty years of suffering were finally over.

F/O Ray English, a Long-Range Navigator on the RCAF Electronic Warfare Unit who actually managed to give me a six-month Long-Range Navigator course in fifteen minutes so I could qualify for employment with Air Canada. Later, when we were at Air Canada, he helped John Caron, Roger Waldman, and me achieve a fair labour contract that permitted our Navigators to transition into qualifying as Pilots, thus continuing our flying careers. The agreement also allowed the rest of our Navigators to either continue their aviation careers or retire with a fair settlement, honour, and respect.

To Andrea Knight, editor of my mom's autobiography, who encouraged me to write this autobiography and advised me to be opinionated. Her punishment was to edit this book!

Thanks also to Robert Young for his invaluable assistance.

My life has been one long terrific educational experience in which I have been fortunate to meet great people, great teachers, great colleagues, and great friends. Writing this autobiography has given me the opportunity to recall these wonderful people and the joy and friendship they have brought to my life and the lives of our family.

I have also been incredibly lucky!

PROLOGUE

This story is about the Voticky family's determination not to be victims of either Fascism or Communism. All that we dreamt of was to be left alone to live normal lives. Adolf Hitler and Joseph Stalin had other ideas for us—the first wanted to murder us and the second wanted to imprison us.

Thanks to the foresight and courage of my parents, we twice fled the terror and fulfilled our dreams. First, we escaped to Shanghai, China, the only place that would give us shelter in 1940. Then, after the 1948 Communist coup d'état, using three-month visitor visas, we escaped to Canada. My father had only USD$3,000 when we arrived in Canada and he had to use half of that to hire a Liberal Party-connected lawyer—the Liberals consider themselves to be the natural governing party in Canada—to get permanent resident status. We had to live on the remainder of that USD$3,000 for the next six months.

Mom and Dad worked hard and had a free and successful life in Canada, fulfilling their dreams of raising their children in a free and democratic country.

My dream was to be a Pilot and I achieved this through determination, hard work, and some luck. My brother immigrated to the United States and fulfilled his dreams there. If we could do it, I believe that everyone can.

Right now, the young undocumented children of illegal immigrants in the USA, mostly from Central America, who are covered by the Deferred Action for Childhood Arrivals (DACA) and are called Dreamers, are under threat of deportation to their so-called home countries. Most Dreamers have no connection to their home country and many do not speak the language. This is not only unfortunate, but probably a violation of the United Nations Convention on Refugees and may even be a violation of human rights. The reason for this mess is a dysfunctional US Congress that is refighting the Civil War at the expense of approximately 1.8 million innocent undocumented Americans. The members of this august body have shown little heart and compassion for the American-educated and loyal young people in their midst.

It is my hope that any Dreamer who reads this book will learn that there are alternatives to the lack of action by the US government. As I explain in the last chapter of this book, Canada and Australia will welcome them. There are precedents for this action. In 1939 to 1941, before the USA entered World War II, young American volunteers came to Canada to join our Armed Forces against Nazi Germany. In the 1960s, young Americans came to Canada to avoid going to Vietnam as cannon fodder. Most of these immigrants stayed and became productive citizens of Canada. The Dreamers can do this too, and I encourage them to read what I have to say in my final chapter.

1

THE BEGINNING

My name is Milan Joseph Voticky. I was born on March 23, 1934, at the London Hospital in Praha (Prague), Czechoslovakia to Arnold and Annamarie (Anka) Voticky, six hours after my cousin Harry Knopfelmacher was born to my aunt Greta, my dad's sister. Mom and Greta shared a room at the hospital. Years later, in Canada, I acquired the nickname "Lou" from my new Canadian friends. The name was derived from the American radio comedy "Life with Luigi" about newly arrived Luigi Basco, "the li'l immigrant." It has stuck proudly to me ever since, even though, in today's crazy politically correct world, it might have ended up with my friends ending up in front of the Ontario Human Rights Commission!

This autobiography is different from those of many other survivors for the simple reason that, despite the best efforts of both Adolf Hitler and Joseph Stalin, I refuse to be a victim. My family beat the odds and we are grateful to everyone who helped us along the way. In addition, this story is not just about me. It's also about the wonderful people I've met during my travels through life. Most of them have enriched my life; I have learned from them, accepted their friendship, enjoyed their kindness, and shared common triumphs and sorrows with them. Most importantly, I matured with them.

My first childhood memory happened during my parents' second honeymoon in Yugoslavia in 1937. They had left me in the care of my beloved aunt Liza (Mom's sister) and one day she took me to a beach for the day. I had just gotten a brand-new fire truck and was pushing it through the sand when I tripped and fell. My jaw hit the truck, which was not good because I had a bad habit of sticking my tongue out of my mouth. The result was a holey tongue that was bleeding profusely. Liza, a lovely twenty-year-old in a black bathing suit picked me up, carried me out to the nearby road, flagged down a car—there weren't many around in those days—and took me to a hospital. They sewed up my tongue, my parents rushed home from Yugoslavia, and for a while I was literally tongue-tied. I couldn't or wouldn't speak for four days but I've made up for that omission over the years. My uncle, Frank Vinson (my dad's American brother) solved the problem by showing up at the hospital with a beautiful pedal car. As soon as I saw it, I said, "Auto!" Brilliant. I haven't stopped talking since.

It was about that time that my parents, aware of Hitler's persecution of the Jewish people across the border in Germany, decided that they had to do something to protect us. They found an (Anglican) Church of Czechoslovakia minister at St. Nicholas Church who was willing to baptize us, so we went to his church and he poured water on our foreheads. This proved to be a life saver because having the baptismal certificates helped my mother get us exit visas three years later—probably because the thug who issued it was not up to date on the rules. In the end, though, the Nazis still considered us to be Jews.

My second memory was of an event that really could have destroyed me for life. When I was four, my mother had the brilliant idea that I should take ballet lessons. But as soon as I found out that I would have to change in a dressing room full of girls, I promptly threw a hissy fit. That was the end of the ballet lessons and I guarantee that the world did not lose another Nureyev!

IN THE MEANTIME, Hitler and his murderous thugs were busy filling concentration camps, persecuting Jews, communists, socialists, homosexuals, Gypsies (as the Roma and Sinti were called then), and every other non-blond, non-blue-eyed minority. Fortunately, my mother, sister, and I all had blond hair and blue eyes, which also helped with the exit visas for our escape!

After World War I, Great Britain and France had signed mutual defence treaties with Poland and Czechoslovakia, guaranteeing that an attack on one of them would be seen as an attack on all of them. But in September 1938, Hitler demanded that Britain and France permit him to take over the Sudetenland, an area that comprised approximately half the territory of the Czech provinces of Bohemia and Moravia and had a large German ethnic population. He claimed that "....the Czechs were slaughtering the German minority in the Sudetenland." It was a blatant lie.

After getting British Prime Minister Chamberlain and French Prime Minister Daladier to agree to the surrender of the Sudetenland, Hitler then proceeded to demand parts of Poland and Hungary. On September 30, 1938, at Munich, Germany, Britain, and France betrayed their treaty obligations and their nations' honour by signing the infamous Munich Agreement. Promised Soviet support also failed to materialize; all the big powers decided that they were not ready or willing to go to war with the newly powerful German Reich over little Czechoslovakia. The Czech goose was cooked, without dumplings or sauerkraut.

On October 1, 1938, the German Wehrmacht swarmed across the Czech border and seized the Sudetenland. That was the day that Prime Ministers Neville Chamberlain and Edouard Daladier joined Hitler and Mussolini in the Hall of Infamy. Hitler had taken the Sudetenland, but when he arrived back in London, Chamberlain declared, "We have achieved peace in our time!"

Then, on March 15, 1939, the German juggernaut comprised of the Wehrmacht, Schutzstaffel (SS), and Geheime Staatspolizei (Gestapo) stormed into Prague and took over what was left of Czechoslovakia. They incorporated part of it into the German Third Reich as the Protectorate of Bohemia and Moravia, while Slovakia was severed to become a separate country. So much for "peace in our time." Our Slovak brethren, under their new President, Roman Catholic bishop Monsignor Tiso, became Hitler's allies in the war and in the persecution of both Jews and Gypsies. After the war, President Monsignor Tiso was hung as a war criminal by the Slovak people—I guess he wasn't able to get to the Vatican in time. After all, the Roman Catholic Pope and Church helped hundreds of other Nazi war criminals escape to Latin America.

A strong Slovak resistance developed almost immediately and together with the Czech resistance harassed the German occupiers for the next six years. In addition, there was mutiny within the Slovak army and, on August 29, 1944, the opposition launched the Slovak National Uprising. Unfortunately, they were betrayed by the Soviet Red Army, whose assistance had been promised, and were crushed by the Wehrmacht. Stalin had ordered the betrayal to ensure that there wouldn't be a strong Slovak resistance to a planned Communist take-over after the Nazi defeat.

My parents watched all these events with great trepidation and made their plans to escape, including moving funds to Switzerland to assist us in our flight. My uncle Vilda (Mom's oldest brother) escaped to Switzerland on a student visa—he was only thirty at the time and a more or less permanent student. He finally graduated from law school in 1948 at age thirty-nine after a six-year interruption to his education while we all were in exile in China. His job in Switzerland was to watch Dad's money!

Dad's plan was to get our family to Italy and from there to a safe haven further away from Hitler. Despite being Hitler's allies, Benito Mussolini and the majority of Italians treated Jews well and certainly did not prosecute or persecute them at that time. It was only after the overthrow of the Fascist dictator and the German occupation of Central and Northern Italy in May 1943 that the Jews were harassed and attacked. Even then, many of the Italian people continued to protect their Jewish fellow countrymen and other Jewish refugees in Italy, who were mostly from North Africa.

Mom, my younger sister, Vera, and I travelled to San Remo, Italy to wait for Dad's escape from what was now the German Protectorate of Bohemia and Moravia. With us were my dad's cousin Nelly Schwarz and her husband, Hugo, two wonderful people and close friends of my parents. As time passed, however, and the Nazi Gestapo—the dreaded secret police—refused to give my dad an exit visa, my mother decided to go back to Prague to get him out. It was an extremely courageous act; there was no guarantee that she could ever get out again herself. She further decided to take Vera and me with her, which was very brave but not too smart. Hugo and Nelly begged her to leave us with them, but my mother responded, "If we die, we die together." The three of us were on the next train back to Prague.

Our immediate family, along with my mother's brother Ernie, his wife, Hilda, and their daughter, Eva, all moved into my grandparent's apartment at 18 Celetna Ulice, on the edge of Staromestecke Namesti (the Old Town Square) in the heart of Prague. To say that it was crowded would be an understatement; we were six adults and three children in a three-bedroom apartment.

In January 1940, under a dark, ugly, cloudy sky, the Gestapo came looking for my dad, Uncle Vilda (who was safely in Switzerland), and Uncle Ernie on the suspicion that they were spying against the German Reich by communicating with Switzerland and enemies of the Third Reich. They were, of course, wrong. What Dad was doing was smuggling US dollars to Switzerland and Uncle Vilda was depositing them and monitoring the money in a Swiss bank. This was our escape fund; we weren't communicating with enemies of the Reich. Dad's mission was simply to save his family, not to start World War II!

Ernie hid in the attic of the apartment building and my dad hid under the bed in their bedroom. The two Gestapo men, in their long black leather coats and fedoras, herded Mom, Hilda, my grandparents, Vera, Eva, and me into the sitting room, which was off the living room and separated by a double door. One of the doors was closed, leaving only a narrow view of the living room. These two Gestapo men must have been the most incompetent members of Hitler's thugs—they would have easily found my dad if they had bothered to look in the bedroom and, with a little more effort, they would have found Uncle Ernie. They were, of course, out of luck with Vilda since he was safe in Zurich. But to meet their arrest quota for that dark and dreary day they decided to arrest my beloved grandfather Maxa. My mother went ballistic and started screaming. Just then, however, she spotted my dad trying to escape through the living room.

To distract the Nazi goons, she picked up a chair and threw it at one of them, which allowed my dad to escape from the apartment. After ducking the flying chair, the shaken example of brave, fascist manhood said to my granddad, "If she does that again, I will put a bullet between her eyes." They handcuffed my granddad and took him away. We all got dressed and went to my Voticky grandparents' apartment on the Vltava

River, about a kilometre away. We spent the rest of the day there and after dark we all returned to the dark apartment at 18 Celetna Ulice.

To our surprise, Maxa was there, sitting in the dark living room smoking a cigarette. The Gestapo had held him all day, forced him to stand a short distance from a wall, then made him lean forward and brace himself against the wall with his fingertips. At the end of the day, they let him go because he didn't know anything and certainly hadn't done anything wrong. A year later, that wouldn't have mattered.

A new family escape plan was hatched and financed by my parents. Dad had enough money in Switzerland to pay for sixteen of our family members to escape:

1. Dad, Mom, Vera, and me.
2. Uncle Ernie and Aunt Hilda Kanturek and their daughter, my cousin Eva.
3. Uncle Armin and Aunt Greta Knopfelmacher, and my almost-twin, Harry.
4. My two sets of grandparents—the Votickys and the Kantureks—as well as Uncle Vilda, and Aunt Liza Kanturek.

My mom set about finding a way to get all the required exit visas from the Gestapo and their Czech collaborators—the police and finance departments. Anyone who has met my mom knows that she was fearless, aggressive, vicious, and, at times, downright obnoxious; she never took NO for an answer. In other words, it wasn't smart to mess with her! The Gestapo thugs and their Czech stooges never had a chance. They no doubt gave us the exit visas just to get her out of Central Europe and allow the German juggernaut to continue with its plans to conquer Poland and the USSR.

Uncle Armin Knopfelmacher was a dentist. He was a good man, who did volunteer work fixing teeth for former German concentration camp inmates who had managed to escape to Czechoslovakia after the brutal treatment that they had received from the Germans. Yet he believed that Hitler and the Nazis would not dare to do the same to foreigners. He refused to join our family in the escape and my mother's success in securing the exit visas had unfortunately created a family crisis. If

Armin, Greta, and Harry were not going, then my grandparents Hugo and Olga Voticky decided that they weren't going either; they couldn't bear to leave their beloved daughter, Greta, behind. Uncle Armin's decision thus doomed his wife, son, and my paternal grandparents to a horrible death at Auschwitz-Birkenau and Treblinka.

We not only had the exit visas from Czechoslovakia, we also had entry visas and boat passage to Shanghai. In the place of the Knopfelmacher family, Mom and Dad offered their closest friends, Rudla and Litka Winter, and their daughter, Eva, a free ride into exile. They jumped at the opportunity and joined us in our exodus. After the war, in July 1946, the Winter family returned to Europe with us, but were then trapped in Czechoslovakia for twenty years until 1968. Rudla Winter was not the brightest man around and upon his return to Czechoslovakia he joined the Communist Party to advance his career. He said that he could see great opportunities with them in the future. When the Communist Party staged their coup d'état eighteen months later, they rewarded him with a good job, which trapped him and his family there. They were finally able to escape when the Velvet Revolution in 1968 temporarily opened the borders until the Soviet Union and their Warsaw Pact allies crushed the revolt. They managed to cross the border to Vienna and went from there to Australia.

Their daughter, Eva, had earned a medical degree in Prague and today, at age eighty, is still a qualified, practicing physician in Sydney, Australia. In January 2012, on a visit to Australia, Catherine and I were pleased to meet her again after sixty-six years. It was a great reunion for me and a wonderful experience for Catherine. We also got to meet her younger sister, Jana, a charming woman who was born in 1946 after our return to Prague. I had never met her.

Shortly before we left Czechoslovakia, another family crisis erupted. My maternal grandparents, Max and Hedvika Kanturek, were refusing to leave because their younger daughter, Liza, wouldn't join us. So, we had to go without them. Fortunately, a year later, when the Nazis got really nasty, my parents convinced them to join us in exile and Dad arranged to get them to Shanghai by the overland route via Berlin, Moscow, Siberia, and Japan. They got transit visas through Japan thanks to the heroic work of the Japanese vice-consul in Lithuania, Chiune

Sugihara, who saved thousands of European Jews. Sugihara issued these transit visas against direct Japanese government instructions and this courageous man is credited with saving more than six thousand Jewish lives by enabling them to get to Shanghai through Siberia and Japan.

My mother, Anka Voticky, and her family. Left to right: (behind) Uncle Vilda; my mother, Anka; and Uncle Erna; (in front) my grandfather, Max (Maxa); my grandmother, Hedvika; and Aunt Liza. Prague, 1929.

A street sign in Prague, across from the new Jewish cemetery, that carries the Voticky name. The photo was taken in 2005.

My parents and their friends Karel and Marta Peka (Pekova), who survived Theresienstadt. Their daughter, Alena, survived the same concentration camp and grew up to become a top ballet dancer. From left to right: my mother, Anka Voticky; Karel Peka; his wife, Marta Peka; and my father, Arnold Voticky. Prague, 1935.

My mother, Anka Voticky (left), with friends Marta Mautnerova, later Pekova (centre) and Litka Smolkova, later Wintrova (Winter) (right). Marta survived Theresienstadt with her family and Litka and her husband and daughter sailed with us to Shanghai. Prague, 1936.

Me at age three at the beach in summer 1937, just before I bit through my tongue, leaving me "tongue-tied."

My first cousin, Harry Knopfelmacher (left) and I. Harry was my "twin," born six hours after me at the same hospital, where our mothers, Anka Voticky and Greta Knopfelmacher shared a room. Prague, 1936.

*My aunt Greta Knopfelmacher, my father's sister, with her son, Harry (right),
and Tommy Voticky, the son of my father's brother Egon. Prague, 1937.*

*St. Nicholas Church, (Anglican) Church of Czechoslovakia, Prague, where my sister,
Vera, my parents, and I were baptized in 1937 in an effort to protect us from the Nazis.
Photograph taken in 2012.*

Me at age four, trying on my gas mask. Every Czech citizen was issued one because of the threat of an attack by Nazi Germany. Prague, 1938.

My maternal grandparents, Max and Hedvika Kanturek, in 1938.

My grandfather Max Kanturek (left) outside the family jewellery store in Prague in 1937.
The store was sold in 1939.

My grandfather Max Kanturek, with my uncle Erna Kanturek (centre), and my father,
Arnold Voticky (right), inside the family jewellery store. Prague, 1939.

The sponsorship document for the Voticky and Kanturek families to go to the United States, arranged by my great-grandfather Emil Kohn. The document also shows the prepaid ticket for our passage. November 29, 1938.

File No. 811.11 JTI/gk.
            AMERICAN CONSULATE GENERAL

        Praha II., Panská ulice 2, May 2, 1939.

Mr. Arnold Votický,
    Celetná 18,
        Praha I.

    The Consulate General wishes to confirm
herewith that you and your family were registered
here under the   Czech   quota on   December 12,1938.
Under the present immigration laws it is assumed
that your turn might be reached within   approx. two years.

    This estimation of your waiting time is given
without any obligation.

                    Yours very truly,
                    For the Consul General:

                        J.Forrest Ingle,
                    American Vice Consul.

A 1938 letter from the American vice-consul in Prague confirming that our family had been registered under the Czech quota for entry to the United States. He estimated that our turn would come up in two years; had we waited for admission to the US, we wouldn't have survived.

Hugo and Olga Voticky, my paternal grandparents, with their grandsons, my cousins Harry Knopfelmacher and Tommy Voticky in Prague in 1939. My grandparents and their fellow victims were taken to the Treblinka death camp, where they were herded into a field, ordered to dig their own graves and strip naked so their clothes could be sent to people in Germany, then shot in the back of the head and pushed into their own freshly dug graves. My grandparents were murdered in Treblinka in June 1943. My nine-year-old "twin," Harry, was murdered in Auschwitz on December 18, 1943. Tommy survived with his parents, who escaped to Chile.

2

ESCAPE AND THE LONG JOURNEY

On April 6, 1940, ten of us—the three Kantureks, the three Winters, and our family of four—departed from Wilson Railway Station in Prague and headed for Trieste, Italy. Our last image of Prague was of Uncle Armin telling my parents that he would be at the same place when we returned from our "vacation" to welcome us back. Armin was proof that you could be both intelligent— as I've said, he was a doctor of dentistry—and stupid at the same time. Our last view of them was seeing Hilda Kanturek's mother screaming uncontrollably as she watched her only child leave. She was certainly prescient—this was the last time that Hilda saw her parents. They both perished in the Theresienstadt concentration camp of malnutrition and disease.

We arrived in Trieste, Italy the day after we left Prague and settled into a small hotel. Our first steps to freedom were complete and we felt relatively safe. Despite having a Fascist government, the Italians did not persecute Jews. Almost immediately, Dad boarded a train to Zurich to pick up our travelling money while the rest of us anxiously awaited his return.

Dad was smart and very fortunate to be able to get all his assets out of Switzerland at that time. After the war, the Swiss banks did every-thing in their power to deny that they were holding any Jewish money and made it very difficult, if not impossible, for Holocaust survivors to retrieve their family assets. Author Tom Bower wrote about this in great detail in his 1997 book, *Blood Money: The Swiss, the Nazis and the*

Looted Billions (published in the US as *Nazi Gold: The Full Story of the Fifty-year Swiss-Nazi Conspiracy to Steal Billions from Europe's Jews and Holocaust Survivors*). Hundreds of millions of stolen Jewish money, as well as gold reserves stolen from the central banks in the occupied European territories and priceless art stolen from the Jews, art galleries, and museums of occupied Europe disappeared into Swiss and German bank accounts, and into the vaults and safety deposit boxes in Swiss banks. This was, without question, one of the greatest bank robberies in history.

The Swiss government and Swiss Bankers Association considered this to be perfectly legal business procedure during wartime and did not feel at all responsible, guilty, or even embarrassed by the looting of European and Jewish property. Most of it was never recovered, but thanks to the work of US Senator Alfonse D'Amato of New York and the patriarch of the Bronfman family, Edgar Bronfman, the Swiss banks were forced to compensate Holocaust victims for a portion of these losses in 1997.

The European Bank gold was also recovered by some of the victimized European central banks and some of the art was recovered by European museums and individuals. However, more than seventy years later, some of the art is still being reclaimed today. The magnitude of the theft by an allegedly neutral Switzerland and its banks and their collusion with the murderous Nazis was unprecedented in history. Their actions added insult to the torture and murder of millions of innocents.

Senator D'Amato, Edgar Bronfman, and the World Jewish Congress had to exert tremendous political, criminal, and economic pressure, as well as considerable moral suasion to achieve this historic recovery of stolen assets of the victims of fascism. They deserve credit for opening a new chapter in international law to protect people whose rights have been violated by governments. In effect, they had to blackmail the Swiss government by threatening to take away the operating licences of Swiss banks in America, where they make most of their profits.

To compound these crimes, the Swiss federal police turned over thousands of Jewish refugees in Switzerland to the Nazi Gestapo during the war. As Tom Bower describes, these refugees were deported to concentration camps and most of them were never seen again.

Despite the many crimes of the Swiss authorities and the Swiss banks, however, this is not the whole story. There was also at least one Swiss hero whose name deserves to be included with Schindler and Wallenberg and Sugihara and Winton but has remained little known. When the Nazis seized control of Hungary in 1944, working in concert with the collaborationist, fascist Arrow Cross to surround Budapest, Carl Lutz, the vice-consul and head of the foreign interests division in the Swiss legation there, quietly but determinedly set about rescuing tens of thousands of Jews.

According to *Under Swiss Protection: Jewish Eyewitness Accounts from Wartime Budapest*, a 2017 book edited by Holocaust historian Charlotte Schallié and Carl Lutz's daughter, Agnes Hirschi, Lutz spearheaded a dangerous operation that between March 1944 and 1945 saved some fifty thousand Hungarian Jews facing certain death. As the Nazis stepped up their raids on Jewish homes and transports to the death camps, he began negotiating with the Nazis—including Adolf Eichmann—and obtained permission to issue "protective letters" giving people permission to emigrate. While he only had authorization to issue seven thousand letters, he expanded the number by putting the names of whole families on each document. Once the papers had been issued, he got permission to move the people holding the papers into safe houses in Budapest, where they remained protected. Conditions were horribly overcrowded and filthy—it was hard to turn anyone away—but it was safe.

Unlike his own government—who initially reprimanded Lutz for his unauthorized actions—and the greedy Swiss bankers, Swiss diplomat Carl Lutz was "righteous among the nations." That was the designation he received from Yad Vashem, the Holocaust remembrance centre in Israel, in 1964. We should all know his name.

AFTER DAD'S SAFE return to Trieste, we all finally boarded the SS *Conte Rosso*, an 18,000-ton Italian ocean liner, to begin our month-long voyage to Shanghai, China via Bombay and Manila. We hoped that the great distance would provide us safety from the horrors of Nazi Germany.

A year after our journey, the *Conte Rosso*—our lifesaver—was sunk on May 24, 1941, by a British submarine, the HMS *Upholder*, sixteen kilometres off the coast of Sicily en route to Tripoli, Libya. It was then being used as an Italian troopship. Of the 2,729 souls on board, 1,291 perished. We found out about this disaster later that year and it was the first time that I, at the age of seven, truly understood the meaning of war and death.

After we passed through the Suez Canal, the temperature increased tremendously every day. One morning, this very adventurous six-year-old awoke at dawn on a beautiful sunny morning—my guess is that it was before 6:00 a.m., and I was extremely hot. I was sweaty and covered in a prickly heat rash, so I decided to go for a swim in the pool, despite strict orders from my parents not to go there alone. The pool was a makeshift affair consisting of a square wooden box made of two-metre boarding covered in waterproof canvas, and no there was no shallow end. It was all one depth—way over my head—and was fed by a fire hose reaching down to the ocean and a pump.

I bravely donned an adult life jacket (there were no small ones), tied it as tightly as I could, and got into the pool. As soon as I hit the water, I promptly slid right out of the life jacket and sank to the bottom of the pool. I was terrified—but it was more of the punishment I would receive when I got out of this mess than of drowning. Fortunately, when I opened my eyes I saw the fire hose in front of me. I grabbed it and pulled myself to the surface. This was the first of many close escapes I have experienced throughout my life. I have to admit that I've been very lucky! I clambered out of the pool and ran to my cabin. I never dared tell anyone for fear of what my mother would do. To this day, I am a lousy swimmer, very uncomfortable in any water deeper than a bathtub.

My next memory of the long journey to Shanghai was our arrival in Bombay (now Mumbai), India. It was so hot that the pavement was very soft, and I felt as though I was sinking into it as we walked along the streets.

We arrived in Shanghai late at night on May 10, 1940. As we disembarked from the ship we saw hundreds of people; about 98 per cent of them were Chinese with a few Europeans in the mix looking for friends or family who had escaped from occupied Europe. My mother stood in the middle of the melee and yelled out in Czech, "Does anyone here speak Czech?" She repeated it a few times and, sure enough, one Czech man, Kurt Reitler, answered among the hundreds of Chinese. He found overnight accommodation for us at the home of the Czech consul—I slept in a hallway—and then Mr. Reitler helped us get us settled in our own place. He was a very nice man and we met up again with him in Montreal after our second escape to freedom—this time from Communism.

My mother's passport photo, 1940.

The travel documents that allowed me to leave Nazi-occupied Czechoslovakia with my family, travel through Italy, and sail to Shanghai. Note the red "J" stamped on the second page—the Nazi government passed regulations in 1938 invalidating all Jewish passports and ordering that any new passports issued to Jews indicate their status as Jews. In order to make this even clearer, all Jewish males had to add "Israel" to their names and Jewish females had to add the name "Sara." Hence, on the second page and throughout the document, I am identified as Milan Josef Israel Voticky.

My family on the way to Shanghai on the SS Conte Rosso, 1940. Left to right (back) my father, Arnold Voticky; my mother, Anka; her friend, Litka Wintrova (Winter); Litka's husband, Rudla; Uncle Erna Kanturek; and his wife, Hilda; (in front): me; my sister, Vera; Litka and Rudla's daughter Eva; and my cousin Eva Kanturek, Erna and Hilda's daughter.

Jewish refugees from Austria disembarking in Shanghai from the Italian ship *Conte Verde.* December 14, 1938.

Jewish refugees disembarking in Shanghai from the Italian ship SS Conte Verde. December 14, 1938.

My reunion, after sixty-six years, with Eva Winter in January 2012, on a visit to Australia, with my wife, Catherine. Left to right (back): the husband of Eva's younger sister, Jana; and Catherine; (in front): Jana; me; and Eva.

3

SHANGHAI

n 1940, Shanghai was an open city divided into areas controlled by the French, Japanese, American, and British authorities. It was also quite peaceful despite being in the middle of a war between China and Japan and surrounded by Japanese Armed Forces. It was also one of the only places where Jewish refugees escaping from the Nazi storm sweeping Europe could find asylum. It was a haven of last resort.

When we arrived in Shanghai, I only spoke Czech, however, I quickly learned German from my playmates (other refugee kids) and Mandarin from my new Chinese friends. My parents registered me in the Shanghai American School and there I learned to speak English— or as my American friends call it, American.

We found a townhouse in the French Quarter, where French law was paramount, and settled into our new home with the Kantureks. It was a little crowded, but that was all we could afford. Unfortunately, the German Nazi consul general lived next door with his twelve-year-old son decked out in his Hitler Youth uniform complete with swastikas and a dagger. I was only six, but I learned an important lesson from this little Nazi bastard. One day I called him a dirty Nazi and he responded by pulling out his dagger and slashing me three times on my left arm. Fortunately, except for the entry wound on my left wrist, where I still have a small scar today, the cuts were mostly superficial, but I still bled quite a bit. I guess in a minor way, I too shed blood to the Nazi swine.

These are the important lessons I learned from this incident:

1. Be careful who you pick your fights with—if they are bigger than you or have a weapon, keep your mouth shut.
2. Never challenge someone who has a weapon—they may use it on you.
3. The Nazis were vicious animals who would kill or maim the weak and the defenseless. They also taught their children to hate and maim and kill at an early age.

These lessons have served me well throughout my life. After wrapping my bleeding arm in towels, my mother took the law into her own hands. She caught the little Nazi and beat him severely enough that he ended up in the hospital. Both families filed lawsuits and charges, but luckily the French judge threw it all out of court.

AS I SAID, my first school was the American School and it was great. In addition to learning English, I developed a love for the American people and their way of life. I found them to be friendly, kind, and generous, not at all like the grumpy and perpetually angry and argumentative Europeans I knew. Later in my life, this affection was more than justified by my experiences with them. They aren't perfect—no one is—however the majority of Americans come close. I am now a very proud Canadian, but my second choice would be to be an American. Regrettably, today the American people are deeply divided, and compromise has become a dirty word.

My uncle Vilda arrived on the SS *Conte Verde* (sister ship of our SS *Conte Rosso*) in September 1940. My mother's parents and her sister, Liza, arrived in January 1941, via Berlin, Moscow, the Trans-Siberian Railway, Vladivostok, and Kobe, Japan. My dad travelled to Kobe, Japan to meet them and bring them to Shanghai. He waited on the dock all day for their arrival and was arrested a number of times on suspicion of being a spy. Each time he provided documentation and was released. Again, my aunt and grandparents owed their survival to my dad and Japanese Vice-Consul Chiune Sugihara. They were also assisted by the US Jewish Joint Distribution Committee, who bought their railway tickets as they had ours.

The remaining fragment of the official resident certificate I was issued when we arrived in Shanghai on May 10, 1940.

The house where my family—the Votickys and the Kantureks—lived in the French Quarter in Shanghai, 1941–1942. Photograph taken in 2012.

*The first school I attended in Shanghai in 1941, the Shanghai American School.
Photograph taken in 2012.*

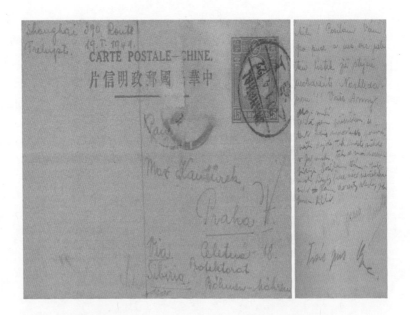

*The two sides of the1941 postcard my father sent to my grandfather Max Kanturek to tell
him that train tickets had been purchased for him, my grandmother Hedvika, and my aunt
Liza to travel on the Trans-Siberian Railway from Vladivostok to Japan
and on to Shanghai.*

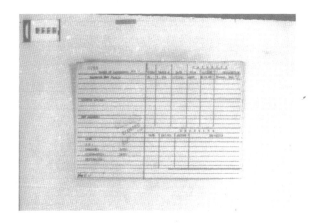

The Trans-Siberian Railway ticket—the $112 cost was paid by the Jewish Joint Distribution Committee—for Max, Hedvika, and Liza Kanturek to travel from Prague to Vladivostok, through Berlin and Moscow, and on to Kobe, Japan. They were met there by my father, who brought them to Shanghai.

JAPANESE CONNECTION: Chiune Sugihara's story will be told in an award-winning documentary film, "Sugihara: Conspiracy of Kindness," to be presented by the Morikami Museum on Sunday. *Submitted photo*

Japanese vice-consul in Lithuania, Chiune Sugihara, whose humanity and decency saved thousands more people from the Holocaust, including members of my own family. Over the summer of 1940, without explicit instructions from his government, he granted about 2,140 ten-day transit visas that would allow the Jewish refugees to leave the Soviet Union from the port of Vladivostok and travel through Japan.

4

PEARL HARBOR

December 7, 1941, better known as Pearl Harbor Day (December 8 at 4:00 a.m. in Shanghai), was the day that Japanese military forces attacked the US itself, the South Pacific territories of the US and other Western countries, and their Asian neighbours in a massive coordinated air, sea, and land attack.

The Allies had evacuated the US Marine detachment in November 1941 to Manila. The only Allied Forces left in Shanghai were the British HMS *Peterel* with a crew of twenty-seven and a sixty-three-year-old Captain, and the USS *Wake* with a crew of twenty-five, these ships were anchored in the Huangpu River opposite the Bund to provide communication links for their consulates. They were surrounded by a large Japanese Task Force, which at 4:00 a.m. opened fire on the lightly armed Allied ships. The British were able to scuttle their ship, but the Americans did not have enough time and were captured. Japanese Marines came off the Japanese Fleet and captured the International Settlement and Hongkou that day.

This was a traumatic event in Shanghai because until that date the 18,000 European refugees who lived there had felt safe and detached from the events in Europe. Communications were slow and difficult. Unlike today's instant communication via satellite and Internet, static interfered with high-frequency radios communications. World War II was no longer 8,000 kilometres away; we were now right in the middle of it. We had no idea how the Japanese would treat the European refugees.

The Imperial Japanese forces occupied all of Shanghai and the approximately half of China that they were able to take from the Chinese government of Chiang Kai-shek and the small Allied force that controlled the International Shanghai Settlement. The French Concession remained under the control of the traitorous Vichy government in France.

The American, British, Dutch, and Belgian residents of Shanghai instantly became enemy aliens and were forced to wear red armbands. The French were exempt because of the collaborationist Vichy government led by Marshal Henri Philippe Pétain (ironically a French World War I hero who had played a large part in defeating Germany). The other European refugees were considered to be stateless residents, as they had no government to represent them.

The Czechoslovak consul, Major Stepanek—obviously looking for medals and a political career after the war—paid a visit to the Japanese Commander in Shanghai and demanded that the approximately 250 Czechs be declared enemy aliens. If he had been successful, we would have been forced to join our Allied friends in Japanese concentration camps. How kind of him to try to condemn 250 of his fellow citizens to more than two years of brutal imprisonment that included both maltreatment and malnutrition—a regular diet of soggy boiled rice and occasional decaying fish—in order to help his postwar political career.

Fortunately for us, the Japanese Commander demanded to know the reason for this brave, generous, and stupid offer. Our consul general gallantly responded that it was because the Czech government-in-exile in London led by President Edvard Beneš had declared war on Japan. When the Japanese officer then asked him how many ships the Czechoslovak navy had, the answer for landlocked Czechoslovakia was, of course, none! (The cruise ships on the Vltava River in Prague didn't count.) The next logical question from the Commander was, "Then how are your troops going to get here to fight the Imperial Japanese forces?" The Czechoslovak consul had no answer for that, so, luckily, instead of declaring him an enemy alien, the Japanese Commander threw him out of his office.

Although the Japanese Commander's action did save the Czech refugees from the brutal confinement that other Allied residents in

Shanghai suffered, however, we were now classified as stateless refugees. This carried other consequences. While the American, British, and Dutch citizens were confined to concentration camps, we, the stateless refugees, were ordered into a ghetto created for us in Hongkou, the poorest part of Shanghai. On November 15, 1942, the Japanese Army decreed that all Stateless Refugees would be confined to a small ghetto in a poor Chinese part of the city—Hongkou. By May 18, 1943, this mass transfer was completed.

The Nazis were pushing the Japanese Commander to turn over control over the Jews to them. The Commander called in the leaders of the Jewish community and asked them why the Germans hated the Jews so much? Rabbi Shimon Sholom Kalish probably saved all our lives when, according to Warren Kozak he answered, "Because we are Orientals." At that, the Japanese Commander's stern face broke into a smile. He didn't accede to the German request and the Shanghai Jews moved into a wall-less, fenceless ghetto in Hongkou.

Our family of eleven was very fortunate, as Dad still had enough funds to build two small semi-detached homes in the ghetto for our family of eleven. We were jammed into close quarters in four rooms, two tiny bathrooms, and one tiny communal kitchen equipped with a Chinese version of a tiny Hibachi for cooking. However, we were fortunate to be able to avoid living in the horrible slum dwellings that filled Hongkou. Most of the refugees had to survive in even smaller living quarters and rely on communal living quarters, kitchens, and bathrooms. These unfortunates survived through the hard work of Laura Margolis, an American angel who represented the Jewish Distribution Committee, and volunteers like my aunt Liza Kanturek. Thanks to Dad's foresight, our family was very lucky; as far as possible in that situation, we were able to control our living conditions and destiny.

That same month (May 1943), the Italian people overthrew Fascist leader Benito Mussolini and switched from the German to the Allied side in the war. The *Conte Verde*—the ship that my uncle Vilda had arrived on a few months after us—had been trapped in Shanghai by the Japanese attack on Pearl Harbor and was docked in the Huangpu River, right across from the stately bank buildings in the waterfront area called the Bund. The Italian crew, relieved to finally be on the right side of the war, scuttled the big ship to deprive the Japanese of its use. The *Conte Verde* majestically rolled onto its side in the shallow river with its smokestacks pointing away from the Bund. For this act, the Italian crew was rewarded with a trip to a prisoner-of-war camp. The Japanese did eventually manage to refloat the *Conte Verde* after a year of extremely hard work and then towed her to Japan for a refit as a troopship. Unfortunately for the Japanese crew and troops on board, on her first sailing as a troopship, she was sunk by an American submarine waiting for targets of opportunity just outside the harbour.

After we moved into the ghetto, Uncle Ernie and my grandfather Max got me involved in soccer and boxing. I could handle the soccer, but after two years of training and one fight (which I lost), I quit the latter. I really didn't enjoy getting punched in the face and still wonder today why anyone in their right mind would. My uncle and grandfather taught me the basics of soccer and helped me develop into a reasonably decent athlete and fair soccer player. It was the start of my lifelong love of all sports—except boxing, that is. They also taught me the basics of sportsmanship: winning is the objective, but always be gracious in victory and generous in defeat. I have governed my life by these principles.

The American School was closed after our American friends were sent to the concentration camps and we were forced into the ghetto. My parents transferred me to St. Francis Xavier School (SFX), a Catholic Jesuit missionary school, which, unfortunately, was outside the ghetto. There were no walls around the ghetto, but anyone wishing to leave needed a pass from the Japanese Commander, Ghoya, who called himself the "King of the Jews." He was a moody and xenophobic little man, who one week might be our generous benefactor, handing out passes to all who applied, and the next week would not grant any passes at all.

Along with fifteen other students, I applied for and received a three-month renewable pass to attend the new school. One of my schoolmates from the ghetto was Michael Blumenthal, who in later life became an extremely successful Wall Street businessman and US Secretary of the Treasury. He also appears to have a short memory. When I attempted to contact him a few years ago, I was brushed off by one of his flunkies who told me that he didn't remember me or the group that travelled to SFX every day for almost three years. Obviously, success had gone to his head and humility was not one of his strong points. In February 2013, Bill Hant of Los Angeles, a successful retired engineer and visiting professor at UCLA, found me and graciously sent me a class picture from our days at SFX.

It has never ceased to amaze me that American liberals have been beating themselves up for interning Japanese residents and even US citizens in California after Pearl Harbor. Yes, it was wrong, but my view is that it was based on fear of the unknown not malice. Meanwhile, the Japanese have shown no signs of regret for their inhumane treatment of innocent American, British, Dutch, Canadian, Australian, and Belgian civilians throughout Asia. These civilians were doctors, missionaries, teachers, and businessmen, and their wives and children, yet they were treated brutally and far worse than actual Japanese prisoners-of-war were by the US forces. They were not combatants and posed no threat to Japan but were treated as such with brutality and contempt. Nor have the Western liberals said anything about the millions of Chinese men, women, and children who were imprisoned, raped, robbed, and slaughtered by the Japanese Imperial Army, starting with the "Rape of Nanking."

St. Francis Xavier College was a great school with dedicated teachers who taught us well, although they also tried to convert us to Catholicism as part of the curriculum. The primary mission of SFX was to spread the Roman Catholic faith and to convert those of us who were not of their faith, and they were very persuasive. My two favourite teachers were Brother John (a tall, muscular Irishman) and Brother Leo (a small, thin German), two kind, helpful, and dedicated men. These two used to play soccer with us at recess wearing their long black gowns.

They almost had me hooked on their religion until a morality question torpedoed any chance of ever getting me to join their church. I was ten years old in 1944 and Brother John was presenting a catechism lesson on ethics. He stated that according to Catholic doctrine, if a doctor tending to a mother at childbirth had to make a choice between saving the life of the mother or the child, he had to save the child. I was not the smartest ten-year-old in the world, but I did have the common sense and courage to challenge what I saw as stupid dogma. I asked Brother John what would happen to the other children the mother had at home. Who would care for them? Brother John, however, completely indoctrinated by his religion and his adherence to blind faith, uttered the fateful words that destroyed my faith in him and his church: "God will provide." Yeah sure, just like he did at Auschwitz-Birkenau.

Even as a child that didn't seem right to me. My ten-year-old common sense kicked in and I said something that was the equivalent of BS. That cost me three whacks of the cane across my bare bottom, but it taught me to think for myself—and taught me to be more discreet. These were two more important lessons that have served me well for the rest of my life. I believe that common sense and thinking for yourself are among the most important keys to success in all phases of life.

One day our small group from the ghetto was sent home during a US Army Air Corps raid; fortunately, we were in an area of open fields when the bombs were dropping. There were no targets in the open fields and we really were not in any danger but having an unobstructed view from ground level of the bombers and fighters challenging them, this was a spectacular show of aerial aerobatics interspersed with anti-aircraft fire. This experience is what fuelled my interest in flying aircraft for the first time.

My afterschool activities then included playing soccer, taking French and Russian instruction, and escorting my sister, Vera, to her ballet lessons. The dance classes were run by a sadistic French ballet master, Monsieur Pascal, who drove the youngsters mercilessly, striking them with a cane if they didn't follow his directions. After every session, the kids' toes would be bleeding from standing on them. Vera was a very good dancer and she even starred in *Die Fledermaus* ballet with a budding Nureyev named Kurt. Watching the torturous training of these kids under Monsieur Pascal, though, turned me off ballet forever.

Among the ghetto residents were all the various nationalities that were not represented by any functioning foreign government and were, like us, thus considered to be stateless. This included the White Russians, who had escaped during and after the 1917 Communist revolution and were certainly not represented by the Soviet government, whose only desire was to persecute them and populate their gulags with them. They were victims of Communism, just as we were victims of Nazism.

One of these refugees was my Russian teacher, a fascinating lady from the court of the Russian Romanov royal family named Madame Szigeti. The story of her escape from Russia was like a fairy tale. She was fortunate to escape; the rest of the Russian royal family was slaughtered by the Communists at Yekaterinburg in Siberia in 1918. She taught me Russian by telling me her life story. She was, she claimed, an attendant (not a member) of the Romanov family; her husband, Major Szigeti, was a dentist in the Austro-Hungarian Army who had been taken prisoner during World War I.

Czar Nicholas II's son and heir, Prince Alexei, was a hemophiliac, suffering from a blood disorder that makes blood clotting difficult if not impossible and puts its victims at risk of bleeding to death from even a small cut. Prince Alexei required dental surgery, which could prove fatal, and it came to the czar's attention that there was a prisoner of war in Russia who was a dental surgeon with experience in treating hemophiliacs. He summoned Major Szigeti to the Imperial Palace to care for his son.

Dr. Szigeti must have been a great dental surgeon because he managed to keep Prince Alexei alive until the Communists murdered him at Yekaterinburg. The poor heir to the Russian throne did not die of hemophilia; he died of massive lead poisoning inflicted by a Communist murder squad in the basement of a hideout in Siberia. Regrettably, no surgeon specializing in hemophilia could have helped him then.

Living with the royal family certainly beat life in a Russian prisoner-of-war camp in Siberia, especially with all the lovely ladies at court. That is how Madame Szigeti met her husband. When the Russian Revolution took place in 1917, the Major escaped with his young love and bride-to-be across Siberia to Manchuria and then on to Shanghai. Madame Szigeti regaled me with stories of life within the royal family in so much detail that we suspected that she was actually the missing daughter Royal Princess Anastasia, whose remains were never found. That was how I learned to speak Russian.

In the summer of 1944, while I was picking up lunch for the family at a small local restaurant, I was attacked by a large German shepherd.

He took a bite out of my right hamstring and I have not liked or trusted a dog since. My list of phobias therefore increased to two—water and dogs. Rabies was rampant in China and it was wise to start the rabies shots until it could be determined that the dog wasn't infected. The treatment was an injection into the area around your belly button every day for thirty-six days.

There was no hospital in the ghetto and so I had to travel to one in downtown Shanghai. I had to make the trip alone because my parents weren't allowed out of the ghetto. My mother felt guilty about that for the rest of her life, even though it was not her fault that she couldn't leave the ghetto. After the tenth shot, we were advised that the dog was not rabid, so I was spared the last twenty-six shots and trips to the hospital. This solo experience greatly helped me grow and mature.

At the end of December 1944, Ghoya, the King of the Jews, decided that the sixteen Jewish students at SFX were now obviously a danger to the Japanese empire and refused to renew our passes out of the ghetto. We were not very happy about it because we now had to go to the Jewish School on the edge of the ghetto. We had become somewhat snobbish and were not impressed with this little amateur enterprise run by well-meaning non-professional volunteers who did their best to educate the ghetto children with minimal qualifications and funds. All in all, they did a great job; my sister, Vera, did not have any difficulty advancing her education after a good start at the Jewish school. The group of us from SFX only ended up attending the Jewish school for six months, as the war ended before the 1945 school year started. After liberation, in September 1945, we were free to return to St. Francis Xavier.

There were very few jobs in the ghetto, so there was a lot of poverty among many of the already poor immigrants who had fled their homes to survive Kristallnacht, the concentration camps, and the persecution in Germany and the occupied countries. The majority survived thanks to the American Jewish Joint Distribution Committee and the fearless Laura Margolis, who continued to raise funds for the destitute residents with help from the Sassoon and Kadoori families and other wealthy Persian and Russian Jews. My aunt, Liza Kanturek, ran a soup kitchen for the very poor on behalf of the Czech community.

All in all, life in the ghetto was fairly normal—except for the fact that we needed permission to leave. The Imperial Japanese Army really didn't bother us; they lived in their barracks and we only saw them when they drove by in their trucks. Since I was one of the fortunate few who could leave the ghetto, I was affected less than the other eighteen thousand residents, including my family.

The Bund, the financial centre of Shanghai, in 1940.

A postcard of the Shanghai Bund in 1940, with the sampans that people lived on in the foreground.

The Bund today. Photograph taken in 2012.

The Waibaidu Bridge across the Huangpu River that links the Bund to Hongkou, where the Jewish ghetto was established on November 15, 1942. Photograph taken in 2012.

My sister, Vera (left); Eva Wintrova (Winter); and me in Shanghai, 1942.

Eva Kanturek (left); me; and Vera (right) in the Shanghai ghetto, 1942.

Aunt Liza in the Shanghai ghetto. Shanghai, 1943.

View of a laneway in the Shanghai ghetto, 1943.

The house that my father built for us in Hongkou, in the Shanghai ghetto. In the left bottom corner of the photo is the bomb shelter that wasn't much help to us in 1945 when the US bombing raid came—with Shanghai's high water table, anything below one metre just fills with water. Left to right: Vera; my father; my mother; and me.

The B'nai Brith soccer team in the Shanghai ghetto, 1943. I'm sitting in front on the left.

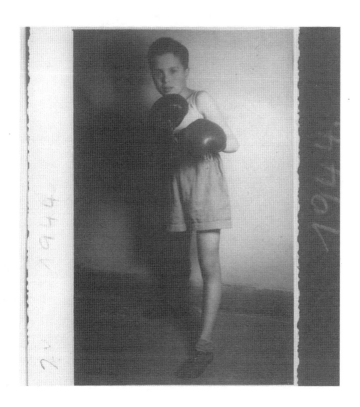

Uncle Ernie and my grandfather Max got me involved in boxing after we moved into the ghetto. It was a brief career to say the least—one fight. I discovered that I really didn't enjoy getting punched in the face. Shanghai, 1944.

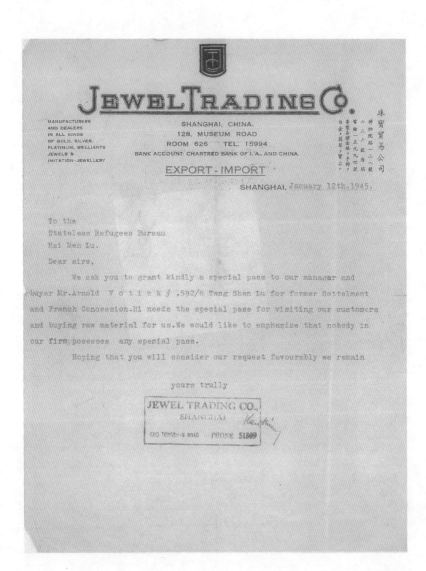

JEWEL TRADING Co.

MANUFACTURERS
AND DEALERS
IN ALL KINDS
OF GOLD, SILVER,
PLATINUM, BRILLIANTS
JEWELS &
IMITATION-JEWELLERY

SHANGHAI, CHINA.
128, MUSEUM ROAD
ROOM 626   TEL. 15994
BANK ACCOUNT: CHARTRED BANK OF I. A., AND CHINA.

EXPORT - IMPORT

SHANGHAI, January 12th. 1945.

To the
Stateless Refugees Bureau
Hai Men Lu.

Dear sirs,

We ask you to grant kindly a special pass to our manager and buyer Mr.Arnold V o t i c k ý ,592/6 Tang Shan Lu for former Settelment and French Concession. Hi needs the special pass for visiting our customers and buying raw material for us. We would like to emphasize that nobody in our firm posesses any special pass.

Hoping that you will consider our request favourably we remain

yours trully

JEWEL TRADING CO.,
SHANGHAI
580 TONGSHAN ROAD   PHONE 51809

A request for a pass for my father to leave the ghetto on business. Shanghai, 1945.

Ghoya, known as the "King of the Jews," the Japanese officer
who administered the Shanghai ghetto.

Ghoya with his staff. Left to right: G. Sherenchevsky, Maurice Feder,
Egon Weiss, and Ruth Kallmann.

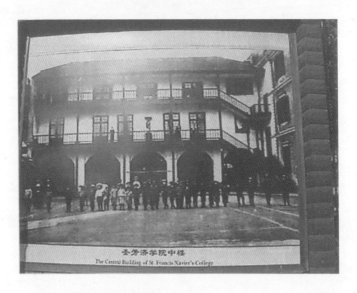

The Central Building of St. Francis Xavier College, where I went to school from 1943–
1943. Shanghai, 1943.

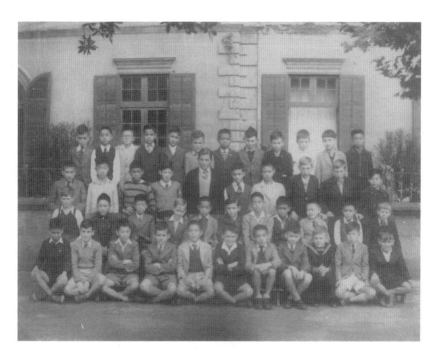

My Grade V class at St. Francis Xavier College, Shanghai. 1943.
I'm in the back row, sixth from the left.

St. Francis Xavier College (Shanghai) today. Photograph taken in 2012.

This two-room building is all that remains of the Jewish School on the edge of the Shanghai ghetto where I attended classes for six months in 1944–1945. Photograph taken in 2012.

Sir Victor Sassoon, a member of the wealthy Baghdadi-Jewish banking and merchant family whose interests spread from Mumbai to Shanghai. Sir Victor, who lived in Shanghai from the 1920s to 1941, was a major funder of the International Committee for the Organization of European Refugees in China (IC). Through the IC, he was the main benefactor of eighteen thousand Jews in the Shanghai ghetto.

5

SEVENTH US ARMY AIR CORPS STRIKES

Shanghai is built on a delta, where the water table is high; if you dig one metre down into the ground, you hit water. It is therefore not possible to build basements or bomb shelters. What passed as our bomb shelter was two tables, one on each side of the living room window, with an old bed and an extra mattress sitting on top of them. If our house collapsed, this was supposed to protect us from being buried alive. In the event of a direct hit, we would be burnt toast, with no chance of survival.

To our knowledge there were at least seven potential military targets in the ghetto, including a military go-down, or warehouse, across the street and approximately three hundred metres (one hundred feet) from our home. All we could do was hope that any potential bombing of that target would be accurate and not too heavy.

July 17, 1945, dawned as a beautiful, sunny, summer Shanghai day, with the temperature rising to about 30°C (86°F). Just after lunch the air raid sirens started to whine, but a lot of people ignored them because there had been so many false alarms and Hongkou had never been bombed. We took it seriously, though. Mom, Vera, and I settled into our shelter while Dad was next door getting an infected foot tended to by Uncle Vilda.

The fun began at approximately one o'clock with the sound of high-pitched whistling as the bombs started to fall. The whistling lasted until just before impact, followed first by a deathly silence and then a very noisy explosion. My mother became hysterical because Dad wasn't with her. Vera and I tried to calm her down to no avail until my dad came skipping into the shelter on one leg between explosions. As soon as she saw him, Mom started screaming all over again, saying, "You're wounded, you're wounded!" Dad calmly responded that he was hopping because he had ointment on his foot and didn't want it rubbed off by walking on it.

The air raid lasted approximately thirty minutes, with lots of whistling sounds, followed by a deathly silence of a few seconds, then loud explosions. One thing I learned about surviving an air raid: as long as you hear the whistling of bombs, you're safe—you'll never hear the one that gets you. Shortly after the bombing stopped, we left our shelter and went out into the street. The military target close to us was a smoking ruin and there were wounded Chinese being transported to hospitals in rickshaws since there were no ambulances. Stunned survivors wandered the streets.

We could see a lot of smoke coming from an area north of us, where Dad's cousin Nellie Schwartz and her family lived. Nellie was the woman who didn't want Mom to take Vera and me back to Czechoslovakia from Italy in 1939. She and her husband now had a daughter, Eva, who was born in Shanghai. Dad said to me, "Let's see if the Schwartzes are alright." We took a bottle of water and headed north on foot. Fifteen minutes later we arrived at the place where their home should have been, but the only thing left standing was their bathroom. The three of them were still in it, looking completely shell-shocked.

Everything in the house was totally destroyed—they had no clothes, furniture, or food—so we took them to our home. Vera and I gave up our room and moved in with our parents, where we slept on the concrete floor in our parents' bedroom until we left Shanghai exactly a year later. We also gave them clothing and the other necessities of life to replace what they had lost. Hugo, Nellie, and Eva moved into our room and stayed there until we left Shanghai.

This turned out to be the deadliest air raid on the ghetto. More than one hundred Chinese and at least thirty-three Jewish refugees were killed, while hundreds of others were wounded. The war in Europe was over and air raids were becoming a daily occurrence as the US Army Air Corps strove to end the war in the Pacific.

Everything changed on August 6, 1945, when Uncle Vilda picked up the news on his home-built illegal short-wave radio that at 8:15 a.m. a US B-29—the Enola Gay—had dropped an atomic bomb equal to twenty thousand tons of explosives on Hiroshima. The entire city was destroyed and there were tens of thousands of casualties. The air raids on Shanghai stopped and the ghetto residents started to celebrate the end of the war.

That turned out to be a little premature. President Truman demanded Japan's unconditional surrender within seventy-two hours or the US would continue to drop atomic bombs on Japan. The stubborn Japanese military government, however, believed that the US was bluffing, that they had only one atomic bomb in their arsenal. Accordingly, they decided to continue the war. All the casualties at Nagasaki were the responsibility of that Japanese military government decision.

Over the next three days, while rumours spread about the devastating new American weapons of mass destruction, the Japanese secret police went nuts looking for hidden short-wave radios. They found our radio, but luckily, they didn't find the attachment that converted it to short-wave, which allowed us to receive the Voice of America broadcasts. Those same broadcasts, however, would later bring us the news from Europe that would devastate every one of us. All too soon we would learn about the horrors of Auschwitz-Birkenau, Majdanek, Dachau, Treblinka, Sobibor, and Bergen-Belsen, along with the countless other horrors that had wiped out so many of our families. Everyone living in the Hongkou ghetto lost family members in the Holocaust.

THE JAPANESE MILITARY government had called the USA's bluff and they lost. The Americans actually had two atomic bombs and three days after the bombing of Hiroshima, a second US B-29 dropped an atomic bomb on the major city of Nagasaki, wiping that city off the face of the earth and killing thousands more. The dead were lucky; the surviving wounded suffered horribly and died slowly. As I said, the dead and wounded at Nagasaki were a direct result of the intransigence of the Japanese Emperor and his military government. Finally on August 15, 1945, the Japanese government decided to surrender and World War II finally came to an end.

There are individuals today who accuse the United States of war crimes for unleashing the devastation of nuclear weapons. They weren't there in 1945 and don't understand the horrors that Japan inflicted on Southeast Asia and their citizens, and the vicious mistreatment and murder of US, Asian, and European civilians and prisoners of war. They also forget that it was the Japanese who started the war in the Pacific with the sneak attacks on Pearl Harbor, Hong Kong, Singapore, and Manila. They conveniently forget the atrocities committed by Japanese forces throughout Asia, the millions of Chinese slaughtered, the Rape of Nanking, and the thousands of Korean and Chinese "comfort women"—women forced to be sex slaves for the Japanese Imperial Army. To this day, the Japanese government has not apologized to or compensated these women.

Critics of the bombings of Hiroshima and Nagasaki also ignore the horrendous Allied and Japanese casualties that would have occurred if the US had been forced to invade the Japanese Home Islands. If the Japanese defence of Iwo Jima and Okinawa is any indication of the fierce determination of the Japanese people, the casualties would have been in the hundreds of thousands or even millions. When faced with defeat on Okinawa, the Japanese Imperial Forces coerced their own citizens into committing mass suicide, herding them over a cliff at gunpoint, pushed forward by tanks and bayonets, rather than have them come under foreign control.

Following the Japanese surrender, the Japanese Imperial Army was still in charge of Shanghai but were now there only to maintain a semblance of order. The defeat was a loss of face for the Japanese military, invoking a profound sense of shame and loss of honour. Some of their officers committed suicide, and the enlisted men sat dejected in their barracks. As a result, we didn't see very many of the occupiers anymore.

My aunt Liza asked me to deliver some food to her British friends in a Japanese concentration camp approximately ten kilometres (six miles) outside of Hongkou. I was picked for the job because everyone thought that, even if there still were Japanese guards on duty, they wouldn't bother an eleven-year-old. My friend Manny and I got on our bikes, our baskets full of food and headed to the camp.

When we arrived at the gates, they were wide open and there were no guards around. We found my aunt's friends and gave them the food, for which they were very grateful. They had been living for more than two years on a diet of cold soggy rice and occasionally cold scraps of foul fish. They had to stay at the camp until the Americans arrived and could evacuate them home because they had nowhere else to go. The Allied concentration camp inmates were all too weak from malnutrition to celebrate the end of the war and their new freedom.

In the ghetto, however, there were tremendous celebrations and we highly anticipated the arrival of the US forces. Every day we waited for our liberators and every night went to bed disappointed as the days dragged on. Distances are great in the Pacific generally and China particularly; the US forces had to come a long way to liberate us.

6

LIBERATION AND THE DAWN OF A DREAM

On the morning of September 3, 1945, we were having breakfast when we heard the roar of powerful aircraft engines over our home. I ran outside and saw the most beautiful sight that I'd ever seen in my eleven years—four powerful P-40 Warhawk fighter aircraft in green-and-brown camouflage colours with a Shark's Jaw (their emblem) painted on the nose. Flying in close formation approximately one hundred feet (30 metres) above our house, they were followed by four more, and then four more, and then four more.

This was a complete famous Flying Tiger Fighter Squadron, by then a part of the 23rd US Army Air Corps, which had been fighting the Japanese Imperial Army under General Claire Chennault since 1937 on behalf of the Republic of China as the American Volunteer Group. They had been volunteer US military fighter Pilots fighting the Japanese for China until Pearl Harbor, when they were transferred back to the US Army Air Corps. The sound of their powerful and noisy engines was the sound of freedom! We were FREE!

As I stood and watched this magnificent air power display, my mother came out and ordered me back into the house to finish my breakfast. I refused and when she asked me why, I said, "Because someday, I'll be flying those airplanes!"

"You are not going to fly anything," my mother retorted. "You would get killed!" My mother was always right even when she was wrong, but fortunately she was certainly one hundred per cent wrong on that statement as my later career proved. I stood outside waiting for more aircraft, but that was all for the day. I have savoured that day all my life and I followed through on my promise, although it was in Canada, not in the USA! In 1991, I retired from Air Canada with more than 20,000 flying hours.

Later in life, I had the honour of flying Canadian CF-100 All Weather Fighters (AWF) during the Cold War and serving in North American Air Defense Command (NORAD), working closely with our American allies and friends for almost ten years. We were successful in helping to deter the Soviet Union from starting World War III. The dream I had on September 3, 1946, became a reality. Mission accomplished!

Shortly after the beautiful display of air power, word spread through Hongkou—which was no longer a ghetto—that American ships were arriving in the Huangpu River and docking all along the shoreline and offshore right up to the Bund, the financial heart of Shanghai. The US Navy's Seventh Fleet was arriving. I still don't know exactly how many ships arrived in the next few days, but the word was that there were more than 140 ships in this flotilla. Naturally, I had to find out for myself and proceeded on foot downtown to the Bund. Thousands of other people had the same idea and by the time that I got there, I was part of a mass of humanity celebrating victory over Japan and the final end of the brutality of World War II.

Lost among the newly liberated people of Shanghai were a few hundred American soldiers and sailors, who managed to work their way through the crowd in their Jeeps and personnel carriers. It was a great day for all of us especially for the young US servicemen who were finally almost out of the line of fire. Not completely out of danger as I found out sixty-five years later. I met one of those young sailors in 2010 while playing golf in Florida and when we discovered that we had both been in Shanghai in 1945, we got together and reminisced.

Dr. Don Hafner was eighteen in 1945, only seven years older than I was at that time. He had been on board a troop ship earning fifty dollars a month, but three months later he'd been transferred to a minesweeper, clearing mines off the Coast of Hainan Island and earning the princely five dollars a month in danger pay.

One day, five months after Japan's surrender, while on shore leave on a beach on Hainan, he and two buddies wandered up a hill to explore the island. While traversing through a cemetery, they came under heavy rifle fire from remnants of the Japanese army. These stragglers didn't believe that Japan had surrendered and refused to give up their weapons—in the Philippines, the last straggler didn't surrender until ten years later, in 1955. Don and his buddies were very fortunate to have been able to beat a hasty retreat and get back to their ship unharmed.

Think about it, this young sailor was only seven years older than me and he was a warrior. Don was discharged from the Navy in 1948, went to medical school, and became a prominent cardiovascular surgeon in Ohio. He passed away in 2016, still trying to improve his golf game.

Don had always thought of Shanghai as a glamorous place to visit, so when his ship left the Oakland Naval Base and the crew was told that they were going to Shanghai, he was excited—he was going to a city that he had only dreamed of. He couldn't wait to go ashore on liberty but was shocked to find the city in almost total darkness at night. There wasn't enough power to light a city of eight million people (now 25 million), and we were rationed to forty kilowatt hours per month. That was not much for ten adults and five children living in four rooms. It was a good thing that we had lots of candles! This rationing persisted throughout the war and for the year we were there after that.

The darkness also inspired fear in the young sailors; they travelled in groups of four to six and all carried blackjacks for self-defence. What they needed was a young streetwise kid to show them around the city—especially the safe bars—who spoke both Mandarin and English. As it turned out, I just happened to fit the bill.

Two days later, when I was heading downtown, I ran into six young American sailors who were having a heated argument with two pedicab (bicycle-powered rickshaws) drivers about the fare. These vehicles, designed to carry two passengers, were a combination of the front half of a bicycle and a lounge chair mounted on two wheels. They were one step up in transportation from a rickshaw, which was a single-seater on two wheels pulled by a running coolie (as menial labourers were called in China then).

Being fluent in both Mandarin and English, I offered to mediate the two-language dispute and the young sailors happily agreed. I asked them and the pedicab drivers where they had come from, then decided that the sailors each owed the drivers fifty cents US. I got that amount from them, paid the drivers, and told my new friends to follow me without turning back. When one of the drivers followed us and grabbed my left arm, I slapped his hand with my right hand and he immediately let go of me. The Chinese were intimidated by both the Europeans and Japanese, even European kids, so the drivers let us go. The sailors couldn't believe their luck—they had found a kid who spoke both English and Chinese, knew the city, and could handle the natives.

One of the sailors asked me if I knew where the nearest bar was, and I told him that I did. When we got there, my new buddies ordered beer and a Coca-Cola for me; this was the start of my lifelong love and addiction to Coca-Cola. We spent the rest of the day wandering through every bar that I knew about. At 8:30 that evening, one of the young men turned to me and said, "Hey, kid, where are the broads?"

Responding like a typical eleven-year-old, I asked, "What's a broad?"

The sailor answered, "Girls, you know, girls."

My stupid response was, "What do you want girls for? We're having a good time. Why spoil it with girls?" The only girl I knew was my sister and, like all eight-year-olds, she was a pain.

This obviously convinced them that I was not a pimp, just a dumb kid, so they gave me four US dollars and told me to go home. This was a lot of money then—remember that their navy pay was only fifty US dollars a month. They invited me to come and see them on their ship, the USS *Repose*, a hospital ship docked near Hongkou. I headed home, fully aware that I was almost three hours late and would face some serious corporal punishment. When I walked through the door I was met by a hail of slaps to the back of the head (*pohlavky* in Czech) from my mother before I could say a word. (To the day she died in 2014 my mother claimed that she never hit me). Finally, I got a chance to explain my day. Mom's first response was to scream, "You are lying!" but when I pulled out the four US dollars, I turned from a lying brat into the family support and hero. That money could feed the four of us for a week and Dad had been unable to earn anything for the previous year.

This was the beginning of my career escorting American sailors and soldiers around the bars and sights of Shanghai. For the next year, in my youthful ignorance, I took these sailors and soldiers to some of the most dangerous parts of Shanghai without realizing the risks. Fortunately, we never encountered any trouble other than the odd drunken bar fight among US servicemen. After a few months, though, I began to recognize the dangers and started to carry a hidden kitchen knife. I have no idea what I could have done with it except to pass it to one of my American friends. Fortunately for us, we usually travelled in groups of four to ten and this provided us with protection.

In turn, I spent days with them in a LST (Landing Ship Tank), delivering mail to the ships of the Seventh Fleet in the harbour. Their idea of fun was to let me drive the LST, which was easy because it had only a steering wheel and a three-position gear shift—forward, neutral, and reverse.

Of all the wonderful American servicemen I met, the crew of the USS *Repose* was my favourite. In October 1945, my beloved grandfather Maxa got very sick. He was suffering from a terminal illness and although his doctor tried hard to ease his pain, none of us had access to the medication or painkillers that would make him more comfortable. I told my closest American buddy, Seaman Clark (nicknamed Clarkie) about our problem and he promised to try to get help. A few days later, Clarkie showed up with one of the doctors from the USS *Repose*, who brought drugs from the ship, including penicillin, painkillers, and a blow-up life preserver that allowed Maxa to use the toilet without aggravating the bedsores and prickly heat rash that he had all over his bottom. My friends continued to provide us with drugs and food until Maxa died in February 1946, but his last five months were made much more comfortable thanks to the wonderful crew of the USS *Repose*.

In 2009, I started a search for sailors from the USS *Repose*. A lot of them had passed away and others were not traceable, but I finally found ex-Bosun's Mate Joe Weinstein in Boynton Beach, Florida. I drove over to meet him, and we had a great reunion, reminiscing for a whole day. Joe had been a successful businessman and after he retired became an actor to keep busy. His most famous role was in *The Godfather* as one

of the men involved in the attack on Luca Brasi, the Godfather's body-
guard, when he was murdered by Bruno Tattaglia in the bar.

Like Don Hafner, Joe was eighteen years old when I met him in
Shanghai in 1945 and only seven years older than me. Regrettably,
Petty Officer Clark, the leader of this group of sailors, who was twenty-
two years old at that time, passed away a few years ago and I never got
a chance see him again.

THE NEXT YEAR was one to remember. I was able to return to St.
Francis Xavier College now that the ghetto no longer existed, and I
also served as translator and tour guide for a lot of great US sailors and
soldiers. I managed to keep them out of the most dangerous areas of
Shanghai where they might get into fights or get assaulted, cheated, or
robbed. In return, they usually tipped me three or four US dollars and
gave me canned food from the ship or base. Most importantly, they
provided me with Coca-Cola.

At this point I was the sole breadwinner in my family. It was hard
for my dad to sell jewellery when people were struggling to get food to
survive. People were scrambling for food and medicine; they couldn't
really afford to care about trinkets. The black market in American cigarettes was king—trading in them was the biggest industry in Shanghai
at the time.

Christmas 1945 was very special in more ways than one. I was invited
by the crew of one of the ships anchored a few miles up the river to
spend Christmas Day with them. Most of them were young men with
younger brothers at home and they wanted a feeling of family—I was
the fill-in. Unfortunately, this ship was anchored a few miles outside the
harbour, as most of the US Seventh Fleet was based in Shanghai and
the ships were strung out the length of the Huangpu River.

It was a great day. From the time that I got on board they fed me
turkey with all the trimmings, and lots of Coke, ice cream, fresh fruit,
and rich cake. They also ran movies all day. I remember at least three
them, including *The House on 92nd Street*, a true spy story about German
agents who were dropped off on Long Island by a German submarine
to spy on America. In the evening, we had another turkey dinner with
all the trimmings, with more fruit and ice cream and another movie. I

had never seen so much food in my entire life and consumed a lot of it, especially the turkey and ice cream.

Just when it was time to end that amazing day, we found out that the launch that was supposed to take me back to the Bund and bring sailors back from Christmas leave in Shanghai had broken down. It was finally fixed late in the evening, but by the time I got back to terra firma on the Bund dock it was midnight. I took a rickshaw home and was again met by a hail of head slaps from my mother when I walked into the house. This was her way of showing her relief and her love for me—I discovered that she'd had the Police, Military Police and Navy Shore Patrol looking for me all evening!

Escorting US servicemen and translating for them became almost a full-time job. As a result, I missed a fair amount of school and ended up failing Grade 6.

In February 1946, my beloved grandfather Maxa passed away, and I learned firsthand the meaning of death and the sorrow that comes with a much-loved one passing on. All too soon, however, we would discover that he was the first of many World War II casualties in our family.

On July 16, 1946, one day short of a year since the devastating air raid that hit us, Dad came home and announced that we were heading home to Czechoslovakia via the Suez Canal and France on the US Troop Carrier, the USS *Marine Angel*. The US Navy was taking 976 French citizens back to France and had offered any Czechs who could be ready by 5:00 p.m. the next day a free ride to Toulon, France.

We were limited as to the number of suitcases per person, so in twenty-four hours my parents sold or gave away almost all of our possessions. Dad managed to sell our home for $6,500 US and bought US cigarettes with the proceeds. We packed enough clothing for the trip and my father converted all his remaining cash into more American cigarettes. American cigarettes and nylon stockings were the most important internationally accepted currency in the world after the war and the best currency available in both Europe and Asia other than US dollars. Men would steal for them and women would trade their bodies for them. You could buy anything with them—they paid for rent, food, and alcohol.

The badge of the famous Flying Tiger Fighter Squadron, by then a part of the 23rd US Army Air Corps, that signalled our freedom when they flew over Shanghai on September 3, 1945. It was the most beautiful sight I'd ever seen, and I knew that day that I wanted to fly those airplanes.

The USS Repose, whose wonderful crew I befriended, especially Seaman Clark ("Clarkie"). They did so much to ease my grandfather Maxa's pain before he died.

Former Bosun's Mate Joe Weinstein from the USS Repose. I reunited with him in Boynton Beach, Florida in 2009. After retiring from a successful business career, he became an actor. His biggest role was in The Godfather.

A memorial to seven Holocaust victims at the New Jewish Cemetery in Prague. Included on the stone are my uncle Vilda Kanturek and his parents—my grandparents—Max and Hedvika Kanturek. Among my relatives, only my grandfather, who died in February 1946, is buried in Shanghai.

The plaque for the Hongkou Shanghai ghetto, then called the Restricted Sector for Stateless Refugees. The Shanghai Jewish Refugees Museum is on the site of the former Ohel Moshe or Moishe Synagogue, in the Tilanqiao Historic Area of Hongkou district, Shanghai. Photograph taken in 2012.

The plaque commemorating the Ohel Moshe or Moishe Synagogue at the Shanghai Jewish Refugees Museum. Photograph taken in 2012.

The joint Israel–China memorial to the Shanghai ghetto. Photograph taken in 2012.

My brother, Michael, and me at the Shanghai Jewish Refugees Museum, on the site of the Restricted Sector for Stateless Refugees. Photographs taken in 2012.

7

THE LONG VOYAGE HOME

Aware that a disaster had occurred in Europe, but with no knowledge of the magnitude of the Holocaust that had devastated the Jewish people, we set sail on board the USS *Marine Angel* at 7:00 p.m. on July 17, 1946, for the thirty-day journey back home. After a hectic twenty-four hours, twenty-eight Czechs had been able to join the French evacuees on the voyage. It would take four weeks because we were travelling at eight knots (15 km/h) and the accommodations were certainly not of the calibre of the *Conte Rosso*. Nevertheless, we were all excited to be going home. We had left everything behind except some clothing and two suitcases full of American cigarettes. Happy as we were to be returning to Europe, our feelings were mixed. We were sad to be leaving our homes and the city and the Chinese people who gave us shelter in our time of need, a time when no one else in the world gave a damn about our fate.

THE USS *MARINE Angel* was a troopship designed to carry five thousand fully armed troops in three huge cargo holds, each containing four to six tiers of bunks. Since there were only 1,004 passengers on board, we had lots of room. Meals were served buffet-style in one huge dining room (the mess hall). The men were billeted in the forward hold (the forecastle, or foc'sle in navy terms), couples without children were in the amidships hold, and the mothers and small children were in the rear hold (the fantail). As a young man of twelve, I was in the forecastle with the men.

At approximately 9:00 p.m. on that first evening out, my uncle Ernie Kanturek burst into the hold looking as though he was being chased by a ghost and called all the Czech men together. He told us that he had found three stowaways on board! They were three young Orthodox Jewish men from the famous Yeshiva School in Shanghai who were determined to walk from the Suez Canal across the vast Sinai Desert to Palestine. At that time, most of the Middle East was under British control—Egypt, the Sinai Desert, and Palestine were British Protectorates, and no one could legally enter these territories without British permission.

The three young men had no papers to enter the British Mandate territories, no survival gear, no food, and—most importantly—no water to take on their venture across the Sinai Desert to the Promised Land. They only had their faith to guide and sustain them. Their chances of making it to Palestine were very slim to none, but when Ernie tried to reason with these young fanatics, they told him that if Moses could do it so could they.

We formed a war council and decided that we had to feed these misguided young men for the three weeks it would take to get to the Suez Canal. I didn't have a vote, but as always, my dad was the brains and the leader. Basically, the other Czech men followed his leadership. Everyone volunteered to help in any way they could. Since I had experience with American sailors, my job was to befriend the ship's crew, distract them if necessary so they wouldn't find our stowaways, and help the young men leave the ship. I was very successful in striking up a friendship with the Third Engineer, Sandy from El Paso Texas, whose last name I have regrettably forgotten. This centre of influence was very important to our plan. Sandy was a great guy and proved to be the key to our escape strategy.

Hiding the stowaways was easy—the ship had five thousand bunks and only 1,004 passengers so no one would notice three more. Accordingly, we hid them in plain sight in our section of the forecastle with strict orders to stay away from the crew and our French fellow travellers (who ignored us anyway). We were concerned that the French passengers might turn them in, like the people of France turned in 76,000 French Jews to the Germans. Unfortunately, the yeshiva students stood out like a sore thumb with their long curly sideburns and fedoras. We had to steal their fedoras so that they wouldn't wear them, but they of course still had yarmulkes so we could be sure that God was not offended. Another part of our plan was that a couple of the men would escort our illegal guests up on deck in the evening, after dark to get some fresh air.

The next morning, three stalwart Czechs were first in line in the mess hall and filled their trays with all the goodies that the US Navy had to offer for breakfast. They then snuck down to the forward hold to feed our hungry stowaways. That is when the next problem arose: our travellers refused to eat any of the food because it wasn't kosher! Uncle Ernie tried telling them that he was a rabbi and it was permissible to eat non-kosher food to sustain life in an emergency, but these guys had spent their lives studying the Torah and knew better. To make a long story short, for the next three weeks they ate nothing, but apples and oranges and they spent a lot of time in the toilets. Fortunately, the USS *Marine Angel* had lots of fruit on board as well as toilet facilities for five thousand men.

I had a great voyage because I spent most of the trip with the crew, from the engine room up to the bridge—I'm sorry to say that they wouldn't allow me up in the crow's nest on top of the mast despite my pleas.

After approximately ten days at sea, we had some real drama. A young French woman on board broke her leg and because she had to have a cast on it, the crew provided her with one of the officer's cabins, with room service provided by a young black steward. Even with my close contact with the crew I have no idea what actually happened in her cabin, but she accused the steward of rape.

The Captain took the charge very seriously and threw the young sailor into the brig in the cold, damp bowels of the ship. Not a great place to travel. Once a day his guards would bring him up on deck in handcuffs for an hour to get some fresh air and exercise. He was just a kid himself and looked like a beaten dog. I felt really badly for him because even the other sailors weren't convinced that he was really guilty, but in those days, it was hard for a black man to beat an accusation of assaulting a white woman. It was an era when white men and women were terrified of black men, making it difficult to determine whether an assault had actually taken place.

I thought about that young sailor for many months after the trip and hoped that he had been treated fairly. I hoped that once all the passengers were off the ship, they had let him go since you can't have a trial without an accuser or a witness. My sailor friends thought that this would be the final outcome.

A week after this incident all hell broke loose in the Indian Ocean. For more than two days we were hit by a huge typhoon, with winds of 100-plus miles per hour (160-plus km/h) and fifty-foot (17 metre) waves. Every passenger on board got seasick except me. The crew took me into the crew quarters because the smell below in the passenger decks was horrendous, and my sailor buddies thought that I would get sick just from the stench. I lived and ate with the crew for three days. Once a day they would go on deck with life jackets on and tied together, then attach themselves to the ropes strung together on deck. They took me with them so I could get some fresh air, but I always had to be tied to them with my life jacket on.

On the first day of the storm, I took a meal down to my mother, who took one look at it and threw up. I didn't do that again. That typhoon was one heck of a ride, better than anything at Disney World. After the storm, the crew had a ceremony making me an honorary seaman in the US Navy for surviving the typhoon without getting seasick!

A few days later we arrived in Suez, the port at the southern end of the Suez Canal. It was extremely hot. We had to wait a full day for our turn to head north and after that it would take another day to reach Port Said at the northern end of the canal. Most of the sailors decided it was time to go swimming and took turns diving approximately thirty feet (10 metres) off the gangplank platform into the dirty brown water on the port (left) side of the ship. None of the passengers joined them, but they did gather on that side to watch the show. Besides sharks, there was also the danger of cholera and typhoid—we hadn't survived World War II in China for nothing: we had learned all about the dangers of contaminated water. We didn't need any advice about the danger of sharks either!

The trip through the Canal was great. It is very narrow, and ships' speeds are limited in order not to collapse the sand berms that form the canal's banks. Fortunately, the USS *Marine Angel* could only do about eight knots (15 km/h), so there was no danger of speeding. It took most of the day to reach Port Said. The crew of the USS *Marine Angel* again took turns diving into the brackish Suez Canal off the left side of the ship.

Now that we were at the north end of the canal, the real drama would begin! My dad hired an Egyptian boatman to take our stowaways ashore, so they could follow Moses to the Promised Land, on foot just like him. With no food, three bottles of water, and dressed as if they were going to synagogue, these religious zealots were about to start a journey of hundreds of kilometres across the Sinai Desert, through hostile Arab Bedouin territory and British Occupation Forces. They were both very brave and very stupid, and the only way they would have made it was if Moses came back to lead them.

Luckily, my buddy Third Engineer Sandy was the Officer of the Deck that day, which meant that he was the acting Captain for the day. My job was to keep him occupied on the port side of the ship while the dozen Czech men surrounded our stowaways and guided them to the starboard (right) side of the ship where our hired boat man was waiting. I was successful in keeping Sandy interested watching his fellow crewmen diving off the gang plank.

Our escape crew threw a rope overboard and the first two successfully made it into the boat, but the third one was a real klutz—he lost his grip and fell into the Suez Canal with a huge splash. Fortunately, no one noticed, and they pulled him into the boat. Then our intrepid bribed boatman headed straight for the British police station on shore, where he got paid a second time for turning the stowaways over to them! The twelve Czech men watched in awe at this betrayal but couldn't do anything about it. All they could do was accept that this was the way things were done in the Middle East.

We later found out that our plucky stowaways ended up in a British camp on Cyprus and finally got to Israel along with all the internees on Cyprus two years later when Israel was declared independent by the United Nations. This was a far better fate than they would have met if they had tried to walk across the Sinai Desert facing hunger, dehydration, and Bedouin bandits. They actually owed their lives to the double-dealing Egyptian boatman and twelve brave Czechs!

Five days later, we arrived in Toulon, France and stepped on European soil for the first time in more than six years. The French Refugee Organization provided buses to take us to a Displaced Persons Camp until we could return to Czechoslovakia. We were offered accommodation in a giant but very clean hall with a couple of hundred camp cots. Needless to say, there was no privacy.

The accommodation had the required facilities, but this was not good enough for my dad. He took a look around and said, "My family is not staying here!" We picked up our suitcases (including the two full of American cigarettes) and headed for the main gate. We caught a taxi (which cost us two American cigarettes) to the railway station and took the first train to Marseilles. The twenty-four other Czechs followed us like a bunch of sheep. Dad must have felt like Moses himself!

I was very proud of my dad; this quiet little man had again proven that he was a leader for the second time in a month. Mom called him Moses (leading his family and friends out of danger), and she was right. Through their courage and foresight, Mom and Dad had saved fourteen lives and were now leading twenty-eight Czechs home.

We arrived in Marseilles and headed for a small hotel that could accommodate the Czech invasion. We spent a week in Marseilles waiting for train reservations to Paris, where a Czech government evacuation train would take us the rest of the way home.

Marseilles was a marvellous city in 1946, a busy port, full of great history, cheap food and lodging, and a friendly population. The four of us—Dad, Mom, Vera, and I—lived there for a week on one carton of American cigarettes, which my mom sold on the black market. She was afraid to let Dad deal with the black marketers for fear that he would be robbed; she felt a woman and a young boy would be safer (assuming that even criminals had a code of honour). Therefore, I became a lookout while she did the selling of those horrible weeds.

One beautiful, sunny afternoon, we were having lunch in an outdoor restaurant when my Mother's ultra-sensitive ears picked up the Czech language being spoken at another table. Sitting there were about a dozen young people conversing in Czech! Mom went over and spoke to them, then came back with some startling information. These kids (sixteen to eighteen years old) were Czech Jewish concentration camp survivors; they told her about how they had survived the death camps and gave us the first eyewitness account of the horrors of the concentration camps. They also told her that the Communists would take over Czechoslovakia within two years (they were wrong, it only took eighteen months). These young people said that they were intent on breaking the British Blockade of Palestine—they were determined to settle there because they were convinced that Europe didn't want any Jews. All Jews seeking safety, they said, should go straight to Palestine. Dad's response was, "No, we are going home! That is where I can make a living."

My most memorable experience in Marseilles was our trip to Chateau d'If with its terrifying fortress prison in the harbour. This visit had a major effect on me. This was the prison where the Count of Monte Cristo was allegedly imprisoned and from which he escaped. I was so taken with the story that I asked my parents to buy me Alexandre Dumas' book and when they gave it to me, I didn't just read it, I memorized it! I learned two things from that book—to always have courage and to remember that revenge is best served cold. Never threaten anyone; just nail the offender when he least expects it.

There were three other books that strongly affected me in later life and they were all about France—*Les Misérables* by Victor Hugo, *A Tale of Two Cities* by Charles Dickens, and *Scaramouche* by Rafael Sabatini. These books taught me about toughness, fairness, perseverance, humour, irony, generosity, courage, unconditional love, sacrifice, justifiable revenge, and to never be a victim. French and English literature helped shape my life, and I am eternally grateful to the authors because reading these works made me a better man and taught me to treat others the way I wanted to be treated. I loved the story of *Les Misérables* so much that I have seen the stage play seven times and hope to see it again at the next opportunity. To this day, I have a copy of these books on my iPad.

At the end of the week in Marseilles we headed for the train to Paris. The railway station was in chaos; we had waited a week for reservations that now appeared to be worthless as a huge crowd mobbed the train when it pulled into the station. My mother led the charge and twenty-eight Czechs swarmed all over the six-seat compartments and filled two of them with Czech humanity and all our luggage! The poor French people in the two compartments didn't stand a chance against this Czech onslaught. When we invaded their compartments, babbling in Czech and piling up baggage, then sitting on top of it, they fled!

Imagine twenty-eight people with their entire worldly possessions jammed into two compartments designed for twelve. I couldn't handle it and escaped into the corridor outside, which, of course, was also full. At least I could stand up there. It was an all-night trip to Paris and I was able to sleep standing up most of the way because the corridor was so crowded that I couldn't possibly fall over. That is where I learned to catnap whenever I was tired.

We arrived in Paris the next morning, found another small hotel, and then Mom and I went to the black market and sold another carton of American cigarettes. That was all we needed for our Paris stay—two cartons of cigarettes had paid the living expenses for four people living for two weeks in France in 1946.

My parents had never been to Paris and therefore Mom decided that we had to do the tourist routine and see all the cultural sites there in one week. We visited the Eiffel Tower, the Louvre, the Place de la Concorde, the Arc de Triomphe, Notre Dame Cathedral, the Sorbonne, Versailles, and almost every other well-known cultural site.

Finally, it was time to go home. The Czech government sent a train with an armed military escort to bring us home through a still unfriendly Germany. The passengers were several hundred Czechs returning from Latin America plus our small Czech group from China. We were escorted by four heavily armed Czech soldiers.

Travelling through a destroyed Germany was a very enjoyable experience—this was certainly revenge served cold. Watching the Germans removing bricks and wreckage and begging for food from us en route felt really good after their rape and massacre of Europe. These people had set out to conquer the world and destroy the Jewish people and now their women and children were struggling just to survive. To this day, I don't feel guilty about my reaction then; they deserved what they got and most members of that generation, with a few exceptions like Oskar Schindler, were responsible for these horrible crimes.

We arrived in Prague's Wilson Station, where we were met by the three family survivors: Arnost and Lotte Suk (Nellie Schwartz's sister), who had survived the concentration camps, and Helena Grossova (the widow of Mom's cousin Army Sergeant Franta Gross, who did not survive Auschwitz-Birkenau). These were the only relatives who had survived; sixty-five relatives did not. Helena had survived a horrible death march ahead of the advancing Red Army and weighed only thirty-five kilos (77 pounds) when she was rescued by US troops at the end of April 1945. The brutality of the Nazi guards knew no limits during the last few days before liberation; among other indignities, the death marchers were forced to survive on cow dung.

We finally land on European soil. Left to right: Vera; Eva Wintrova (Winter); Litka Wintrova; Rudla Wintrova; and me. Marseille, 1946.

On the right is my mother's cousin Sergeant Franta Gross. He was captured while fighting with the Czech army and, instead of being interned in a POW camp, he was sent to a concentration camp because he was Jewish. He survived a death march near the end of the war, but died in hospital not long after liberation. In the centre is his wife, Helena Grossova. Following her internment in a concentration camp, she also survived a death march, weighing only 35 kilos (77 pounds) at liberation. On the left is my grandmother, Hedvika Kanturek, who fled with us to Shanghai and immigrated with us to Canada.

8

HOME, A COUP D'ÉTAT, AND ANOTHER GREAT ESCAPE

We moved into the Astor Hotel, again using American cigarettes as currency. An apartment in Prague was difficult to
find and almost impossible to secure. To get around those
difficulties, my dad placed a want ad in the newspapers for an apartment, stating that price was no obstacle—all those American cigarettes
probably made him feel rich. The same day it appeared we got a two-
room apartment at 30 Ovenecka Ulice in the very nice district of Letná.
There was only one catch: we had no kitchen because our new landlady
had converted it into her own quarters. So our bathroom, with the addition of a hot plate, did double duty: we used it for both bathing and
cooking. And the bathtub, along with bathing, also served to hold the
live carp before my mother cooked them; it was one of her favourite
foods. The two-piece bathroom—bathtub and toilet in separate small
rooms—had to serve the sanitary needs of the four of us (not to mention
the cooking!). Toilet paper was not available right after the war, so we
made do with newspapers.

The apartment was a little tight, but it was reasonably comfortable.
There was no telephone, but with a bribe to someone at the national
telephone company, we managed to get one. My grandsons all have
iPhones, iPods, and iPads, but I didn't see that first telephone until I
was twelve years old.

Food was still scarce and was rationed on a per capita basis. For
breakfast every morning, I had to line up at the bakery across the street
at 6:00 a.m. for our ration of four rolls (one per person and no butter).

The food rationing was probably why we ate so much damn carp; we bought it directly from local fishermen and it wasn't rationed.

My mom was very insistent that I go into Grade 7 in a Czech school, even though I had never been to a Czech school and had failed Grade 6 at St. Francis Xavier in Shanghai. As usual, Mom was very persistent, and the school principal never had a chance. So, needless to say, I found myself in Grade 7, studying unfamiliar subjects in an unfamiliar environment (history, geography, math—which used metric in place of English measurements—and, of course, literature and spelling).

One day as I was boarding the streetcar to go home from school, one of my classmates yelled, "Goodnight, China!" A man boarding the same streetcar asked my friend why he had called me China and my friend replied, "It's his nickname because he just came from there." The man, who turned out to be a Boy Scout leader, caught up to me and asked if I had ever been a Boy Scout. When I responded in the affirmative, he asked me whether I was willing to do an interview for the Czech Boy Scout magazine. Wow! Twelve years old and I was going to be interviewed for an article about Boy Scouts in China. I was going to be famous, so how could I refuse?

In the article, the author described me as a member of the only Czech Scout Troop in China, and probably the only Czech youth my age who was fluent in Chinese. He gave my account of the Japanese attack on December 8, 1941, and the Japanese occupation thereafter. He also included the fact that my dad wanted me to train in Belgium and become a diamond cutter. I was too respectful of my dad to argue or publicly contradict him about my future, but I would have rather joined the circus and become a tightrope walker without a net (and I was afraid of heights) than a diamond cutter.

IT WAS SOON after our return to Prague that we learned the details of my paternal grandparents' horrible fate. We were told that they had first been sent by cattle car from Theresienstadt concentration camp, a "model" concentration camp used to corral Czech Jews and show a benign face of the Third Reich to the International Red Cross. Catherine and I visited it in 2013. From there, they were sent to Treblinka, Poland, a notorious death camp.

Upon their arrival in Treblinka, my grandparents and their fellow prisoners were herded into a field and ordered to dig their own graves. Imagine, two elderly people in their sixties, who had never done any manual labour, being forced to dig their own graves in hard soil. When they finished their ghoulish task, they were ordered to strip naked, so their clothes could be sent to people in Germany, then they were shot in the back of the head and pushed into their own freshly dug graves. And why were they so brutally murdered? Because they had made the horrible mistake of being born Jewish.

When my dad heard about these gruesome events, he said, "There is no God! I never even saw my mother in her underwear and those bastards saw her naked!" That day my father renounced God and religion, and I did the same. I could not worship a deity that would permit such obscene brutality.

Many years later, in the fall of 2002, Catherine and I visited Auschwitz-Birkenau. The original part of Auschwitz (Auschwitz I) had been used primarily as a prison camp, while Auschwitz II (Birkenau) was deliberately designed and built to be used as a mass death camp. While we were there, we learned the details of the brutal murders of one and a half million innocents including Uncle Armin and Aunt Greta Knopfelmacher, and their nine-year-old son, my cousin Harry, who was born the same day as I. They had arrived at the death camp at Birkenau on December 18, 1943, jammed into a freezing cattle car with dozens of others after a three-day trip from the Theresienstadt concentration camp. They too were forced to strip naked, then herded into the gas chambers, where they took approximately fifteen minutes to die. Their bodies were removed by *Sonderkommandos*, fellow Jewish prisoners who were forced to do this dirty work for three months until they too ended up in the same gas chambers and taken to the ovens for cremation. Before being consigned to the crematorium, their bodies were stripped of any valuables; even their gold teeth were removed and added to the Nazi riches in Switzerland (the Nazis' enthusiastic enablers).

Despite steeling ourselves for the horror of Auschwitz-Birkenau, nothing could prepare a decent human being for this nightmare. Nothing can prepare you for the torture chambers or the execution courtyard, the gas chambers and ovens, the descriptions of the medical experiments of Dr. Mengele in the "hospital." Nothing can erase the memory of one room filled with the victims' eyeglasses; another with battered suitcases; another with the discarded artificial limbs and wheelchairs of the helpless victims.

What kind of animals could inflict these atrocities on innocent fellow humans? So many of these criminals escaped justice by making deals with the victors, the Vatican, or Latin American countries in exchange for money or information. The survivors' cries for justice have been too often ignored and now, with the passage of time, those cries are fading away as the survivors succumb to age and death. Where was the loving and all-merciful God that we hear about on every Sabbath (Jewish, Christian and Muslim)?

Catherine and I spent approximately four hours at the two camps, which was all that we could take; the horror still lingers in the air sixty years after the fact. Even now, when I close my eyes, I can smell the burning flesh. I was devastated, and Catherine was in total shock as she witnessed the horrible crimes against humanity that were committed while she was growing up in Canada. She did everything she could to keep me reasonably calm and, fortunately, she had help from our good taxi driver. Seeing our distress, he offered to take us to a magnificent Roman Catholic Cathedral on the other side of Cracow. The longest operating salt mine in the world, the Wieliczka salt mine dating back to the thirteenth century and operated as a working mine until the twentieth century. Inside, a massive series of underground chapels, complete with altars, statuary, and chandeliers—now known as the Underground Salt Cathedral of Poland—was carved out of the rock salt more than five hundred metres below ground by the generations of Polish miners who worked there. Seeing this spectacular work of dedicated humans who were building instead of destroying made our day tolerable.

If there is a God, where the hell was he when millions of innocents were tortured and slaughtered in the German death camps? If there is a God who is so cruel as to permit this kind of pitiless and barbaric savagery, I do not wish to worship him. Where was God when "His Chosen People" were slaughtered? Probably the same place as Pope Pius XII, who watched from his Vatican windows as Italian Jews were rounded up and shipped to the gas chambers of Auschwitz-Birkenau.

Pope Benedict XVI, at the same time that he prepared to canonize Pope Pius XII, finally declared that "the Jewish people are not responsible for the death of Jesus Christ." Isn't that nice? After two thousand years of vicious antisemitism, he finally admitted that the Jewish people did not kill one of their own. After all, Jesus Christ was a Jew, not a Roman Catholic. There was no "Christian religion" at the time of his crucifixion. He was executed by the Roman Legionnaires under Pontius Pilate—who was certainly NOT a Jew—most likely because Christ was a charismatic Jewish leader and a threat to the Roman hegemony. Yet for two thousand years Roman Catholics blamed the Jews for his death, fanning the flames of antisemitism and hatred that culminated in the Holocaust that cost millions of innocent people their lives, including most of our family.

To make matters worse, the Vatican assisted thousands of Nazi war criminals to escape justice after World War II, helping them get to Latin America, where they paid off the local dictators with the loot stolen from their victims. But all is well—Pope Pius XII is now a saint of the Roman Catholic Church, regardless of his complicity with Hitler and his war criminals, and the assistance that the Vatican provided to allow Nazi murderers to escape justice in Latin America.

Ultimately, I cannot believe there is a God when the greatest wars and crimes against humanity in history have been committed in God's name from the Crusades to the modern-day jihad. Even now, in the twenty-first century, fanatics are blowing up innocent people in the name of their God. Sunni and Shia Muslims both slaughter each other in the name of Allah and their particular sect, the violence fanned by religious zealots. "God" is a handy fall-guy for the inhumanity of man to man (women are rarely the instigators).

ON APRIL 16, 1947, my aunt Liza married Captain Franta Vilim, a Czech army veteran who had escaped to Great Britain in 1939 and was then sent to join a Czech infantry regiment based in Russia as a company commander. The Czech forces in Russia fought under Russian command all the way back to Prague through the Ukraine and Slovakia.

When Captain Vilim reached Slovakia with his unit, he heard about the horrors of Auschwitz and Birkenau. The death camp was not far from where he was based and had just been liberated by the Soviet Red Army. He immediately took a three-day leave and drove a Jeep to the remains of the camp, where, to his amazement, he found his nephew, his sister's sixteen-year-old son, alive. He learned that his sister had died there and that the rest of his entire family had been wiped out except for this nephew and his niece in Theresienstadt. Franta took his nephew and a friend back to the Czech base, dressed them in Czech army uniforms and made them orderlies. They accompanied him all the way to Prague and liberation—he was not about to lose the boys so close to the end of the war.

IN THE POSTWAR era, the Czech parliament was split four ways, among the Communists, the Social Democrats (Socialists), the National Socialists (Conservatives), and the People's Party (Liberals). The four parties in the Czech coalition government, led by the Communist leader Clément Gottwald, were almost equal in strength, but the Communist representation was slightly higher than that of the other parties. Despite a non-Communist majority, however, the other three parties spent more time fighting each other in hopes of increasing their representation in the next election than fighting their common enemy—the Communist Party that was directed from afar by Joseph Stalin.

The non-Communist leaders knew that the Communist vote was solid, so the only way to increase their vote in the coming May 1948 elections was to steal it from the other anti-Communist parties. In their thirst to govern, these anti-Communist parties—representing 75 per cent of the population—took their eyes off the ball. While they were bickering amongst themselves, the minority Communists were preparing a coup d'état. By putting their own party's interests ahead of the welfare of the country, the Social Democrats, the National Socialists, and the People's Party were all complicit in the Communist seizure of power.

In mid-February 1948, the Czech police uncovered two huge weapons depots belonging to the Czech Communist Party. There was a national uproar, but instead of arresting the Communist plotters, the anti-Communists resigned from the government en masse on Friday, February 23, 1948, assuming that this would trigger an immediate election in which the Communists would be soundly defeated. They all had complete faith in the democratic process and expected Prime Minister Gottwald and the Communist cabinet members to resign as well. How naïve! Prime Minister Clément Gottwald was not a democrat; he was 100 per cent in the Communist camp and had a surprise in store for the people of Czechoslovakia. To the Communists, the end always justified the means; playing by the rules was an alien concept to them. The Communists did not resign; they stayed in power and filled the vacant Cabinet seats with their own henchmen. Essentially, they were now the government.

On Sunday, February 25, 1948, I went downtown to see a movie in at the Luxor Theatre just off Václavské náměstí, Wenceslas Square, Prague's main boulevard. The movie was over at approximately 3:30 p.m., and as I walked toward the boulevard, I saw a large crowd on the street ahead of me. I pushed to the front of the throng and saw hundreds of Czech Communist militiamen marching up the boulevard wearing red armbands and carrying brand-new rifles with unvarnished stocks. At the age of fourteen, I witnessed the second occupation of Prague in eight years. This time, however, we were not being occupied by an enemy force but by our own traitorous countrymen representing a foreign power.

This coup d'état had been brought forward due to the discovery of the weapons depots and the resignation of the non-Communist members of the Czech government. Two weeks later, Jan Masaryk, the son of the founder of Czechoslovakia and the country's very popular Foreign Minister allegedly committed suicide. Although it was never conclusively established—the police doctor who ruled Masaryk's death a suicide himself died an apparent suicide a few weeks later—most Czechs had no doubt that Jan Masaryk was murdered by Communist thugs who threw him out of his own apartment window.

The scheduled election was held in May 1948, but it was neither fair nor free. Secret ballots were not allowed; people marked their vote on top of a desk in the open and had to hand their ballots to the Communist goon acting as a scrutineer. He or she would inspect it and then place it into the ballot box. In other words, the Communist Party knew whom everyone had voted for!

Gusta Mrachek, the son of our building superintendent on Ovenecká ulice, and I were close friends. We were in the same class and played soccer together; we were inseparable. We were also politically compatible in our hatred of the Czech Communists. My buddy Gusta and I spent the day going to polling stations and harassing the goons running the show. To this day I don't know why we weren't beaten or arrested. However, we had to make a few quick escapes to avoid mayhem. This was our way of protesting the coup and the phony election that followed.

ONCE THE COMMUNISTS had seized power, my parents decided that it was time to emigrate again—easier said than done. Like the Soviets, the new regime sealed the borders and it was very difficult—if not impossible—to leave legally. Among other restrictions, all emigrants had to pay an "education tax"—that is, to compensate the Czech (now Communist) government for the emigrant's years of free education—before they could even apply. Their passports needed to be signed by the Minister of Finance, certifying that all of their debts (including schooling) had been paid to the government. We also needed documents showing that another country was willing to accept us before we could leave, which put us back into the same situation that we'd been in during World War II: no one wanted us. We couldn't get an immigration visa from any of the countries that we applied to. We were forced into subterfuge.

Dad owned a jewellery store in Karlovy Vary, a famous spa resort, which was managed by his partner, Uncle Ernie Kanturek. As it turned out, the store's one female employee, Louise Deutsch, became our conduit out of Czechoslovakia and into Canada. Her sister, who worked at the Canadian consulate in Prague, introduced Dad to the Consul General, Mr. Irwin, and through him, we got three-month Canadian visitor visas for the entire family. Now came the hard part—getting exit visas signed by the Czech Minister of Finance.

Dad had an old friend and schoolmate, Jan Pachl, who was a wealthy heir to one of Czechoslovakia's largest chocolate manufacturers. Mr. Pachl, who wasn't Jewish, had hidden a leading Jewish Communist, Otto Fishl, from the Nazis on his country estate during the war. Fortunately, when we were trying to get our exit documents, Jan Pachl and his family were also trying to get out of the country. Mr. Pachl went to see Otto Fishl, the man whose life he had saved during World War II; as luck would have it, Fishl was now the Communist Minister of Finance. Mr. Pachl got his exit visa certified and signed and then requested that Mr. Fishl also sign our family's exit visas, which he did for all the twelve members of our family who had survived the war.

Unfortunately, Otto Fishl later got caught up in a purge and show trial of Czech Jewish Communists that emulated the infamous "Doctors' Plot" in which Joseph Stalin accused a group of mainly Jewish doctors of having participated in the murder of a leading member of the Soviet General Committee. Along with eleven other Communist Jews, Fishl was executed on December 2, 1952. We were very lucky to have escaped four years earlier, before the Communists turned on their Jewish friends. History repeats itself, when any government anywhere in the world has problems—they usually turn against the Jewish people first.

ON JUNE 10, 1948, we again boarded a train at Wilson Station in Prague to start our second trip into exile, safety, and freedom. On board that train bound for Brussels were eight passengers—our family of four; my mother's sister, Liza; her new husband, Franta Vilim; their six-month-old daughter, Helenka; and our grandmother Hedvika Kanturek.

Six hours later we arrived at the Czech border city of Cheb, where it took the Czech border guards more than six hours to search a train with eight passengers. They went over us with a fine-tooth comb, but they did not find my mother's jewellery hidden in the pillow that my eleven-year-old sister, Vera, was sleeping on or the jewellery that Mom was wearing in plain sight. Finally, the whistle sounded, and the train started to slowly move toward West Germany and freedom. This was great for us, but sadly my friend Gusta ended up as a political prisoner in a Czech uranium mine. To my knowledge he never came back.

Those last two hundred metres (650 feet) to the West German border seemed to take an eternity. At last, there was a squeal of brakes and the train ground to a halt. A tall African-American Military Police Sergeant boarded our car and announced in a booming voice, "Welcome to freedom, folks! Is there anything that I can get for you?" Having survived two years in Czechoslovakia without a Coca-Cola, I asked for one. (Wouldn't that make a great ad?) The sergeant replied, "You got it, son!" and he got it for me! It really tasted great—freedom and my first Coke in two years. My withdrawal symptoms ended immediately.

We travelled through a still-devastated Germany to Brussels, where the Vilim family left us and headed to Canada via Amsterdam. We spent two days in Belgium while my dad retrieved some jewellery from professional smugglers who had brought it out of Czechoslovakia for him—for 25 per cent of the value. We then continued on to London, where we spent a week before proceeding to Liverpool for our sea voyage to New York on the luxury liner MS *Britannic*.

Since my dad had been able to pay the fare in Czech crowns, we travelled in first-class. He hadn't been allowed to exchange the crowns for US dollars in Czechoslovakia and no one wanted them in the free world, but Cunard was happy to accept them. There is nothing like going into exile in first-class style, even if you arrive poor. My grandmother had a ball—food was served twenty-four hours a day and she didn't miss a single sitting. She made up for five years of forced dieting in Shanghai in five days.

We arrived in New York and sailed past the beautiful Statue of Liberty, then were processed through Ellis Island. We quickly moved on to New York City because we were in transit and not staying in the US. My parents contacted my dad's brother Frank Vinson (he Anglicized his name when he immigrated to the US) and we had a great family reunion with him and his wife, Vlasta.

This reunion ended a family feud regarding Uncle Franta's supposed unwillingness to help his parents—my grandparents—escape the Holocaust. They resolved the situation by blaming their other brother, Uncle Egon (he was also innocent), who had escaped to Chile! Aren't families great? There always has to be a scapegoat. You can solve one problem by creating another. In fact, the truth was, as I've said, that my grandparents wouldn't leave Czechoslovakia without their beloved daughter, Greta.

My Grade 7 class after our return to Czechoslovakia.
I'm in the front row, third from the left. Prague, 1947.

MALÝ ČESKÝ CHLAPEC,

který vykonal velikou cestu

Odjezd do ciziny v roce 1940

Japonci přicházejí...

Nálet na Šanghaj

A zase Američané!

Nejkrásnější chvíle Milanova života

Návrat domů

Jaké jsou tvoje plány do budoucna

My interview for Boy Scout Magazine at age twelve. The author described me as a member of the only Czech Scout troop in China, and probably the only Czech youth my age who was fluent in Chinese. He gave my account of the Japanese attack on December 8, 1941, and the Japanese occupation thereafter. Published in Prague, 1947.

9

MONTREAL, FRENCH CANADA, AND REDEMPTION

O ur destination was supposed to be Toronto, Ontario, but while we were in New York, a friend of my parents from Shanghai, Baruch Petranker (a high-rolling blowhard, whom I never trusted or liked), called from Montreal and convinced my dad that we should go to Montreal instead. As far as he was concerned, Montreal was the only city in Canada worth living in. That would have been great, except for three things:

1. My dad would have had more opportunities in Toronto because there were more European immigrants to deal with.
2. Toronto real estate outperformed Montreal's by approximately five to one in the next thirty years.
3. Mr. Petranker moved to San Francisco three weeks after we arrived in Montreal, never to be heard from again. He left us to fend for ourselves. With a friend like that, who needs enemies?

To top it all off, Dad didn't know that he could get a refund on the Montreal-Toronto portion of the train tickets and therefore did not redeem them. Because there were no refunds in Europe in those days, Dad didn't ask for it. The CNR still owes us!

We arrived in Montreal's Central Station on the morning of July 1, 1948; we joined Confederation on Canada Day, one year ahead of Newfoundland. Montreal, the second-largest French-speaking city in the world, was bedecked in British Union Jacks. When we met

Canadians, their first question to us was "What religion are you?" After years of persecution and still in fear, we denied being Jewish.

My first question to Canadians was "Don't you have your own flag?" Their answer was simple: "Of course we do. We have the Union Jack!"

As someone who grew up believing in my country, my flag, and my national anthem, I was startled to discover that Canada had no national anthem or flag. The country used the British national anthem, "God Save the Queen," and the British Maritime flag of a Union Jack on a red field—it was the same flag used by the British Merchant Marine.

I could not believe that French-Canadians, who made up a third of the country, did not demand a flag and an anthem of their own. It took them another ten years to ask the same question and when they did, in the late 1950s, the seeds of the Quiet Revolution were sown. The movement towards secularization and political realignment blossomed under Jean Lesage, premier from 1960 to 1966, and generated the Quebec separatist movement led by René Lévesque. Along with a determination to break the Roman Catholic Church's grip on the francophone population, the desire for major changes to Quebec society was fuelled by the many indignities that French-Canadians suffered from their English-Canadian "masters." When the Canadian National Railway (CNR) opened a luxury hotel at Central Station in 1958, in the heart of Montreal, and named it the Queen Elizabeth Hotel, that was one insult too many. Even in my early twenties, I was disgusted by the insensitivity of the stupid Anglo establishment.

We crossed Dorchester Boulevard—now named René Lévesque Boulevard—and walked diagonally across Dominion Square to a small hotel, the Bell Lodge Inn, where the five of us checked in for eleven dollars a night; today there is a huge Sheraton Hotel on the site and rooms run to three hundred dollars a night.

Dad had USD$3,000 to start a new life in Canada. He had to pay half of it to a Liberal party–connected lawyer in Ottawa to change our visitor visas to immigration visas and permanent residence. The balance, together with the jewellery he had brought with him, was all there was for us to live on and to start Dad's business.

Two weeks after our arrival, we were in our own apartment on Ridgevale Street in the Côte des Neiges neighbourhood and the next day, I had my first job delivering the daily *Montreal Gazette* on two routes. I had a total of 110 customers and was earning the princely sum of five cents per customer per week plus meagre tips from the more generous of them.

A week later, I had another job, working Fridays after school and all-day Saturday for the Steinberg grocery chain as a wrapper at forty cents per hour. Six months later, I got a five cent per hour raise and was promoted to the vegetable and fruit departments. I wasn't a vegetarian, but it was obviously my duty to eat all the fruit that I could without getting sick. In September, I started Grade 9 at West Hill High School (WHHS).

Dad, with my uncle Franta Vilim as his partner, opened European Art Jewellery on Mountain Street—around the corner and two blocks from Peoples Credit Jewellers, a large Canadian jewellery chain. He did no market research and probably didn't even know what it was. While Peoples was selling jewellery and watches for one dollar down and one dollar per week—and collecting kickbacks from the finance company that charged the suckers 29 per cent interest—my dad was trying to sell jewellery the European way—for cash with no credit facilities. As a result, my dad ended up with a large unsellable inventory.

In December 1948, Uncle Ernie Kanturek left Karlovy Vary and showed up in the immigration prison in Halifax with his wife, Hilda, and their daughters, Eva and Jana. They were in jail because Ernie was afraid to tell Canadian immigration that he had USD$3,000 cash on him. He thought that Canada was like Czechoslovakia and he would be arrested for smuggling; he didn't realize that all that he had to do was to declare the funds. But once he had already denied having any funds, he couldn't change his story. Therefore, my dad borrowed USD$3,000 from his brother Frank Vinson in New York and went to Halifax to bail out the Kantureks. The family was released from jail and the money was sent back to Uncle Frank.

European Art Jewellery was not doing well and Uncle Franta left to become partners with Bill Klusachek in the manufacture and sales of ladies' hats. This proved to be a highly successful venture, as no respectable woman would go anywhere without a hat in those days. Over the next fifty years they built a great successful and diversified business. I did not like or trust Bill Klusachek and in later life he proved me right.

The jewellery store lasted eighteen months, and closed with CAD$1,500 in debts, which my dad repaid over two years. He didn't know that when you went bankrupt in Canada, you didn't have to repay all of your debts; he was a man of great courage and honour. My dad was the gentlest, nicest, and most honest man I have ever met. His biggest weakness in business was that he was not mean enough; he always paid his debts but did not always collect what was owed to him.

IN THE MIDST of the brewing family financial crisis, on October 12, 1949, a surprise package arrived at St. Mary's Hospital on Lacombe Avenue in Montreal—his name was Michael Peter Harry Voticky. He had been conceived to ensure that the Canadian government would have great difficulty deporting our family (who were still on visitor visas) if my parents had a child with Canadian citizenship. Mike was our anchor baby and our parents' response to the antisemites in the Canadian government and civil service who truly believed, as Irving Abella and Harold Troper documented, that when it came to Jews, "none is too many."

The bad news was that Michael was another mouth to feed; the good news was that he was satisfied with mother's milk and Mom got a baby bonus cheque of twelve dollars a month from the federal government. In order to survive, our family had to take extreme measures in the summer of 1950. Mom took in sewing that she could do while looking after the new baby and Dad got a job selling Swiss and German chocolates to immigrant delicatessen owners.

MY FRIENDS AT West Hill High School, had great difficulty pronouncing my name and tagged me as "Luigi the little immigrant" after the popular radio program *Life with Luigi*. My friend Sonny Evans cut the name down to Lou and, since I preferred it to Milan, it has stuck with me ever since.

We had two Europeans on the school junior soccer team—Malcolm Hughes, a British lad, and me. Because we were the most experienced soccer players on the team, we were, of course, the stars, not necessarily through great ability, but just through experience. We were good enough that the senior team used to bring us up for games to help them out. One of my teammates on the senior team was Kenny Burnham, who in later life worked with me as an Air Canada Pilot, was a fellow member at the Summerlea Golf and Country Club, and also became a client of mine in business.

I also played goalie for the Côte des Neiges Midgets, Juveniles, and Junior "C" hockey teams. I ended up as the goalie because I was the worst skater on the team and had experience playing that position in soccer. When we finished playing Juvenile hockey at age nineteen, our options were to either quit playing the sport or form our own team. No one would do it for us. This was my first crack at organization—we all chipped in the registration fee and I approached the NHL Montreal Canadiens to sponsor us, which they happily did at the price of signing ourselves to a "C" contract with their team forever. Luckily, none of us were good enough for them to really want us. Their sponsorship consisted of fifteen old Canadiens sweaters; no skates, pants, shoulder pads, gloves, pucks, or even old sticks. We had to provide these ourselves, but we were the Côte des Neiges Junior "C" Canadiens! I wish that I'd kept my sweater; it would be worth a lot today and my grandsons would love it.

I also found time to play soccer for the Montreal Maccabees senior team. I was a reasonably good athlete because I worked very hard, not because I had a lot of talent. I practiced a lot and most of all, I never quit—you could knock me down, but you couldn't keep me down! The dressing room was a babble of languages—just like Babylon.

I got a job for the summer of 1950 as a counsellor at Camp Lewis, a camp for underprivileged children from the slums of Griffintown and Point St. Charles in Montreal. These were tough, streetwise kids right up to my age of sixteen. I was responsible for a cabin of twelve of these kids and, while the majority of them were good kids, one fifteen-year-old (we'll call him Punk) was a problem. He thought he was a tough guy and he was certainly a bad influence.

One day, I caught half my campers smoking a cigarette behind our cabin and asked the one holding the cigarette to give it to me. He started to pass it to me when Punk said, "Give it to me." The scared thirteen-year-old did as he was told. Punk put the cigarette into his mouth, sucked in the smoke deeply, then blew it right into my face. The smokescreen was great—he never saw my right cross headed for his big mouth. He went down as if he had been drilled by Rocky Marciano (the undefeated World Heavyweight Boxing Champion at that time), and immediately burst into tears. He wasn't as tough as he thought he was.

Naturally "tough guy" reported me and I was called in by the camp director. I was advised that my behaviour was not acceptable and if I did it again, job action would be taken against me. I told this dumb bleeding-heart social worker that Punk was terrorizing the other kids in the cabin, but he would not get away with it again as long as I was there. Then I told the camp director that I really did not wish to be part of his social experiment and I was quitting. They gave me a bus ticket back to Montreal but didn't pay me as I hadn't stayed for the season. The pay was only five dollars a week plus room and board, so I didn't lose much. This was the beginning of the era where Canadian justice was overrun by bleeding hearts and social workers, and criminals were mollycoddled instead of punished. Convicts today only serve one-sixth of their sentences in Canada as long as they behave—there is no truth in sentencing. I had no desire to be part of it even at the age of sixteen.

I had just finished Grade 9 and started looking for a full-time job for the rest of the summer to help out my family. When I got back to Montreal, I got a four-day-a-week job delivering ladies' hats all over Montreal for French Feather and Flower, Uncle Franta Vilim's company, and another two-day-a-week job working for Steinberg's grocery chain. I worked this six-day, fifty-two-hour schedule for a total of twenty-two dollars per week.

One day, while delivering hats, I ran into my classmate and good friend Ron Freeman. We talked about going back to school and he told me that he wasn't going back to West Hill High School. He had just been hired by the Canadian National Railway as an office boy at twenty-five dollars for a five-and-a-half-day, forty-six-hour week. That was three dollars a week more and a half a day less than the two jobs that I was working. On one hand, I knew that I needed more education to fulfill my dream of becoming a Pilot; on the other, my family needed an additional income.

I asked Ron, "What about school?"

"I'm going to evening high school classes at Sir George Williams," he replied.

I went straight to the CNR employment office and was immediately hired as an office boy at twenty-five dollars for a five-and-a-half-day week, then went to Sir George (now Concordia University) and signed up for Grade 10. Since Mom and I were the sole sources of income for the family—Dad's earnings, such as they were, went to paying his debts—the three-dollar increase was important.

I went home and told Mom and, as usual, she went ballistic until I told her that I had signed up for night school. It took Ron Freeman and me six years to finish high school at night (two or three courses at a time), but it was well worth it. Fortunately, I also learned to type there, which served me well in the computer age that arrived forty years later. The schooling provided for my eventual entry into the Royal Canadian Air Force (RCAF) Flying School and the start of four great careers.

After a one-month bout of pneumonia, to which I have been susceptible for the rest of my life, I reported to the Auditor of Passenger Accounts at Canadian National Railways on October 2, 1950. The offices were in the viaduct underneath the CNR railway tracks running into Montreal's Central Station. It was a terrible place to work—it was very noisy and dusty, and every time a train passed overhead, the place would shake, and the dust would rise up in clouds. There were a couple of thousand employees working in these horrible conditions and most of the old-timers there had severe lung problems. Mr. King, the chief clerk, had even had a lung removed. The horrible working conditions and the snooping straw bosses were an added incentive to get my education completed and get out of that terrible sweat shop.

For me, as I've said, this was a way to support my family and get an education at the same time, so I could fulfill my dream of flying and build a better life. The pay was awful; out of my starting salary of twenty-five dollars for a five-and-a-half-day work week I kept two dollars a week to pay for the streetcar (the fare was five cents at that time) and dinner three times a week on school nights—a hot dog,

French fries, a May West cake, and a ten-ounce Pepsi was twenty-five cents at Johnny's greasy spoon right next door to the office. The rest went to Mom for rent and food. At this point, my social life consisted of playing soccer, football, and hockey, and hanging out at the local drug store and drinking Pepsi (six cents for ten ounces) rather than ten cents for six ounces of Coca-Cola—which I preferred—when I wasn't playing sports.

One of the men that I met at the CNR was a large and impressive man named Ralph Diplock. He was a World War II army veteran and now a Regimental Sergeant Major in the Victoria Rifles Reserve Regiment. After I turned eighteen he recruited me into his regiment, and I got my first taste of military life and discipline. I loved it; I was now a member of an elite military and the twenty-dollar monthly stipend was a bonus! They taught me how to shoot and operate a radio.

What I did not enjoy was summer camp with the regular army at Camp Val Cartier, where a handful of soldiers from the famous Royal 22nd Regiment (the Van Doos) Regulars took turns beating our battalion's brains out at war games. They trained me to operate a forty-pound radio and I became the headquarters company radio man. However, sleeping in a foxhole with two inches of water in it and eating cold rations was not my idea of fun. This only further inspired me to finish my evening high school, so I could try for Pilot training and sleep in clean sheets in a bed and be fed hot meals.

The commanding officer of the Victoria Rifles was Brigadier General Aird Nesbitt, the rich inherited owner of Ogilvy's, a famous department store in Montreal—his main qualification other than his wealth—who attended the war games not in a Jeep, but in a chauffeur-driven black Rolls-Royce with a fully equipped bar in the back seat! He would drive around the simulated battlefield and invite the young junior officers into the Rolls-Royce for a drink. And the young officers were flattered. Shades of the "Charge of the Light Brigade" in the Crimean War. As a lowly corporal, I was never invited into the Rolls-Royce—just as well since I had acquired a taste for beer, not hard liquor. No wonder the Van Doos made us look like the amateurs that we were during the simulated combat; our Commanding Officer covered his incompetence with alcohol.

Basically, while the officers were drinking, Sergeant Major Diplock had to run the battalion as best he could just to ensure that we weren't all captured or simulated as killed. I learned the meaning of leadership from him, and that if you ever have to go to war make darn sure that you have a crackerjack non-commissioned officer with you. It will improve your survival chances considerably. This reinforced my belief that I needed to be a regular, an officer, fly aircraft, sleep in clean white sheets and be among men of equal qualifications and training; that is, to not go to war following an alcohol-fuelled Rolls-Royce.

I graduated from Sir George Williams high school four years later at the end of May 1954 and immediately proceeded to the Royal Canadian Air Force recruiting station to start my career as a Fighter Pilot—nine years after I had told my mom that was my objective. I underwent one week of intensive medical, physical, coordination, psychological, and intelligence testing. I passed all of them with flying colours, then reported for my final interview with F/L (Captain) Turenne. He informed me that although I had passed all the tests, since I hadn't taken high school physics, I wasn't qualified for aircrew! All I could do was sign up as an airman and after one year apply for aircrew.

I was stunned, and I asked him, "Sir, since you've known from the day that I came in that I didn't have physics, why did you let me go through all the testing without telling me this at the beginning?" He had no answer for me. "Do you think that I'm stupid?" I continued. "You're looking for airmen not aircrew and the stunt you just pulled proves that I can't trust you!"

I walked out of the recruiting unit with smoke coming out of my ears, vowing to forget about becoming a Pilot in the RCAF. Joining the Royal Canadian Navy (RCN) to fly was out since they preferred young men with British accents (this is no joke; the way to promotion in the RCN was a mandatory British accent). At that time, the Canadian army had no aircraft, therefore that option was out, too.

There was no way that I was going to continue at my dead-end CNR job under the railway tracks. I had other options. I was a very good football player and could take a run at a Canadian professional football career despite my five-foot-seven and 155-pound body (a wee bit small even then). I had learned to play Canadian football while at West Hill

High School and I fell in love with the sport. I turned out to be a pretty good and small offensive left guard and defensive centre linebacker. After leaving WHHS, while I was attending Sir George Williams at night, I played football for the North End Rams Juveniles, then for the Lakeshore Flyers Juniors, and finally for the Côte des Neiges Gremlins Intermediates, founded, organized, and run by Mickey MacDonald, a rabid fan and organizer.

In late June, I attended the Montreal Alouette professional football tryout camp at the Westmount Athletic Grounds. After all, Canadian football players could earn almost twice my pay at the CNR for five months of fun! The coach was an American Southerner from Wake Forest in Winston Salem, North Carolina, "Peahead" Walker. In response to Canadian sports writers' accusations that he was prejudiced against Canadian and black athletes, he recruited a black Canadian Olympic track star, Ivan Livingston, and tried to turn him into a running back. That way, he would get a two-for-the-price-of-one stopper for the journalists.

Ivan was a great young man, but he should never have been on a football field because he had three weaknesses: he did not catch the ball well, had no football experience, and, fatally for a running back, he wouldn't follow his blockers out of the backfield, which exposed him to great danger from defensive ends and linebackers like me. We linebackers feasted on poor Ivan as we waited for him to break out. He was very fast, but he had to cross the line of scrimmage to advance the ball and we waited there for him and the ball like four hungry predators. Since this did not work out, Peahead tried him out at wide receiver—the good news was that he could outrun everyone in camp; the bad news was that even when he was wide open he had difficulty catching the ball. Ivan was just not a natural football player and the experiment came to an end. Coach Peahead Walker continued to get hounded by the media to find a Canadian or a black player for the team.

After two weeks of heavy workouts came the big day. The Alouette Inter-Squad Game was upon us, my big chance to play with the professionals and impress the coaches. We Canadians were the cannon fodder for the real football pros—the Americans, who played both offense and defense. The Canadians would battle it out for a chance with the Varsity team, hopefully without getting killed. I was on the Red Team, in the second row of receivers for the White Team's kick-off.

The kick came to me and I advanced the ball ten yards before I was tackled. Since I was a defensive player and we had the ball, I left the field. Our offensive team came on but could not move the ball, so we were forced to punt. I went back on the field and on the second play from scrimmage, the line in front of me opened up and through it came the biggest fullback that I had ever seen. This was Harry Haukkala, a McGill University Collegiate All Star weighing approximately 230 pounds (104 kilos). He was moving at great speed and I figure that his kinetic mass must have been four times his weight. (I guess Captain Turenne was right—I should have taken physics in high school). I was a good football player because I never hesitated and always hit the opposing player first, the secret of survival in football. This time, surprised by Harry's size and speed, I hesitated. He ran right over me and left his footprints as a memento. I woke up in the locker room, with the team trainer leaning over me with four fingers in my face.

"How many fingers?" he snapped.

"Four!" I answered.

"OK," he said. "You can go back out there."

"Are you nuts?" I retorted. "I almost got killed out there. I quit!" Anka Voticky did not raise a dummy. I was a very good football player for my size, but I was just too small for these guys and out of my league. It was one of the smartest decisions of my life, especially after seeing all the crippled and brain-damaged former professional football players. At age eighty-four, my knees are fine and my brain is still working well!

Fifty years later, I ran into Harry Haukkala in the elevator at the Vaudreuil Inn in the Montreal suburb and accused him of wrecking my potential professional football career. At first, he was startled because he didn't remember the incident or me (of course not—he ran right over me!) and then I broke up laughing and told him the story. I said that I was very grateful for his running over me that day as it led me to the one career that I really wanted. We enjoyed meeting again, mainly because he didn't run over me this time.

NOW IT WAS time to reassess my career opportunities since I still had no intention of spending fifty years working under the tuberculosis-inducing, slave-labour conditions at the CNR. The union-controlled seniority system dominated conditions at the CNR, destroying any incentive for promotion. Getting maimed playing football was also a bad option. I knew that I had to give flying another chance, so I headed back to Sir George Williams and signed up for Grade 10 physics.

One day, my friend, Herb "Sonny" Evans, who was training for a commercial Pilot license, called me and invited me to go flying with him on a Saturday morning. He was doing a three-leg navigation exercise and wanted company. When my mom found out about Sonny's training, she had warned me never to go flying with him because he would crash and kill me. Naturally, though, I didn't follow her advice and, since she didn't remember my intention to become a Pilot, I didn't mention my planned adventure. One beautiful Saturday morning Sonny and I headed for Laurentian Aviation at Cartierville Airport, climbed into a Cessna 152, and headed for St. Jean, Quebec, with Sonny in command on one of his mandatory cross-country navigation flights. We landed safely to find that there was no one around. Finally, Sonny found one lonely watchman on duty and had his log book signed by him.

We climbed back aboard the Cessna, fired up the engine and took off. Right after takeoff, however, the engine started to sputter and instead of landing straight ahead as he was supposed to do, Sonny decided to go around and land on the runway that we had just left. The rule for single-engine aircraft is that if the engine fails on takeoff and you cannot restart it, land straight ahead; you will never make it if you turn back as you lose too much airspeed and altitude in the turns. A lot of dead Pilots prove this theory.

I guess Sonny had slept through that lesson or decided that he was smarter than more experienced Pilots throughout aviation history. The engine quit on final approach and our luck ran out at approximately sixty feet (the height of a six-story building) as Sonny tried to extend the glide by pulling back on the yoke, losing airspeed and stalling the aircraft into the ground. It is truly amazing, but when an aircraft hits the earth, it is the aircraft that shatters. We hit short of the runway like a ton of bricks. I covered my face as we crashed and could feel that it was very warm and wet. I opened my eyes and saw that my hands were covered in blood—my blood! The aircraft was destroyed. I was strapped in and trying to get out when Sonny asked, "Holy shit, what happened to you?"

"I think we crashed, asshole," I answered, "and I am trying to get out of here before it blows up!" After undoing our seat belts (this was before car seat belts and they saved our lives), we easily got out of the wreckage and then walked around the airfield looking for help. Sonny didn't have a scratch on him! My mother's premonition had been right, but my good luck held—I had escaped death again.

We finally found the watchman and he called for an ambulance, which took us to the nearest hospital. I was covered in blood, but not seriously injured. They bandaged my head and sent me by ambulance to St. Mary's Hospital in Montreal. I was more concerned about my mom's reaction (I was in no shape for more head slaps) than my injuries and called my Aunt Liza and her husband, Franta. Instead of calling my mother, she called my dad, who got Mom out of the way by sending her to the park with my brother, Michael. Uncle Franta picked me up at the hospital and drove me home, my head wrapped in bandages.

After I got home, my dad parked me in the living room to await Mom's arrival. As soon as she walked in the door and entered the living room, she immediately screamed at me, "I told you that he would crash and kill you if you went flying with him!" The good news was that due to my head injuries, I didn't get whacked!

None of this discouraged me about flying; with the little knowledge of flying that I had, I knew that the accident was Sonny's fault not the aircraft's. Sonny should have landed straight ahead and not made the fatal error of pulling the nose up hoping to extend his glide. He did the opposite, losing airspeed and stalling the aircraft, and dropping sixty feet (18 metres). I didn't know much about flying, but I knew that in a gliding situation you must push the nose down to maintain flying airspeed and land straight ahead, with no turns.

After successfully completing Grade 10 physics, I signed up for Grade 11 physics. Sonny should have too, as he had a very short career in flying.

Uncle Ernie Kanturek (left); with my father (centre); and Uncle Franta Vilim in front of their jewellery store, European Art Jewellery, on Mountain Street. Montreal, 1949.

The West Hill High School Junior Soccer team.
I'm in the middle row (centre). Montreal, 1949.

A shot of me (left) running track at West Hill High School. Montreal, 1949.

10

MY LIFE CHANGES FOREVER

n September 1955, I attended at the Montreal courthouse to be sworn in as a brand-new Canadian citizen. This was a very proud day in my life. I had finally found a country with laws and equality, where I need not fear being persecuted for my beliefs or speech, and anyone who was not treated equally could fight for their rights.

But it was on May 21, 1956, just after finishing my Grade 11 physics at Sir George Williams that my life really changed forever. I was going on a double date with my buddy Bob McKee and we stopped to pick up his date on 18th Avenue in Lachine. When we got there, we met Bob's date's sister and her best friend—a gorgeous blue-eyed blond with a ponytail and gorgeous blue eyes. Her name was Catherine Shapcott. I shook her hand, and when I looked into those smiling blue eyes, I saw a beautiful soul and was smitten. As they say, the eyes are the reflection of the soul and hers were beautiful; she was the most beautiful woman I had ever met. I fell madly in love right then and there.

As we were leaving I asked Bob to get me a date with the beautiful Catherine and he asked me why.

"Because I'm going to marry her!" was my response.

"You're nuts, buddy!" was all he could say, but he did as I asked. Eighteen months later, he was the best man at our wedding.

Years later, Catherine admitted to me that the main reason that she had agreed to our first date was because my date on the night we met had once taken a boyfriend away from her. As I said earlier, "Revenge is best served cold." It reminded me of the *Count of Monte Cristo* and

Scaramouche. Luckily, this time I was the beneficiary of this act of revenge. I must have done something right on that first date because we have been together through thick and thin, poverty and success ever since—for sixty years.

I couldn't afford a car in those days, but I had saved enough of my army pay to buy a BSA 350cc motorcycle. It wasn't great transportation, but it allowed me to court my future wife. Catherine and I saw each other every day thanks to my BSA motorcycle, although I'm sure I woke up half of Lachine when I went home very early every morning because the bike had a bad starter and I had to jumpstart it.

I was weakening in my resolve to join the RCAF because it would mean eighteen months away from Catherine while I trained in Western Canada. But she believed in my dream and encouraged me to go for it; she told me that she would wait for me to graduate. Her support has been a driving force in my life ever since, especially when things got really tough. I had passed Grade 11 physics and quit the CNR—despite my superiors' attempts to give me a leave of absence instead, saying that I could return always to the CNR if I failed. I, however, was determined not to fail and there was no way that I was going back to the CNR slave-labour office if I did. I went back to the recruiting unit, went through all the tests again (fortunately F/L Turenne was no longer there) and was accepted for aircrew selection and training.

On July 20, 1956, I boarded a CNR train for the No. 2 Officer Selection Unit in London, Ontario with two other prospective Pilots. Mike Stephenson was a cocky seventeen-year-old sponsored by No. 401 Reserve Squadron in Montreal, which guaranteed him a Pilot slot if selected for aircrew training because that squadron didn't need Navigators. The other recruit was a brash ski instructor who guaranteed us that he would be selected for Pilot training (he wasn't). I was older than both of them, quietly confident in my ability, but afraid of failure, so I kept my mouth shut.

There were 110 eager Pilot wannabes at the No. 2 Officer and Air Crew Selection Unit in London culled from more than two hundred applicants at the recruiting units across Canada. We underwent three weeks of extensive testing for leadership, hand-eye coordination, motion sickness, intelligence, team cooperation, team work, physical strength, mathematics, physical and mental endurance, and ability to run one mile (1.6 kilometers) in under six minutes.

The most interesting part of the selection process was a day trip to the RCAF Medical Testing Centre at the Downsview Air Force Base in Toronto. We were all fed a sumptuous meal—our first good one in almost a month—and then subjected to medical testing that included various orientation and disorientation tests and attempts to stimulate air sickness in all of us. This test was after being fed the biggest and best lunch in three weeks. Most of us survived, but a few were eliminated right then and there due to a susceptibility to motion sickness. Then we went through two weeks of intensive testing.

Finally, the day of reckoning came. On August 10, 1956, more than one hundred anxious young men were seated in a gym and called out one by one in alphabetical order to learn our fate. Naturally, with my surname, I would be one of the last called and I had to wait almost two hours to hear my name. I marched into the Flight Commander's office, snapped off a spiffy newly learned salute and heard the magic words, "Congratulations, Flight Cadet Voticky, you have been selected for Navigator training!" I was speechless. I hadn't been chosen for Pilot training, but I was one of only thirty-three young men who had made it out of the Selection Unit. Most importantly, I had a job as long as I worked hard and passed dozens of tests.

It turned out that eighteen out of the thirty-three flight Cadets had been selected as Navigators on this course—the RCAF mostly needed Navigators and Radio Officers for the Argus anti-submarine aircraft at that time. All I could say, with great relief, was, "Thank you, sir!" I saluted again and then proceeded to the barber shop for a military haircut. This was followed up by being sworn in, getting our military gear at supply, changing into our new uniforms, and then heading straight back to our classroom.

Mike Stephenson did make the cut for Pilot training; he graduated eighteen months later to fly in the RCAF reserves and was hired by Trans Canada Air Lines (later Air Canada) as a Pilot. I met him again ten years later when I also joined Air Canada. Shortly thereafter, he had a major heart attack, which, under the medical standards at the time meant permanent grounding and the end of a flying career at a very young age. Air Canada kept him on as a ground-school and simulator instructor. That was really hard for someone who had gone through a tough selection process, trained and flew for ten years, and then lost it all for medical reasons before his thirtieth birthday.

Needless to say, the ski instructor went back to make a living on the ski hills.

Everybody in the classroom was buzzing with excitement. Then, F/L (Captain) Boyer—he looked like Captain Steve Canyon, the comic strip character—walked in with his officer's hat on the back of his head and started our indoctrination by announcing, "Gentlemen, welcome to the Royal Canadian Air Force. We are going to spend the next year and a half training you to be killers. For those of you who are feeling queasy about that word, don't worry. You won't be here for graduation. At least half of you will have been CTed (Ceased Training) by then." And he was right!

None of us had joined the RCAF to become killers, but his words made us realize that this was serious business. In order to defend Canada, we might be forced to kill or wound an enemy, so if we wanted to survive, we'd better learn how to do it effectively and efficiently or we would become the casualty. To quote General George Patton, "A hero is not a man who dies for his country; it is a man who makes another poor young man die for his country." We had to become good Pilots and Navigators to ensure that we and our country would not lose out if the Cold War got hot. The Soviet Union was a threat to all Western democracies and it would be our job to defend Canada.

The next day, thirty-three newly minted Flight Cadets, as super-numerary officers wearing Pilot Officer Uniforms with white patches on our wedge airmen's caps to distinguish us from real commissioned officers, boarded a bus and headed for Pre-Flight School in Centralia, Ontario. We had officer privileges, but not rights—we had to salute real officers, but no one saluted us.

Pre-Flight School entailed three more months of intensive school-ing, exercise and military drills. There was a lot of pressure from 6:00 a.m. until lights out at 10:30 p.m. every weekday. Scholastic work was interspersed with gym, drilling, and marching—there was lots of home-work at night and on weekends—and we also had to wash and press our uniforms. We got only one weekend off during the whole three months. All of this psychological pressure was designed in part to make us voluntarily CT (quit). The RCAF didn't want quitters flying their aircraft, so the objective was to make us quit before we ever got near an aircraft.

In addition to the physical and mental regimen I've just described was the need to learn and pass Junior Matriculation-level trigonometry to pass Ground School. I had never taken this type of mathematics before, but I quickly learned the secret. There are six formulas that are the key to passing a trig exam. I memorized these formulas and passed the exam with flying colours. F/L Turenne had never mentioned trig, even though it was a required course and much harder than physics. As it turned out, I never needed trig during the rest of my Air Force or civil aviation career. It was just another hurdle that the RCAF put in our way.

The drill instructors were very tough; they usually picked the oldest or toughest man in any given course and proceeded to do everything they could to break him. I seemed to qualify as the oldest and F/C Ian McMahon, a grumpy, unpleasant Scotsman, qualified as the toughest, therefore, we got the treatment. The instructors thought that if they could break us, they could break the rest of the Cadets on the same course. I think they got bonuses for voluntary CTs. It was my misfortune to be picked as the pigeon for Course 5611 by Corporal Nowell, but it was his tough luck that he picked the wrong guy. He did everything in the book—and a few things not in it—to make me quit.

The Gestapo couldn't break my mother and I carried her genes. Corporal Nowell didn't know that he never stood a chance trying to break me. It wasn't for lack of trying. He charged me for long hair almost every week when I was getting my hair cut two and three times a week. Every time he charged me, I had to march (not walk) a mile every evening after class to the guardhouse and back in full uniform. When I finally got the barber to shave my head (long before it was fashionable), Corporal Nowell then charged me for illegally shaving my head! Back to the guardhouse I went every night. It was a period of tough character building.

We did our gym workouts, including sit-ups, in an old hangar with an ice-cold concrete floor during October and November. We had to do more than one hundred sit-ups every day. Not surprisingly, I developed a severe case of bleeding hemorrhoids; I had great difficulty walking and certainly couldn't march. Fortunately, the base doctor excused me from drill and gym for the last week of the three-month course. My temporary disability permitted the sadistic Corporal Nowell to believe that he had made me quit. Since I couldn't march at our Pre-Flight School graduation ceremony at the end of that week, I had to sit with those unfortunates who had either failed or quit. When Corporal Nowell passed me sitting among the former Flight Cadets (who had failed), he smiled from ear to ear—he thought that he had beaten me! Again, he had underestimated my determination and ability. The rest of the Cadets in my course received their diplomas and then the school Commanding Officer (CO) called my name to receive mine. Despite being in a lot of pain, I snapped to attention, marched up as best I could—it was more like a faster shuffle—to receive my diploma, saluted the Commanding Officer, accepted my diploma, saluted again, and marched back to sit with my unfortunate former course buddies. As I passed the corporal, I gave him a big smile and then I gave him the bird!

My grandmother, Hedvika Kanturek (centre front), with all her grandchildren.
I'm standing behind her. Montreal, 1955.

Here I am as a proud Flight Cadet in the Royal Canadian Air Force. January 1957.

GRADUATION CLASS
5614 AI

LAC Don Parker

Standing, left to right: F/C Smith, F/C Stewart, F/C Fink, F/C Barr, F/C Michaud, F/C Berlanguet.
Seated, left to right: F/C Chase, F/C Voticky, F/C Terry, F/C Beal, missing F/L Douglas, (Course Director).

44

My graduation as a Flight Cadet—I'm in front, second from the left.
Winnipeg, Manitoba, 1957.

11

FLYING SCHOOL

WE DID IT! We were headed for Flying School, the Pilots to Claresholm, Alberta and the Navigators to Winnipeg, Manitoba. Out of the original thirty-three, fourteen Navigator and twelve Pilot trainees made it through Pre-flight School. No. 2 Air Observer School at RCAF Station Winnipeg was commanded by Wing Commander Danny Williams, Distinguished Flying Cross and two Bars (which was equivalent to three DFCs), a World War II hero who had flown as a Lead Navigator for the Royal Air Force's famous Dambusters. This experienced and highly respected officer was a role model for all of us.

Right after we arrived in Winnipeg on a Saturday, I got in touch with a friend of my sister whose father was Minister of Labour in the Manitoba Provincial Government. Her mother invited me to their home for Sunday dinner, where I met a young RCAF Pilot based at the Navigation School. He was tall and good-looking—he looked like an advertising poster for the typical Air Force officer—and very pleasant. He was also newly married and was there with his new wife. I enjoyed a wonderful evening with these wonderful people.

The next morning, the first Monday of our course, fourteen budding Canadian Navigators arrived in our classroom to find fifteen British Royal Air Force Acting Pilot officers in the room. Their education and training were equivalent to ours, and they were only commissioned officers for pay purposes, to provide them with a liveable income while in Canada. They were also draftees, whereas we were all volunteers.

The seating had been arranged in an alternating Canadian/British pattern. In a typically friendly Canadian gesture, I extended my hand to the mustachioed RAF Cadet sitting behind my seat, and said, "Hi, I'm Lou Voticky." This little pipsqueak looked me up and down as if I was below his class and from another planet, and then in a fake snobbish upper-class accented voice, looked down his nose at me and said, "I am Acting Pilot Officer Humphrey. We are commissioned officers, you know."

"Frankly, Humph," I retorted. "I didn't know and what is more, I really don't give a shit. You are a guest in my country now, so try to behave like a Canadian while you're here." I was glad that this jerk was not old enough to have been in the Battle of Britain because if he was, we would probably be speaking German.

At dusk that evening, approximately 5:00 p.m., just as classes were ending, the emergency sirens sounded. Fire engines and ambulances were roaring toward a runway. There had been an aircraft accident and two young Pilots who were practicing touch-and-go's—landings immediately followed by takeoffs—had been killed. One of them was the nice young man I had met at dinner the night before. My thoughts were with his family and I was badly shaken that night. The only RCAF Pilot I knew was dead the day after I had met him. I found myself re-evaluating my desire to be an aviator, but fortunately my inner strength came through; I decided that I could not and would not quit my dream. I had come too far, worked too hard, and I wanted it too badly.

We spent the next seven weeks in Ground School working hard to learn the basics of flight and especially navigation. Interspersed with gym and drill, swimming was part of the delights. That required us to walk through the snow at -40°C wind chill (also -40°F) to and from the pool. Then came the real fun—night guard duty in the four navigation schools on base, once per month duty, and no time off to sleep before, during, or after. Going straight back to class after guard duty was the routine, so trying to stay awake all day and study was even more character building. If you were lucky, you got guard duty on the weekend. At least then you could get some sleep the next day. The British Acting Pilot Officers (APOs) were lucky; they didn't have to stand night guard duty. I assume it was below their class and dignity.

Finally, Week 8 arrived on January 11, 1957, and with it our first chance to actually fly. Our Pilot, Flying Officer (F/O) John Weir, one Navigator instructor, Flight Cadet Gord Simonson—a six-foot-five-inch gentle giant from Saskatchewan—and I flew together in our bulky World War II winter flying suits in a little twin-engine Beechcraft C-45 (Wichita Bug Smasher). We sure filled the aircraft. The Cadets would each navigate half the flight with the instructor supervising. We must have been successful because we found our way back to Winnipeg and then they scheduled our first solo flights for a month later. On that solo flight, we would have just one young brand-new Pilot straight out of Flying School for company. Talk about the blind leading the blind! It was truly amazing that we didn't all get lost.

My first solo flight was on February 12, 1957. My Pilot, F/O (1st Lieutenant) Pickard, and I flight planned our trip, checked out our aircraft, then launched at 9:00 a.m. The Pilot took me to the initial point (IP) over Lac Labiche and then it was my turn to show what I had learned. I gave the Pilot a heading to fly due east to the first turning point, then checked my equipment for my first sun astronavigation heading check in an aircraft moving at 120 mph (200 km/h). I had to make sure that we were flying in the right direction and our compass was working correctly—in those days, they weren't always very accurate.

I took my first heading sun shot five minutes after the IP and to my horror discovered that instead of being on a heading of 110 degrees magnetic (east south east), we were heading 170 degrees magnetic (south)! My first thought was that I had made a mistake. Trying not to panic, I told F/O Pickard to turn 60 degrees port (left). This would only parallel our desired track direction, but it would give me time to recheck my heading without over-correcting, and then to reset the compass.

I took another heading check and, believe it or not, we were now heading 110 degrees. So I then recycled both the magnetic and gyroscopic compasses, took a position fix and found that we were thirty miles (forty-eight kilometres) south of our desired track and running parallel to it. I had my Pilot turn 45 degrees port (left) and, to my great amazement, we hit our first turning point bang on but twelve minutes late. It must have been a combination of sixth sense and pure luck! I had to be running out of miracles.

The rest of the flight was uneventful, but I was sure that shortly after landing I would be Ceased Training and thrown out of the RCAF. Terrified, we went into debriefing where a real Navigator went over my flight and F/O Pickard's report of it. To my amazement, the Pilot praised me for the wonderful job that I had done, how I had immediately recognized a mechanical failure of the compasses and taken corrective action without hesitation. He also reported that—to *his* amazement—I had not panicked, had taken immediate corrective action, and, after all that had happened, I had hit the first turning point bang on. The only person more stunned by these miraculous events than the Pilot and Navigator instructor was me!

I got 96.5 per cent on my first solo navigation flight, the best mark out of twenty-nine Canadian and British Cadets who completed that first exercise that day. I learned that anyone can make mistakes due to mechanical or human error, but that what counted in aviation was to stay calm and correct the error. This gave my confidence a tremendous boost; in the next year and a half of flight training no Cadet ever beat me in flying training. I remained No. 1 right until the day I graduated from the Operational Training Unit on CF-100s at Cold Lake. My Ground School performance was not that great, but my flying marks kept me on top all the way through training.

At the end of January 1957, the top three Canadian Cadets on each of the eight courses in Basic Navigation School got a seven-hour ride to North Bay, Ontario in a creaky old World War II Douglas C-47 Dakota (the civilian version was the DC-3) for an introduction to jet flying. One of our group, Flight Cadet Alistair (Scotty) MacKay was airsick all the way to North Bay, a great start to an introductory flight in a jet fighter.

We arrived at RCAF Station North Bay on January 25, 1957, attended a short familiarization course on flying the CF-100—mainly emergency, oxygen, communication, and ejection procedures. We were being prepared to ride in 414 AWF Squadron's brand-new CF-100 All Weather Mark V (MK V) fighter! The CF-100 MK V was much lighter than the MK IV because eight fifty-calibre machine guns had been removed, it had added wing and horizontal stabilizer extensions (controls that climb and descend of aircraft), and it had more engine power than the MK IV. It could get up to 52,000 feet (16,000 metres), or 7,000 feet (2,000 metres) more than the MK IV. We were highly motivated to not go any higher than 45,000 feet (14,000 metres) because, unfortunately, we didn't have any pressure suits. We needed them to go any higher because, in case of a loss of cabin pressure, the pressure suits would prevent our blood from boiling. I guess they had spent all the money on extending the wings and tail. Sometime later, one of my Pilots, F/O Wayne Foster and I did take the CF-100 up to 52,000 feet and once was enough!

There was another performance enhancement with the new configuration: a Pilot could hold the aircraft at low level by holding the yoke (stick) forward, trim the aircraft nose up, build the speed up to 400 knots—aircraft speeds are measured in nautical miles—which translates into 460 miles or 736 kilometres per hour. When they released pressure on the yoke, the aircraft would go vertical and climb straight up like a rocket. This was phenomenal performance for that era. At that time, no one even considered the cumulative stress that this applied to the extended wings and tail. Aviation had a lot to learn in the new jet age.

At 10:40 a.m. on January 26, F/L Spencer and I went out to aircraft No. 575 to carry out a pre-flight inspection, climbed aboard, got strapped in tight, fired up the two giant Canadian Orenda jet engines and taxied out to Runway 27. At 11:00 a.m., after receiving takeoff clearance, F/L Spencer applied takeoff power. I had never experienced such a surge of power! I sank back into my ejection seat and thirty-five seconds later we were airborne.

Gear up, flaps up, level off at 1,500 feet (457 metres), hard left downwind, and then request clearance for a low-level high-speed pass over the east-west runway. Tower responded, "Black Knight 7, you are cleared for a high-speed low flyby!" F/L Spencer instructed me to accept the clearance and, in my first use of an RCAF aircraft radio, I responded—in what I'm sure was a voice three or four octaves higher than normal, "North Bay Tower, Black Knight 7 cleared for high-speed low pass."

We flew approximately twelve miles (twenty kilometres) downwind, then came around base leg onto final and went down to fifty feet (15 metres) above ground with 95 per cent power to perform our low pass.

As we flew down Runway 27, F/L Spencer applied maximum continuous power, held the joystick full forward, and trimmed the nose up, reaching 410 knots (470 mph or 810 km/h). Then, when we flew by the control tower, he released the forward pressure on the joystick and we rocketed straight up!

I was breathless; this was the greatest experience of my life. We reached 18,000 feet (5,500 metres) in one minute, then he then rolled the aircraft upside down and, looking down, I could see that we were still over Runway 27. WOW! This was why I wanted to fly. This was certainly not a noisy propeller-driven aircraft chugging along at 120 mph. The deal was sealed—I wanted to fly jets. This was better than the Flying Tigers' Warhawks, which had made me fall in love with flying and aviation in the first place.

We flew around North Bay for an hour and F/L Spencer demonstrated the capabilities of the CF-100. But I was already sold; this was the aircraft that I wanted to fly. The only problem I encountered was clearing my ears in a 10,000-foot (3,000 metre) per minute dive, but that wasn't enough to discourage me.

The next day, we flew back to Winnipeg in the creaky old C-47 and poor F/C MacKay was again sick all the way home; the smell in the aircraft was awful. The amazing thing, though, was that with courage and determination he eventually overcame air sickness. He learned to fly jet fighters and out of all of us non-university graduates at the Air Navigation School at the time, he attained the highest rank. He made it all the way to Brigadier General!

Unfortunately, unknown to the Pilots or aircraft designers at that time, these violent manoeuvres also greatly overstressed the CF-100 Mark V aircraft wings and tail. That summer two CF-100 Mark V's performing this same manoeuvre at air shows in London, Ontario and Madison, Wisconsin crashed after their wing and horizontal stabilizer extensions folded up under the accumulated stress of the manoeuvre and broke off. All four crew members died in these two accidents. After that, the CF-100 was restricted to 300 knots below 10,000 feet and that corrected the problem; we didn't lose any more CF-100s due to wings or tails breaking off until they were retired fifteen years later.

In February, I caught an extremely bad cold, but unless it was bad enough to be hospitalized, this didn't excuse me from the pleasures of drill or gym; it did excuse me from swimming. I still had to attend the swim session and wear a bathing suit in the cold pool area. I sat on the sideline freezing while my buddies swam in the relatively warmer water (at least there wasn't any ice on top of the water), thus exacerbating my illness.

It was really cold in the pool area. My nemesis from day one at the Air Navigation School, A/P/O Humphrey of the RAF, found a new sport; every time he went by me, he splashed me with the cold water. I warned him off twice, but the third time, I leaped into the pool on top of him, grabbed him by the throat, and took him to the bottom. It took two of my classmates to get me off him. Amazingly, I never had a problem with APO Humphrey or any of the British Cadets after that.

In March 1957, as we were completing our basic navigation training, we made our requests for advanced training. We had three choices: Long-Range Navigator (Transport or Maritime Command), Radar Navigator (Fighters—Air Defence Command), or Radio Officer (Maritime Command). Most wanted Long-Range for career reasons and the rest opted for Radar Navigator. No one volunteered for Radio Officer—Morse code was not our friend. I picked CF-100s and Radar Navigator despite my course director's pleading for me to go Long-Range. "You'll be a great Navigator," he said, "and, if you go for Long-Range Navigator, you'll have great career opportunities in civil aviation after you leave the air force. With CF-100s, there will be no post-RCAF flying career and you have a good chance of dying young. Those aircraft are widow makers!"

Despite his no-doubt sage advice, deep down I knew that I had made the right choice. As the top man on my course, I got my first choice—CF-100s—and sixty years later I'm still here. I guess the course director and my mother were both wrong. Later on, I was still able to have a second career as both an airline Navigator and Pilot with Air Canada. Flying then became my route to a successful third career in the financial industry because of the trust and networking within the Pilot group.

DURING THE WINTER of 1957, while I was the goalie on the Flight Cadet hockey team, we won the Station Winnipeg Championship. That entitled us to represent Station Winnipeg in the Western armed forces finals at Portage la Prairie. The tournament highlight was what happened with our star player, whom I'll call JP. He didn't show up for the bus at 6:00 a.m. on Saturday morning for the ride to the tournament, so we had to go to his room, gather his equipment, roll him out of bed, dress him, and carry him to the bus. He'd had a hard night and slept all the way to Portage La Prairie—one hundred kilometres (62 miles). In the arena, we got him dressed in his hockey gear and he slept through the first two periods on the bench. After two periods, we were down 4–0 despite my goaltending, and JP was sick all over the dressing-room floor between periods! Miraculously, he came to and scored five goals in the last period. That was our only victory in the tournament and as far as we got; he was so tired that he couldn't repeat that performance in the next game.

In April, we graduated from Basic Navigation School and were granted two weeks leave. This was great as I was able to return to Montreal and spend time with Catherine after months of separation. I brought one of my roommates, F/C McNally, home with me to Montreal as he wanted to visit his sister, who was attending McGill University. He spent three days with my family and accidentally got me into trouble by discussing our flying training at dinner.

I had told my mother that I was going to be a Ground Officer because she sincerely believed that aircraft were designed to kill people. After hearing the training stories from McNally, she went ballistic at dinner and told me that I was not going back to the RCAF. I got around her by telling her that if I didn't return, they would come after me, court-martial me for desertion, and that the maximum penalty was the firing squad. Fortunately, because of her European background, where this kind of justice was quite normal, she believed me. Good thing that Corporal Nowell wasn't there to tell her that he would be very happy to accommodate her if I did not go back (he might have even sent her flowers).

I returned to Winnipeg in early May to attend the Advanced Airborne Interception School along with fourteen other Cadets. Our course director was a really good officer, F/L Douglas; he was friendly and helpful. The only one problem was that he forgot to teach us the Ground School part of Airborne Interception Theory and Techniques, which is why we were there. We were all able to learn the techniques in flight training in our venerable World War II B-25s converted to interceptors with the addition of an old radar set but needed the correct background and technical terminology for the written exam. We had to attend Ground School again, this time for five weeks, and then we were checked out to fly the converted B-25s.

This aircraft was made famous by Colonel (later Lieutenant General) Jimmy Doolittle, Congressional Medal of Honor winner, when his small squadron of sixteen B-25 aircraft launched off the USS *Hornet* in a horrible rainstorm to attack mainland Japan just five months after Pearl Harbor. The B-25 was not designed to fly off an aircraft carrier and none had ever taken off from one before this. In one of the great feats of airmanship and courage in World War II, the overloaded B-25s launched off a wildly pitching three-hundred-foot (ninety-one metre) flight deck in a terrible storm to attack the enemy that had just destroyed a large part of the US Navy. The aircraft reached Japan, dropped their bombs on military targets, and then tried to make it to Chinese territory controlled by the Nationalist Chinese government. None of them made it; they were either shot down or ran out of fuel. Some of the crews did make it to China and were rescued by Chinese civilians; more than half of them died or were taken prisoner and tortured by the Imperial Japanese Army.

Our course of fifteen Cadets flew through the summer and successfully qualified on this aircraft to become Radar Navigators. With three weeks to go to graduation, a problem arose—F/L Douglas remembered that he had not given us the course on Radar Intercept Theory, which was not quite the same as actually doing intercepts. He told us that since we had done the flying part of radar intercepts successfully, we would have no problem writing the theory exam. After all, he said, the pass mark would only be 50 per cent. However, he neglected the fact that the theory exams were prepared by people who had learned intercepts from books not from actual flying experience. Any similarity between the two was purely coincidental.

We ended up writing an exam that bore little relationship to what we had done in flight; the theory part of the test was sadly out of date. Eleven out of fifteen of us failed. I got a mark of 49 per cent and the high man on the course got 54 per cent. In the US Air Force they would have used a bell curve to adjust the marks and only one of us would have failed. That was not true of the RCAF and, in this instance at least, they preferred to protect one of their own officers who had screwed up and then lied to cover it up. They proceeded to make an example of us by issuing a Cease Training for all of us. After spending approximately $150,000 and eighteen months training each of us, they were willing to sacrifice eleven young men three weeks from graduation and useful service to save one lousy officer three years from retirement.

The eleven of us who had failed the exam had to face a Cease Training Board consisting of three fellow officers of F/L Douglas. We told our story truthfully, but the Board either didn't believe us or didn't want to believe us. They completely ignored the fact that there is no way that eleven witnesses to the same event could concoct the same story without errors. Clearly, in the end, the CT Board had to protect their fellow officer and instructor and the truth didn't matter. We were all Ceased Training and recommended for release from the service.

We had one last chance: an appeal to School Commander W/C Danny Williams, a World War II hero from the RAF Dambusters. Eleven concerned Cadets gathered in the waiting room outside his office on Monday morning. My roommate, Jean Michaud, was the first Cadet in the Commander's office, and came out smiling, he had got a recourse back to the next course. I knew that there would only be one more recourse available to us, so when the Commander's secretary said "Next," I dove for his office. When I got inside, I snapped to attention and threw him the best salute in my repertoire. He acknowledged the salute and got right to the point, asking me, "Why did you fail?"

My response was a total lie: "Sir, my fiancée and I were planning our wedding after my graduation and I was so focused on that that I wasn't paying attention to my studies." I knew that this was what F/L Douglas's fellow officers wanted to hear. Then I laid it on thick. "Sir, if you give me another chance, you will not regret it; I will succeed, graduate, and become an officer that you and the RCAF will be proud of!"

School Commander W/C Danny Williams rocked back and forth in his chair for what seemed an eternity—it was really only about three minutes—then finally looked me in the eye and said, "Recourse granted, but you had better not fail me!"

"I will not fail you, SIR!" I responded. And I definitely did not. I kept my promise to W/C Danny Williams and became an excellent officer, a superb Navigator, and a dead-eye Top Gun in Air Defense Command.

I hated to lie to this good man and war hero, but I had no choice; it was the only way to save my career. Senior officers would almost always protect their junior officers, even if eleven flight Cadets testified and contradicted that officer. Besides, F/L Douglas had lied at my Cease Training (CT) hearing, claiming that he had given us the missing course and would lie again. I'm sure that he did the same at all the other Cadet's hearings to save his career.

The other nine Cadets went into the Commander's office and told him the same truth. They were all Ceased Training and released from the RCAF less than three weeks from graduation at a cost of $1,350,000 to the Canadian taxpayer because of one lying officer. These were good guys and would have been good Navigators and officers, but they were thrown out to protect an incompetent officer because they told the truth. Two of us got another chance because we played the game and lied to satisfy the military ethos.

NAVIGATION CADETS HERE FOR WEEKEND TRAINING

A North Bay airman, Flight Cadet Robert Hutson, 1302 High Street, second from right, is welcomed to RCAF Sta- North Bay along with three of his buddies by SL K. C. Mason, CD, right, chief of operations. The airmen, part of a oup of 20 who arrived here yesterday from the RCAF's basic navigational school at Winnipeg, will spend the week familiarizing themselves with an operational station and will check out for the first time in a CF-100 all-weath ter plane. The cadets attended a formal mess dinner at the officers' mess Friday night and started their round kend lectures, tours, and flying this morning. Shown left to right, are Flight Cadets P. A. Upper, 19, Toronto; M icky, 22, Montreal; Robert Hutson, 21, North Bay; and SL Mason, the officer who will be in charge of the cac iliarization weekend. Flight Cadet Hutson is a former member of 547 Air Cadet Squadron of North Bay, and ident of the North Bay Collegiate Students' Council last year.

—Nugget Staff

Preparing for my first flight in the 414 AWF Squadron's brand-new CF-100 All Weather
Mark V fighter. I am second from the left. North Bay, Ontario, January 25, 1957.

12

FAMILY CRISIS, THEN A WEDDING

Three weeks after I had been granted the recourse, in Montreal on Friday, October 27, 1957, at 5:30 p.m. Eastern Standard Time, my dad finished work in downtown Montreal and headed home to Decarie Boulevard. He felt uncomfortable, was sweating, and had severe chest pains. His route home went past our family doctor's home in Outremont and fortunately, he decided to turn into Dr. Kraft's driveway. He got out of his car, went to the front door, rang the bell, and collapsed. The doctor answered the door to find my dad lying on his doorstep. My dad had had a massive heart attack and Dr. Kraft saved his life.

Many years later, I met Dr. Kraft's widow, thanked her for her husband having given my dad an extra sixteen years and seven days of life. She replied that her husband was never usually home that early, but that night was Friday night—Shabbat, the Jewish Sabbath—and she insisted on him being home at sunset for dinner. My dad lived an extra sixteen years because of a woman's insistence that her doctor husband come home early for Sabbath dinner (maybe God was making it up to him for his parent's brutal execution).

Two hours after that dramatic event in Montreal—not knowing anything about my dad's close brush with death, I marched onto the Parade Square at RCAF Station Winnipeg for Wings Parade. This is the ceremony in which aircrew Flying School graduates get their Officer's Commission and their respective wings. I was headed to Fighter School at the No. 3 Operational Training Unit at Cold Lake, Alberta. Out of my original intake of more than two hundred potential aircrew who arrived with me in August 1956, only fifteen Pilots and Navigators were left to receive our wings that night. It was the proudest moment of my life up to that point.

An Army Major General pinned on our wings, presented our commission scrolls from Queen Elizabeth II, and we removed the white tabs from our hats. We were now Flying Officers (1st Lieutenants) and gentlemen—the Queen's Commission says so—in the Royal Canadian Air Force. We were granted five-year short-service commissions. The best part was that the British APOs were only promoted to Pilot Officer (2nd Lieutenant) and P/O Humphrey now had to salute me and my fellow Canadian graduates.

When I proudly received my Navigator wings it boosted my maturity, pride, and self-confidence tremendously. The next evening, I hitched a ride to Montreal on the accursedly slow and noisy but reliable Douglas C-47. I arrived at midnight to discover that Dad was in the hospital in very poor condition after his heart attack and my mom was staying with her sister, Aunt Liza.

When I visited Dad the next morning, he looked awful. I had never seen anyone in such horrible condition before and for a while it looked as though he wouldn't make it. He spent five weeks in the hospital and needed another couple of months to recover. During those agonizing weeks and months my parents had no income, so I was granted emergency leave to help them. Dad had commitments to his clients, mainly small delicatessens in Montreal and Toronto and also had outstanding credit with most of them (they were notoriously slow payers). I stepped in and helped my mom deliver orders and collect the overdue invoices; the first was easy, the second was not.

Knowing that European immigrants and refugees had a fear of uniforms, I donned my brand-new officer's uniform and drove around downtown Montreal delivering chocolates and collecting debts. This proved very effective and I collected enough to pay Dad's medical bills—no, there was no Medicare then; it didn't come until 1966. We had to pay my parent's rent as well as their living and medical expenses (my income was only $300 per month upon graduation).

During the time I was in Montreal I got the news that I wouldn't be going to Cold Lake for Operational Training on the CF-100 All Weather Fighter until August 1958 and would therefore be assigned ground duties in Winnipeg until then.

November 21 was Catherine's birthday and on that day I asked her to marry me. We were in the Garden of the Maples Inn in Pointe Claire, our after-football-game hangout. I thought it was very romantic, although she did not agree. When she said yes, that moment made me as proud as getting my wings.

We had intended to get married in the summer of 1958, which would now be impossible, so we decided to move our wedding forward to the end of December 1957 and live in Winnipeg until my transfer to Cold Lake in August. Ever practical where money was concerned, I realized that this had the added benefit of my being able to deduct her from my income tax for all of 1957. It saved us a total of $180—that was big money in those days.

On December 28, 1957, Catherine Shapcott became Catherine Voticky at St. Andrews Church in Lachine, Quebec. It was a great day for me and we even got some sunshine, which is unusual in Montreal at the end of December. We had a total of $400 to pay for the wedding, which had to cover the cost of using the beautiful old St. Andrews Church in Lachine, Quebec, and its wonderful minister, Reverend John Patterson, along with forty guests. Fortunately, we got $400 in cash as wedding presents and this funded our honeymoon trip to Winnipeg via New York City and kept us going for three weeks until my next payday (my long-range financial planning was non-existent at that time). We stayed at the celebrated Plaza Hotel in New York.

The highlight of the trip to New York for me—the incorrigible sports fan—was dinner at Jack Dempsey's Restaurant on Broadway; my new bride was not impressed. Neither was the waiter when I only gave him a two-dollar tip for a nineteen-dollar dinner. He was pretty surly about it, so I took the tip back and amazingly wasn't mugged on my way out. The two dollars may not have been much for him, but it was a lot for me.

We spent New Year's Eve in New York and then drove west across Pennsylvania, Ohio, Indiana, Michigan, Illinois, Iowa, and the Dakotas to Winnipeg. We had a memorable night in Iowa when the heating in our motel failed—the outside temperature was -10°F (-23°C)—and we had to get dressed to survive in bed (not very romantic!). The next morning, our 1955 Green Studebaker, my pride and joy, wouldn't start because of the cold. It took most of the morning to get it going so we could head out on the final stretch to Winnipeg.

The Studebaker was an aerodynamic gem that could do 90 mph (150 km/h), once you got her started in the cold weather. I was a bright new officer headed to Jet Fighter School and I was fearless—and also very reckless. We were driving up through North Dakota in the late afternoon, with the sun setting on our left in the west. The gas pedal was to the floor and we were smoking north at the Studebaker's maximum speed when I hit a patch of black ice and went into a horrendous skid.

I steered with one hand and used the other to push Catherine's face into the space between us. Fortunately, I was a good enough and lucky enough driver to steer into the skid and got us out of this mess with no injuries or damage to our car. My beloved wife has never forgotten or forgiven this dumb youthful transgression (women never forget). She still thinks that I'm a lousy driver, but my argument is that if I had been, we wouldn't have survived that horrible skid.

We arrived in Winnipeg on the evening of January 7, 1958. It was very, very cold—the chill factor was -40° (both Fahrenheit and Celsius), and it stayed that way for the next two weeks. We checked into a prearranged boarding house, where we had two rooms, a small kitchenette, and a small communal bathroom. There was a plug-in for the car's block heater, but it didn't help much, so we ended up taking the battery out every night and bringing it to the apartment. That was the only way the car would start in the morning. We spent the next ten days shopping for necessities and going to movies at night (needless to say, there was no TV or Internet).

I reported for duty at RCAF Station Winnipeg on Monday, January 20, 1958. I was expecting to be assigned to some office duties until I was due to go to Cold Lake for Fighter School (No. 3 Operational Training Unit) in August, but I got the shock of my life when I was told that I had to be in Cold Lake by the following Sunday, January 26, for a CF-100 course the next day. I was elated, but I had a problem. I had brought Catherine out to Winnipeg, but I couldn't take her to Cold Lake. There were no spousal accommodations there.

As a result, on Friday, January 24, I bundled Catherine on board a Trans-Canada Air Lines North Star for her return flight to Montreal. The ticket cost us $93, which hit our budget pretty hard (no credit cards then). It was Catherine's first flight ever and she was pretty nervous (since then she has flown a couple million miles and she's still nervous). The sight of the flames coming from the exhaust of the noisy Merlin engines did little to reassure her.

Catherine returned to Lachine, Quebec to live with the Simard family in the house where she had lived before we were married and went back to her old job at Decca Records. She didn't last long at the job, though. She started waking up every morning with morning sickness, which heralded the arrival of our first child. The Simards were great and treated her as though she was one of their own.

Catherine's pregnancy was great news and inspired me to work harder as our family was growing and had to be taken care of. I wanted to get back to see Catherine, but the distance was great, and we never had more than a day or two off at a time.

13

ALL WEATHER FIGHTER SCHOOL COLD LAKE

The Saturday morning after Catherine returned to Quebec, I set off in my Green Hornet across the snow-covered Canadian Prairies for Cold Lake with my other surviving course buddy and roommate, Jean-Yves Michaud. We shared the driving and arrived at RCAF Station Cold Lake on Sunday afternoon. We plugged in my car, then checked into the bachelor officer quarters, cleaned up, got into uniform, and headed for the officer's mess. That was the last time that I drove that car until the thaw in May; it was frozen solid until then. When they named it Cold Lake they weren't kidding!

The first thing we checked was the notice board for the next day's course information. To our dismay, our names were not on the course list. Monday morning, bright and early, we reported to station headquarters to see the Station Chief Administrative Officer (CAdO). After a half hour wait, he deigned to see us; we entered his office and threw him snappy salutes.

"Sir," I said. "We just checked the board in the mess for the new course starting today and noticed that our names are not on the list."

"Of course not," he replied. "I didn't bring you here to start the course. I brought you here because I'm the coach of the officer's hockey team, and I need a goalie and a forward. You two fit the bill."

This officer had dragged me away from my honeymoon, not to perform my Air Force duties, but to help his damn hockey team! I was flattered by his opinion of my hockey ability, but not amused by having to leave my new bride and spend extra time in this frozen northern wilderness. Talk about abuse of authority and taxpayer funds. Right then I decided that I was not going to play for this jerk. There was no way I could refuse a direct order, so therefore, I would have to outsmart him.

"Sir, you've got the right goalie, but Jean-Yves can't even skate."

"Are you kidding me?" he snarled. "How come he was on the Winnipeg Flight Cadet Team roster?"

"No, sir," I responded. "He was on the roster because he was our equipment manager."

"Great! I need an equipment manager too!" Talk about covering your behind—administrative officers are famous for that.

"We have another problem, sir," I continued, thinking fast. "I just got married and now have new responsibilities. I have to take care of my new wife and if I get injured playing hockey, I'll lose my flying pay. I can't afford that, so I have quit all body contact sports." Put that in your pipe and smoke it, mister! I thought to myself. I wouldn't disobey an order, but I could protect my health and income. Flying pay was 28 per cent of my income.

The CAdO, however, managed to get the last word. "Fine, F/O Voticky. I have just the job to keep you busy until the next course starts in three weeks." The three station messes (for officers, sergeants, and airmen) produced a lot of waste food every day, which was sent out as pig swill. At least it was organic, though this was long before anyone was using that term. The CAdO provided me with a car and driver, and for the next three weeks I had to peddle pig slop to the farmers for fifty miles (eighty kilometres) around. Amazing. The RCAF had spent $150,000 teaching me to shoot down Soviet bombers and this jerk turns me into a pig-swill salesman. He sure got his revenge! The good news was that his team was terrible because they had a lousy goalie.

This was the only time in my life that I refused to play any sport. The good news is that he had to get me on the next course to cover his tracks and three weeks later I was in the CF-100 Ground School with seven other new Navigators and eight new Pilots. Our first job was to marry up with a Pilot with whom we would crew for the next three years. There was Bob MacWilliams, a tall good-looking, cocky, and a little arrogant new Fighter Pilot, and Bob Bennedetti, a short, very cocky young guy with a Napoleonic complex and an ego the size of a CF-100.

Don't get me wrong, these comments are not meant to be derogatory; to be a good Fighter Pilot and survive it helps to be a bit cocky, a bit arrogant, and have a large ego and a Triple A personality. If you don't fit that profile, your career as a Fighter Pilot in combat will be very short. However, these two had a little too much of these qualities, so I decided to strike them off my list. Bob MacWilliams teamed up with Gerry Finch and they were like a real married couple—they fought all the time, once even physically.

Bob Bennedetti teamed up with my then-roommate Ross Stevenson, a superb athlete and physical specimen. Bob Bennedetti had a reckless streak in him when flying. After two years and many dumb flying stunts, Ross turned him in for violating regulations and Bob Benedetti was released from the service. Ross left the RCAF a couple of years later, went home to Cranbrook, Alberta, a mining town, and applied for a job at the local mining company. The employment manager asked him for his qualifications and experience.

"Killing Russians" was Ross's snappy reply.

"I am afraid we don't have any need or vacancies for those skills," the interviewer responded. But he hired him anyway, just in case the Russians showed up in Cranbrook, I guess.

I got lucky, one of the new Pilots was a very nice, quiet French-Canadian, Onil Lacharité (we called him Lach). He could barely speak English, but I figured that if this guy could get through Flying School with his limited English, he had to be one hell of a Pilot. I was right. We got "married" and became one heck of a skilled crew together, eventually becoming the Top Gun crew on our Fighter Squadron.

It was during the course that Catherine told me she was pregnant and that I would be a father sometime in October. Now I had to work that much harder to ensure that I didn't fail and could take care of my family.

All Weather Fighters, like the CF-100, were twin engine jets with a two-man crew: A Pilot and a Navigator Weapons Officer. The original CF-100 MK IV armament was fifty-eight World War II US Navy free-flight 2.75-inch rockets that were fired with one squeeze of the trigger to ensure the destruction of the target—we had to be ready for nuclear-armed Soviet bombers—and eight 50-calibre machine guns.

Four squadrons of these aircraft were based in Europe as part of the North Atlantic Treaty Organization (NATO) Force. Nine Fighter Squadrons and one Training Squadron of the newer MK V aircraft were based in Canada as part of the North American Air Defense Command (NORAD). As I've said, these aircraft had extended wings and horizontal stabilizers, and the machine guns had been removed to reduce weight; this enabled the MK Vs to operate up to seven thousand feet (2,300 metres) higher to an altitude of 52,000 feet (15,850 metres), which was thought to be the maximum altitude for any Soviet bomber.

The Pilot's job was to fly the aircraft and follow the ground controller's instructions to bring the fighter to within thirty nautical miles of the enemy target (called a bogey). It was then the Navigator's job to acquire the target on his radar and vector the Pilot into position to attack the bandit (a bogey became a bandit when it was identified as hostile). The Pilot did this by following the Navigator's instructions for compass heading, airspeed, and altitude until twenty seconds before the kill (called a splash). At this point, the Pilot took control by flying the dot on his radar scope to maintain it in the crosshairs and squeezing the trigger on his yoke. As long as the trigger was depressed the rockets would fire automatically. All our attacks were from the ninety-degree beam to eliminate any possible speed advantage for the bomber. After the rockets fired, we would pass behind the target or through the debris (in practice and in the real thing).

After three weeks of more Ground School and a checkout on the CF-100 for both of us, we became a crew. We worked well together and by the end of the Operational Training Unit (OTU) course, we were the No. 1 crew on our course. At that time, we had nine CF-100 All Weather Fighter Squadrons in Canada, one Training Squadron (the OTU) in Cold Lake, and four AWF Squadrons in Europe (two in France and two in Germany).

As the top crew on our course, we had first choice of available postings. Onil wanted to stay in Quebec so he could be near his fiancée. I didn't mind because I didn't want to bring my family to Western Europe; I didn't want them anywhere near the Red Army. The Cold

War was on and we all knew it could turn hot at any time. The memory of the brutality of rape and plunder by the Red Army in World War II was still too fresh. I didn't want to be fighting the Soviets in the air while the Red Army overran Western Europe and my family. We both wanted to go to one of the Montreal Squadrons based at St. Hubert on the South Shore of the St. Lawrence River, but there were no vacancies there, so we ended up on 432 AWF Squadron (Black Cougars) at RCAF Station Bagotville outside Chicoutimi in the Lac St. Jean area of Northern Quebec.

14

432 ALL WEATHER FIGHTER SQUADRON

ach and I arrived in Bagotville in June 1958 and were welcomed by another living legend, our new Squadron Commander, Wing Commander (Lt. Col.) John Braham. He had three Distinguished Service Orders (DSOs), three Distinguished Flying Crosses (DFCs), and three Air Force Crosses (AFCs). The top Royal Air Force Night Fighter Pilot in World War II, he was credited with thirty kills against the Luftwaffe bombers in the Battle of Britain at night, working with a very primitive radar set. Toward the end of the war he was shot down over the North Sea and spent the rest of the conflict as a prisoner of war (POW) in Germany. After his capture, he and his Luftwaffe opponents had a three-day wild party in the Luftwaffe Officer's Mess in Denmark—Fighter Pilots have great mutual respect for their buddies and foes alike.

As it turned out, W/C John Braham was a brave man, a great leader in combat, and a superb Fighter Pilot, but he was not a very good officer. Most of his squadron worshipped him because of his reputation, his bravery, his deadly skill, his leadership, and his legendary drinking bouts. To be recommended for a permanent commission or promotion on his squadron, you needed to both be a good Pilot or Navigator and go to the bar with him at the end of your shift. One of his qualifications for officers was being able to party and drink a lot. If you didn't join his drinking sessions, your career wouldn't be long or memorable. Neither Onil nor I fit into that category; we were a good fighter crew but did not meet the alcoholic criteria of our Commanding Officer. This ended up serving us well since we both went on to great careers in civil aviation with Air Canada.

At Bagotville, Onil and I became Rhino 29—our call sign for duty rosters and while flying—and were immediately placed into Combat-Ready Training, the final phase of the two full years of training required for being allowed to defend our country. Six weeks later, after my check ride with the legend and Lach's with the Navigation Radio (Nav Rad) Leader, S/L John Boby (known as Mother Boby, due to his meticulousness in everything that he did), we were declared combat ready. After two years of very hard training, we were ready to fire live rockets and defend Canada. Our reward was being advised that we were headed back to Cold Lake to actually fire live rockets at a target drone trailing behind a tow aircraft.

The Lac St. Jean area, where Chicoutimi and Bagotville are located, is a beautiful part of central Quebec that is 98 per cent French-speaking. Great—my wife was seven months pregnant and I had to go back to the end of the world in Northern Alberta to play war games and fire live rockets. Fortunately, Catherine speaks French fluently because she'd been educated in French schools in Ste. Marguerite, north of Montreal, and we'd met two great people during our first six weeks at Bagotville, F/O (1st Lieutenant) Walt Niemy and his wife, Donna. While I was back at Cold Lake, they kept Catherine company and made her feel welcome. In fact, they became our close friends and remained so until they passed away. Our kids grew up together, we vacationed together, and then we grew old together.

Walt Niemy was a Pilot (call sign Rhino 25) with an electrical engineering degree, a Royal Military College graduate with a great career ahead of him. He was six-foot-three, two hundred pounds, and looked as if he had just left the Royal Military College Parade Ground in his sharp uniform. He was very bright, aggressive, cocky, abrupt, and ambitious. In those days he made it very clear that his objective was to be Chief of the Air Staff (the top man in the RCAF). This did not endear him to his fellow officers, but I thought it was great because here was a bright young officer with the guts to express his ambition. He and I both respected the legend (W/C Braham) for his accomplishments but were not impressed by his officer qualities or his personal behaviour. We had a common bond—we were in the minority on 432 AWF Squadron and even on the entire Bagotville base because we did not participate in the hero worship of our Commanding Officer.

The Base Commander at RCAF Bagotville, was Group Captain (Colonel) Ashman, a World War II veteran who, despite never having qualified to fly jet aircraft, was theoretically the Wing Commander of the two All Weather Jet Fighter Squadrons and the Battle Commander at the base in case of war. Under normal circumstances, to be a real Wing Commander, you had to be qualified to fly the aircraft flown by your wing in order to make proper and sound judgments and decisions on conducting an air battle. The Base Commander, however, was not qualified to fly the CF-100 or any jet fighter; he was only qualified to fly as a Second Pilot in the same small two engine propeller aircraft that I learned to fly on in Navigation School at RCAF Station Winnipeg, the C-45. No one dared let him go flying without another Pilot along to ensure his safe return. Fortunately, we were only involved in a Cold War and his ability to conduct an air battle was not put to the test. His main skills seemed to be golf and spending time in his private suite in the officers' quarters, at the bar stocked with booze paid for by the junior officers.

ON OCTOBER 1, 1958, beautiful Linda Florence Voticky arrived on schedule at 4:30 a.m. at St. Jean de Dieu in Chicoutimi. An hour later, I went home to our little basement apartment in Chicoutimi North, got two hours sleep, finished packing, and an hour after that, the movers arrived to move us to our new apartment at 90 rue des Hospitalières. When I arrived at the apartment, I met our new wonderful neighbours, F/O Elwood Shell and his spouse, Loretta Shell. Elwood came from Edmonton, Alberta and his background was a mix of French, German, Ukrainian, Native Canadian, and a few more nationalities mixed in; he was basically a Heinz (57 varieties) and embodied all the good qualities of his various ancestries. He had played professional hockey in the United Kingdom and then got a hockey scholarship to the University of North Dakota, where he was an All-American defenseman.

These two great people met at university and got married. When their first two sons, Kevin and Curtis, were born, Elwood needed a steady job and ended up as an RCAF Accounting Officer. Loretta was of pure Czech descent and came from a small town in Minnesota. These two amazing people with totally different genetic backgrounds eventually ended up with five children, all of whom were born with severe physical defects or disabilities. Their case was unique in terms of genetic probability and history—the usual odds for a couple with one child with disabilities was that three out of four children would be born without any disability.

After helping me to install our meagre furniture and belongings, Elwood invited me to watch the baseball World Series on his tiny black-and-white TV; we didn't have a TV at that point. There was only one French TV station in Chicoutimi then; no cable, just a rabbit-ear antenna on top of the TV. Every time a car passed outside we got static. For the next six years in Chicoutimi and Moisie, Quebec, all we could watch was French TV.

Kevin and Curtis Shell were both born with club feet, which at that time was considered a lifelong disability. While the Shells were in Chicoutimi, they found a Dr. Lévesque who had developed a surgical procedure for treating club feet. They had learned of the doctor when Elwood picked up a disabled hitchhiker on the way home one night and his passenger mentioned that he had seen Dr. Lévesque for his own rehabilitation—one good deed spawned another. Dr. Lévesque operated on both boys and corrected the problem; his procedure became the world standard for this disability. Chicoutimi had great medical facilities and some of the best doctors anywhere. Both boys grew into healthy young men and played hockey with a lot of success well into their fifties.

LIFE ON THE Fighter Squadron was exciting. There were two Fighter Squadrons at RCAF Station Bagotville: 432 AWF Squadron and 413 AWF Squadron at the other end of the flight line. We conducted friendly competitions on flying training and large-scale exercises. Each squadron had eighteen aircraft, twelve of which were usually available for flying, the rest being in maintenance. We shared the duties and responsibilities equally, including the need for two aircraft and their crews to be on constant alert, prepared for instant scramble to intercept and identify any unknown aircraft within our area of responsibility. Each squadron was divided into two flights, with each flight on duty twenty-four hours, then off for the next twenty-four hours. Two aircraft were on ten-minute alert standby—the crews had to be airborne fully armed and ready for combat within ten minutes from the time the telephone rang in the Alert Quarters, twenty-four hours a day, 365 days a year. Each squadron had to maintain this ten-minute alert for two weeks at a time.

These aircraft were armed with fifty-eight 2.75-inch free-flight rockets that were fired in one salvo. The rockets were not very accurate, which is why we had to fire fifty-eight at a time in order to ensure that we hit our target. We had inherited these rockets from World War II US Navy supplies because they were cheap. The issues with them limited us to a one-attack capability; after that, we had to hope that our base was still there, so we could land, refuel, and rearm. The only other alternative was to ram into a nuclear bomber's tail—not a great choice for anyone! We had a great firing platform, but the one-attack capability was not good enough, especially when we were facing a nuclear-armed enemy bomber force.

We learned how to attack low-level targets—it is very difficult to find these targets on radar due to ground interference—targets that were equipped with electronic and mechanical jamming equipment, and targets that took evasive action. We learned how to track targets with limited broadcast control, using commercial radio station frequencies. Every practice mission was a learning experience and we got better as time went on. It took two to three years to get really proficient for our assigned mission and just when you got really good at it, the Air Force, in its bureaucratic wisdom, would transfer you to a lousy ground job, where all that training was wasted.

During my time on 432 AWF Squadron, Lach and I had two close calls. The first was during an exercise against US Strategic Air Command (SAC). In our first night mission against SAC B-47 bombers, two young and inexperienced fighter jocks came very close to "buying the farm" and not making it home for breakfast. Under the rules of engagement, the SAC crews were permitted to use electronic warfare against us, but they were not permitted to use evasive action such as climb or descend, nor could they turn once they were under attack. In addition, they had to keep all their lights on so that we could see them at night. We didn't have communication with them because we had old very high frequency (VHF) radios and they had new ultra-high frequency radios (UHF), which are not compatible.

On our first major night exercise against SAC Bombers, we attacked the B-47 from 90 degrees on the beam as our speeds were very similar; if we got behind the target, we would never catch up to it because they were faster. Scabbard Control vectored us into position for the attack beautifully and I saw my target 45 degrees left at eighteen miles (thirty kilometres) on my radar at 35,000 feet (10,700 metres). We had a closing speed of 700 knots (1,200 km/h). I called "Judy," taking control of the attack, directing Lach to stay on target.

Everything looked great, we maintained our position until eight miles (thirteen kilometres), when the target started to drift further left toward 50 degrees. I instructed Lach to turn 10 degrees left to regain our position, the target kept drifting left, and we kept turning left too. My eyes were on the radar and I kept asking Lach if he could see the target. He responded negatively, but this was soon easily explained when we almost collided with it—the bomber's aircraft lights were all out, a gross violation of the rules. We kept turning into the target until the overtake speed reached 900 knots (1,600 km/h)—our combined speeds meant that we were now flying head-on toward each other at a speed of one mile (1.6 kilometres) every four seconds. I yelled, "BREAK DOWN AND HARD LEFT!" Lach reacted instantly, pushing the joystick straight down and to the left. If it had not been for his quick reaction, we would have been buried in the right wing of the B-47 bomber.

That was when I knew for sure that I had picked the right Pilot as my partner. Our mutual trust was the key to our ability to avoid a hor-rific accident. Most importantly, it made it possible for us to go home for breakfast later that morning. We had learned a valuable lesson that night—not everyone plays by the rules, even our friends and allies.

I looked up and saw the No. 6 engine approximately three feet over the canopy and my head. As I've said, we called a confirmed kill a "splash"—well, we almost had one in real life. If Lach had not reacted as fast as he did, we would have been "splashed" all over Northern Quebec.

This splash was without the use of rockets or gun camera film; it would have been the result of one huge explosion. We would have had no chance of survival, but the two Pilots and Navigator of the B-47 would probably have been able to eject and survive because the B-47 was a much bigger aircraft than ours. Then they could have blamed us for their illegal behaviour and their serious violation of Air Defense and Strategic Air Command rules and regulations and rules of engagement.

As it was, it turned out that the B-47 Pilot had turned 45 degrees right into us and then turned off all of their external lights in order to ensure that we didn't see them, just to deprive us of a splash. In addition, our own fighter controller either missed or ignored the evasive action and had not warned us. On our side, if we had been more experienced and less focused on getting a splash, we could have recognized the danger sooner. Nor did we ever think that a highly trained SAC Pilot would ever violate the rules of engagement and endanger five men and two aircraft—including himself—so recklessly, just to avoid being beaten in an exercise.

Lach and I were both badly shaken, but it was an important learning experience and it never happened again. That is how fighter crews learn to avoid making dumb mistakes that can kill them. As a general rule, if you survive the first year on a Fighter Squadron, you will complete your tour safely. The way you survive is by not making the same mistake twice or repeating a mistake that one of your squadron buddies has made. All good Pilots benefit from reading accident reports in order to learn from the errors of others.

Another close call came in early April 1960, this one weather-related. Baie de Ha-Ha was directly lined up with the end of our Runway 11, which was great for our airborne radar-assisted approaches in bad weather, but not good when the fog rolled off the water onto our home base at Bagotville.

Eight aircraft from both Bagotville Squadrons had just finished a late-night exercise and were returning to Bagotville for recovery. Rhino 25 with F/L Walt Niemy flying was the first of the eight CF-100s returning from the mission to do the approach; we were following him as his No. 2. The Bagotville Tower gave us the weather at Bagotville as 2,500 feet (762 metres) overcast and three miles (five kilometres) visibility—basically visual approach requirements. We were all under the guidance of our Bagotville Ground Control Approach, our guardian angels in bad weather. When we were under their control, we could only receive their instructions. We couldn't respond or transmit out to them or anyone else, and we only had one radio.

Walt did his approach and, as No. 2 five miles (eight kilometres) behind him, we descended through the alleged ceiling and still could not see the ground—we continued down to our minimum permissible height of two hundred feet (61 metres) with no visual contact with the ground. At two hundred feet, Lach applied go-around power, pulled the nose up, raised the landing gear and flaps and proceeded into the missed approach climb-out. I immediately checked our fuel and determined that we had just enough fuel to reach our alternate of St. Hubert outside Montreal. I gave him a heading to St. Hubert, and we did a right turn direct to the southwest toward St. Hubert while climbing to 33,000 feet (10,000 metres) for the journey to save fuel—the CF-100 burned 6,000 pounds (2,700 kilograms) of fuel per hour at low level, but only 2,000 pounds (900 kilograms) per hour above 30,000 feet (9,000 metres).

It would normally take a maximum of forty minutes to reach St. Hubert from Bagotville, however, on checking our position and ground speed, I discovered that we were right over the St. Lawrence River and flying straight into an extremely strong and ugly jet stream in excess of 150 mph (240 km/h). This meant that our flight might require almost an hour to arrive at St. Hubert, by which time we would be out of fuel. To add to our concern, the St. Lawrence River was full of large ice floes caused by the spring breakup. Not a great place to go for a midnight swim.

The thought of our fourteen-ton fighter running out of fuel and becoming a glider did not appeal to us. We would have had two choices: crash land at night or eject over the St. Lawrence and hope to survive among the ice floes. Neither idea was very appealing.

After we overshot Bagotville, I advised Bagotville Tower to warn the other aircraft behind us and to divert them to St. Hubert. The Bagotville Tower warned them off immediately, allowing them to maintain a higher altitude and thus conserve fuel. The six other aircraft from our exercise then bypassed the approach to Bagotville and followed us on to St. Hubert. As they came on our radio frequency, I warned them of the strong head-on jet stream that had not been forecast by our meteorologists—just like the fog—and suggested that they take diversion action around it or divert to another alternate. Every captain of an aircraft has the right to make his own decision.

Lach and I discussed the pleasures of a midnight swim in an ice-choked St. Lawrence River and whether we preferred to drown or be crushed to death by the ice floes. We decided neither option was a good idea, so I suggested that we turn left to the South Shore where, if we ran out of fuel and had to bail out, our biggest danger was landing in a soft snow bank. Lach agreed and turned 40 degrees left.

We thus crossed over to the land mass of the South Shore of the St. Lawrence, away from the strongest part of the jet stream. This manoeuvre saved our aircraft and saved us an unpleasant night in the wilderness at the cost of extra fuel burn. As we crossed out of the strongest wind and our ground speed increased, the estimated time of arrival at St. Hubert decreased, permitting us to land safely. As we taxied off the runway to our ramp parking location, however, our right engine ran out of fuel and quit; there was very little left in the left fuel tank as well. We were very lucky that night. Seven Bagotville crews got to spend a night in the St. Hubert Officers' Quarters and returned safely to our home base the next morning.

My luck was still there—I had survived two more close calls!

Included in our group of diverted crews were our Wing Commander (Lt. Col.) Joe Schulz—by now we had a fully qualified Wing Commander at Bagotville who was a Fighter Pilot—and his Navigator, Squadron Leader (Major) John "Mother" Boby, who had survived a midair collision just eight months earlier flying with W/C John Braham. When it became apparent that we had to spend the night at St. Hubert, Wing Commander Schulz got upset, complaining, "If we don't get back to Bagotville tonight, who is going to take care of my work in the office tomorrow morning?"

S/L Boby, his deputy, responded with the greatest putdown ever: "Don't worry, sir. The Corporal will take care of it!"

When we returned to Bagotville, our Section Leader, Walt Niemy, told us that when he had broken cloud on his approach at two hundred feet (sixty-one metres) and landed the day before, he could see the fog rolling down the runway toward him so fast that when he lowered his nose wheel and applied the brakes, he found himself in thick fog with zero visibility. That's why we couldn't see or land even though we were just forty seconds behind him.

THE RCAF DIDN'T permit us to play Canadian football because the chances of injuries were too great. However, when the French-Canadians in the Lac St. Jean area decided to form a Senior Canadian Football League in 1959, and requested our assistance, the RCAF permitted us to coach and play to enhance community relations. Naturally, with my love of football, I was one of the first in line to join the new Chicoutimi Labatt Cinquante (50) team. Loaded with Air Force talent and football experience, we were by far the best team and won the local championship that year.

Unfortunately, I sustained my worst ever sports-related injury when a big professional wrestler who was trying to learn football and make it to the Canadian Football League stepped onto my left foot, crushing it. It was swollen and blue for a month; I couldn't run or even walk on it.

Flying was difficult as well because my swollen foot didn't fit my flying boot and I couldn't run to my aircraft when we scrambled. In order to be able to fly, I got a left flying boot two sizes bigger than my right one. I didn't dare report the damage to the Medical Officer because I would have been grounded, which meant that I would have lost my flying pay because the Air Force would have considered this to be a self-inflicted injury. We definitely couldn't afford to lose a quarter of my salary. I was able to keep flying by going to the aircraft long before our takeoff time, inspecting the aircraft, then climbing aboard and strapping in, waiting for the scramble call.

My football performance that year got me another invitation for another tryout with the Montreal Alouettes professional football team. I thanked them for their interest and turned them down. I now had more important responsibilities: one daughter and another child on the way.

Life on our squadron was busy and exciting because there were always new exercises with new wrinkles and there was always a lot to learn. In mid-1959, I was appointed Flight Radar Navigator Leader, a job that involved running courses and examinations on new equipment in both NORAD and Soviet Long-Range Aviation, on the rules of engagement (the pass mark was 100 per cent), and on changing air regulations for both Pilots and Navigators. In addition, I administered the Navigator examinations that went with the training.

La gent enfantine découvre le monde

"Combien coûte un avion T-33", a demandé un jeune garçon à un officier-pilote de la base de Bagotville. "Trois quarts de millions de dollars", lui a-t-il répondu. Voilà une des innombrables questions qu'ont posée les 1,000 garçons et fillettes des écoles de Jonquière, Kénogami, Arvida et Chicoutimi, qui ont assisté samedi après-midi à la journée de l'aviation pour les e͏ la région en collabo le démontre cette ͏ supersonique, à la attractions de l'apr͏ au bruit infernal. (Photo "Le Soleil a͏

Demonstrating a CF-100 All Weather Fighter with Onil (Lach) Lacharité (right) while we flew in the 432 AWF Squadron (Black Cougars) at RCAF Station Bagotville. I'm on the left. Lach was my Pilot on the CF-100 for three years, from 1958 to 1960. Bagotville, Quebec, 1958.

The 432 AWF Squadron (Black Cougars) at RCAF Station Bagotville, 1959.

432 AWF Squadron Top Guns Onil Lacharité (right) and I en route to the 1960 Rocket Meet —the Top Gun Competition for All Weather Fighters.

A portrait in courage. Brigadier General Walter Niemy, my oldest and best friend and the bravest man I ever met. After a horrendous skiing accident and seven hours of surgery, he persevered for the next twenty years as a quadriplegic without complaint or self-pity and learned to walk around the block.

15

THE U-2, THE CANADIAN TOP GUN COMPETITION,

AND SURVIVAL SCHOOL

n early March 1960, W/C Braham called Lach and me into his office and advised us that, as the Top Gun scoring crew (assessed by camera film) on 432 AWF Squadron, we had been selected to represent our squadron at the Annual Rocket Meet Competition—the Canadian version of the US Top Gun Competition. The competition, which was scheduled for late May in Cold Lake, would use live rocket firing. This was the highest honour available in the Fighter environment and allowed us to test our skills against the other very best Fighter Crews in the rest of Air Defense Command.

One reason that we were the top fighter crew on the Squadron was because Lach had a little trick homing in for the "splash." Instead of steering the dot on his scope by using his yoke and ailerons, which tended to lead to over-control when homing in on the target, he controlled his lateral control by a gentle application of the rudder, which resulted in a smooth final twenty seconds of the attack and no over-controlling. As I said, he was an excellent Pilot.

The prize of this honour was that W/C Braham again sent us to Cold Lake for more live rocket firing as practice for the Rocket Meet Competition. We arrived at Cold Lake a few days later, just in time for a lockdown of the entire air base. A top-secret US U-2 spy plane had run out of fuel over Northern Alberta and made an emergency crash landing with wheels up on nearby Montreal Lake, which was covered with a deep layer of ice and snow. It seemed as if half the US Air Force then descended at Cold Lake to recover their top-secret aircraft and make sure that no one got a good look at it.

The U-2 was basically a glider with a fuel-efficient single jet engine, very fragile and relatively slow (400 mph or 644 km/h) aircraft with long wings. It was full of cameras and radio/radar detection equipment and had the ability to fly above 80,000 feet (24,384 metres)—well above any Soviet fighter aircraft or missiles at that time. It had done yeoman service for the Central Intelligence Agency for years, flying high over Cuba, China, Vietnam, as well as the Soviet Union and its Warsaw Pact allies. As I said, it was also very top secret. We'd been hearing rumours about this wonderful aircraft for a few years and now we were among the first to have its existence confirmed.

The entire Cold Lake base was locked down and the whole hangar line was off limits. Everyone on the base now knew that the US secret spy plane was for real and it was here in our backyard! It took the US Air Force a few days to recover their aircraft, repair it, and get it out of Cold Lake. Since we weren't allowed to practice our rocket firing, we spent the time reading and playing billiards in the Officers' Mess.

Five weeks later, on May 1, Gary Francis Powers had an engine problem while flying high over Sverdlovsk in the Soviet Union, which turned his U2 into a severely damaged glider. As he descended to a lower altitude in an attempt to restart his engine, a Soviet S-75 SAM anti-aircraft missile hit the aircraft. Two other missiles missed, but one of them shot down a Soviet MIG-19 that had also attempted to intercept the U-2. A third Soviet fighter, an unarmed SU-9, tried unsuccessfully to ram the U-2 but missed. I guess the Pilot's heart wasn't into committing suicide.

Gary very wisely did not attempt to use his ejection seat; he climbed out of the cockpit and jumped without activating the aircraft's self-destruct system. The word among U2 Pilots (whether true or not) was that firing the ejection seat would blow up the aircraft and kill the Pilot in order to leave no witnesses and provide the president of the US with plausible deniability as to who was responsible. Not destroying his U-2 did not endear Gary Powers to the CIA. He further aggravated them by writing his autobiography ten years later. In 2015, the excellent movie *Bridge of Spies* was made about this.

Unfortunately, President Eisenhower assumed that Gary Powers was dead when his plane disappeared and denied that it was a US spy plane. He was very embarrassed when Comrade Nikita Khrushchev produced a live Gary Powers at a press conference complete with a full confession. Gary Powers was charged with espionage against the USSR and sentenced to ten years hard labour. He served only one year and nine months in a Soviet jail until he was exchanged for a top Soviet spymaster, Colonel Rudolph Ivanovich Abel. Gary Powers was not treated very well by the CIA on his return.

A few years later, on August 1, 1977, while he was working as a helicopter traffic reporter in Los Angeles for station KNBC, he ran out of fuel, crashed, and died. This was a Pilot with over twenty years' flying experience, who had flown dozens of eight-hour-plus missions over hostile Soviet territory without refuelling or having a place to land. It is hard to believe that he ran out of fuel during a ninety-minute flight over Los Angeles in a high-quality Bell Jet Ranger, flying over a city with hundreds of possible landing spots for a helicopter—shopping malls, parking lots, schoolyards, playgrounds.

The CIA was upset with Gary Powers for confessing to the Soviets and then writing about it. But he was tortured by the Soviets and abandoned by the CIA on his return; he felt that the CIA had betrayed him and left him to dangle in the wind. You decide whether you believe that Gary Francis Powers' death was an "accident." Whether he ran out of fuel or whether it was sabotage.

IN LATE MAY 1960, Lach and I, as the No. 1 Top Gun crew on 432 Squadron, were accompanied by a second crew of my buddy F/L Walt Niemy and his Navigator, F/O Ed Lanfranconi, at the Cold Lake Rocket Meet. The competition, comprising eight missions, lasted five days; it was a test of aircraft, radar, weapons systems, aircrew, and ground crew. The secret of success in this competition was that the aircraft, radar, and air and ground crews had to be perfect; any failure of any of these components basically eliminated the crew from any chance of winning.

Unfortunately, both of our crews ran into radar failures, which destroyed one mission for each of us and, therefore, any chance we had of winning the Rocket Meet Competition. If you missed on one mission due to aircraft or radar problems, you scored zero. Because both our crews had to abort one mission each, we had to watch one crew from 416 AWF squadron walk away with the Rocket Meet Trophy. They managed to complete all eight missions with no equipment failures. Walt Niemy did us proud, however, by actually hitting the eight-foot target with one of his rockets.

I HAD ONE of the great experiences of my life in late August 1960. I was flying on the Trans Canada Air Lines milk run, Bagotville–Montreal–Toronto–Windsor–Lakehead–Winnipeg–Regina–Edmonton,   for Survival Training in Edmonton. It was an all-day journey in those days, with the benefit of time zones extending the day. In Toronto, a very nice older gentleman boarded the flight and travelled in the seat beside me in the economy section as far as Regina. He turned out to be the premier of Saskatchewan, the Right Honourable (and one of the few Canadian politicians in my lifetime I consider deserving of this title) Tommy Douglas—the Father of Canadian Medicare. As I watch the mess in medical care in the US sixty years later, I realize that Canada owes him a lot.

It was a long flight with three stops to Regina and we had a great conversation in which my interest in political science and world affairs came in handy. Spending time with this brilliant and energetic man who would have and probably should have been Prime Minister of Canada made it the most educational and interesting flight of my life—other than actually flying the aircraft, that is. Every Canadian owes this great man a debt of gratitude.

Regrettably, Douglas was the leader of Canada's third political party, the Co-operative Commonwealth Federation (CCF), later the New Democratic Party (both Socialist). They have always been a minority party in the country due to some of their wacky ideas on the economy. At least until 2011, when Jack Layton led the New Democrats to greater electoral success and the party became the Official Opposition in the Canadian federal government for four years.

It was an honour to spend a day with the Right Honourable Tommy Douglas, MP, Leader of the CCF; he taught me a lot about the reality of government and political activity in Canada.

The Survival course was also great. After three days of Ground School, we were taken into the Rocky Mountain Foothills and taught how to survive in the wild. We learned some very important lessons from our Indigenous Canadian guides and instructors. A person can survive a long time in the wilderness as long as he or she follows a few simple rules:

1. Stay calm and take an inventory of your assets.
2. A knife, matches, lighters, bottles or cups, and dry socks are vital. Humans need water and fire to survive in the wild.
3. Humans can go without food for three days and continue to function normally. We had twelve high-energy Jelly Beans in our seat packs that would keep us alive and functioning for another four days.
4. Change your socks often and keep them dry. We had two extra pair of woollen flying socks in our seat pack, so we could do just that.
5. Do not exert yourself unnecessarily. Our Indigenous guide stressed this by pointing out one of the differences between Indigenous and non-Indigenous people. The latter waste a lot of effort and time gathering a lot of wood, building big fires, then sitting far away from them. Indigenous people gather a small amount of wood, build small fires, and sit close to them.
6. Set up camp near an open area and prepare signal fires in a triangle in this open area to alert aircraft flying by.
7. Trap rabbits and catch fish to survive.

All in all, it was a great experience and helped me considerably years later in my escape from the People's Republic of China in 1993. I also lost seventeen pounds that I had accumulated in the past two years; luckily, I have been able to keep them off ever since.

16

RCAF STATION MOISIE-CROWBAR SEVEN

n October 1960, my buddy F/L Walt Niemy was transferred to RCAF Station Moisie in the northern wilds of Quebec, fifteen miles (twenty-four kilometres) northeast of Sept-Îles, as their new Chief Administration Officer (CAdO). We all thought it was very funny until a month later I was transferred to the same place as a Fighter Controller. Guess who had the last laugh. Another buddy, F/O Bud Bernston, a six-foot-five gentle giant from Saskatchewan laughed even harder when I got transferred there.

Three months later, when Bud arrived at the front door of our motel in Mexico Beach, Florida, where I was on the Fighter Controller course, his first sentence was, "I'm going to Moisie too. One smart crack out of you, Voticky, and I'll deck you!" I couldn't make any cracks because I too busy laughing. He hadn't said anything about laughing. Bud was there because he was joining me on the Fighter Controller course with the USAF at Tyndall Air Force Base in the Florida Panhandle.

Catherine—pregnant with our second child—was with me in Florida and on the evening of February 5, 1961, at 10:00 p.m., she went into labour. We deposited Linda with our neighbours at the motel and I rushed Catherine to the Tyndall Air Force Base Hospital. Two and a half hours later, at 12:30 a.m. on February 6, 1961, a beautiful, scream-ing Elizabeth Anne Voticky made her global debut as a dual Canadian/US citizen at the base hospital.

IN APRIL 1961, I reported to RCAF Station Moisie, which was pretty well the end of civilization at that time. The only way to get there was either by air from Montreal or by ferry from Matane on the South Shore of the St. Lawrence River, although a road was being built to cover the last 150 miles (240 kilometres) from the Saguenay River to Port Cartier and Sept-Îles. The posting at Moisie was only for one or two years because it was considered an isolated location, which it certainly was.

I arrived on a flight from Montreal with my new boss and Chief Operations Officer, F/L Paul Apperley. We were the first replacements for the mass changeover that was due that summer; most of the officers were preparing to leave at the end of their one-year (singles) or two-year (married) isolation tours.

We had three operational flights to man the Radar Site on a twenty-four hour per day, seven day a week basis, consisting of three officers, two non-commissioned officers, and fourteen airmen each. Paul, an old F-86 Sabre Pilot, and I became good friends as we were both living in the bachelor officer quarters until our families could join us later in the summer. When the Flight Commander of "B" Flight transferred out, Paul appointed me as the new Flight Commander rather than a more senior officer whom he didn't trust.

Three months later, to great fanfare, the Quebec government announced that the new highway was now open all the way to Sept-Îles. I flew down to Montreal to pick up my family and bring them back to Moisie. We packed most of our belongings into our old 1958 Chevrolet and headed north. We crossed the mighty Saguenay River on a ferry at Tadoussac and drove through the town only to discover that three miles (five kilometres) later, the new highway was nothing but gravel, rocks, and dirt! We managed to plow our way through that mess for 150 miles (240 kilometres), until we grounded our old car on a hilltop, where we left our muffler. We then chugged on to Port Cartier at which point we found more paved road for the last stretch into Sept-Îles and Moisie.

A few weeks later, F/O Midge Pennington arrived at Moisie, which was good news for our planned soccer team. Midge was a World War II Fighter Pilot, who also happened to be the finest soccer player developed in Canada up to that time. When the war ended, and he was demobilized, he stayed in England and was the first Canadian-born-and-developed player signed to a professional soccer contract in England (then the mecca of football, what North Americans call soccer).

Midge and I created a team consisting of five real soccer players and ten athletic young men who had not played before and proceeded to teach them the finer points of the game. I was also the team manager, Midge was the coach and captain, and F/L Doug French, our Accounts Officer, was our forty-two-year-old goalie. Along with our Physical Education Corporal, we were the heart of the team, surrounded by young well-conditioned airmen who were keen to learn.

Long hours of practice and entering a local league sharpened us into a very good team over the spring and summer. There were three teams in the Sept-Îles league and we won the local championship in 1961. A year later, with the arrival of two more experienced soccer players, we were even better and won the Sept-Îles Championship again in 1962. We also won the Quebec Armed Forces Championship in 1961 and 1962.

In the summer of 1962, we drove almost four hundred miles (640 kilometres) to St. Jean, Quebec in one long day. In the first game, we played the RCAF St. Jean base and beat them 3–2. I scored our second goal and pulled up lame just before halftime with a pulled hamstring. The pain was so intense that I couldn't continue to play; I couldn't even walk and had to watch the rest of the game from the sidelines. That night I spent the evening applying Rub A535, which eased the pain enough for me to walk.

The next day, we played RCAF Station Bagotville, but I wasn't able to help my team in their 4–2 victory because I still couldn't run. That night I intensified the massaging with the A535—it really works—and the next day, after exercising and applying more of the ointment, I was able to run for the first time in two days. We played RCAF Station St. Hubert and I played the game of my life. I scored four goals and we won again, this time 4–0. As a result, we won the Quebec Armed Forces Championship.

Midge Pennington was the best soccer player I had ever seen or played with. He was also an excellent Pilot, a very kind and gentle man who never raised his voice. All our opponents knew that to stop the

Moisie team, they had to stop our star, coach, and captain—Midge Pennington. While they were double-teaming and watching Midge, they ignored the little guy (me) playing next to him. Our strategy was simple; Midge would feed me the ball and leave the scoring to me.

St. Hubert had a big red-headed Irish centre back who decided that he would stop Midge all by himself, by whatever means necessary. He fouled Midge three times in the first half with intent to injure. I told Midge that we couldn't afford to lose him and that I would take "Big Red" out; if I got thrown out, so be it. Midge quietly shook his head and said, "Leave him to me. We can't afford to lose you either!"

The next time that Midge had the ball, he headed right for Big Red and beckoned for him to come and get the ball. Big Red fell into the trap and when he charged Midge recklessly, Midge stepped aside and brought up his right elbow and smashed it right into the middle of his face. A broken nose and two missing teeth later, they helped Big Red off the field never to be seen again. Fortunately, the referee ignored the offence.

This was a great achievement for our team because we came from a small Air Force base of 250 men and each of the bases that we beat could choose their teams from more than a thousand men each. Not only that, we accomplished this feat in three straight days! We were welcomed back to Moisie as heroes—almost everyone who wasn't on duty showed up to greet us.

In August, the Moisie soccer team flew out to Victoria-Esquimalt Naval Base in British Columbia to represent Quebec in the National Armed Forces Championship. This tournament was a reward for two years of hard training and winning the Quebec championship. It was a vacation. Our three officers on the team—F/O Midge Pennington, F/L Doug French, and I—were treated like Royal Canadian Naval (RCN) officers. This meant that we each had a personal batman (flunky) for the week, who shined our shoes and soccer cleats, pressed our uniforms, and served us breakfast in bed. A much better standard than we ever had in the RCAF and we got this treatment without even needing a British accent!

However, we soon discovered that our Navy brethren were treating our twelve airmen like their own swabbies. They were told that they had to pass inspection every morning and on Wednesday night had to wash the floors and windows. As soon as I heard that, I headed straight for the tournament's Officer-in-Charge, a Lieutenant Commander (a Major—two ranks higher than me). I informed him in no uncertain terms that our men, as well as the Nigerian Flight Cadets from RCAF Station Penhold in Alberta—there were no officers on that team, only the Cadets—were the guests of the Royal Canadian Navy. They were on a well-deserved vacation, I told him, and were going to be exempt from the Navy's house-cleaning, not treated like part of the Nanaimo base.

The Officer-in-Charge blustered in his best phony British accent that all other ranks are equal and will carry out their duties according to Standing Orders of Her Majesty's Naval Base Esquimalt. As I've mentioned, naval officers, especially those from Alberta and Saskatchewan, acquired the fake accent they needed to get promotions. My response, however, was simple and straightforward. "Fine, sir. Please remove RCAF Stations Moisie and Penhold from the tournament and provide us with an aircraft to return to our bases immediately, as we do not wish to break any of your Standing Orders and my men are not washing your damn floors and windows. We are here to represent Quebec and Alberta; Air Force Headquarters did not send us here to do your menial work!"

Knowing that this would not look good on his service record, the Officer-in-Charge suddenly lost his phony British accent and said, "OK, I will amend the Standing Orders to reflect your request. Now get out of my office!"

"Thank you, sir!" was my proper and sarcastic response.

We didn't last long in the tournament unfortunately. Our first opponent was a team of British Royal Navy submariners temporarily based in Halifax, Nova Scotia. They were a bunch of ringers and shouldn't even have been in the tournament; this was a Canadian Forces Tournament. Every British kid plays soccer and is very good at it. It would be like a Canadian Forces hockey team playing in the British Forces Ice Hockey Tournament—the Brits wouldn't have stood a chance. As a matter of fact, at the 1948 Winter Olympics, a team of twelve Royal Canadian Air Force hockey players (the RCAF Flyers) won the Olympic Hockey Gold Medal against the best European and American hockey teams available.

To make a long story short, we were tied 2–2 late in the second half when Midge Pennington was seriously injured. At that time, replacements and substitutions were not permitted, even for injuries, so we had to play with only ten men and without the heart and soul of our team. The Royal Navy team scored in overtime to eliminate us. We had come a long way and had fought very hard but had nothing to show for it except pride in our young men who were only in their second year of playing soccer. They had shown courage, skill, and determination against great odds.

The good news for us was that the Air Force had our own ringers—the fifteen Nigerian Flight Cadets from RCAF Station Penhold were far better than the Royal Navy team. They were fast, could run at full speed all day, were used to high temperatures (it was very hot), and were very skilled. They beat the Royal Navy British ringers in the final to win the championship for the Air Force.

We were very proud of how far we had come, but also heavyhearted as we flew back to Moisie and reality. When we landed at the Sept-Îles airport, however, we were amazed to find our whole base there to welcome us home with flags and music. Everyone who was not on duty was there—officers, airmen, wives, and children, except for my family who couldn't be there because our daughter Linda was in the hospital after surgery. Our team was treated as if they had won the World Cup of soccer and they deserved it. I am and always will be very proud of being a part of this team and proud of every one of the players. I will never forget that courageous group of wonderful athletes.

IN OCTOBER 1962, Nikita Khrushchev, First Secretary of the Communist Party in the Soviet Union, decided to place IL-28 bombers and medium-range and intermediate-range ballistic missiles (MRBMs and IRBMs) in Cuba, ninety miles (145 kilometres) off US shores. This was a major threat to the safety of American cities and civilians that precipitated a thirteen-day global crisis, bringing the world to the brink of a nuclear World War III and Armageddon. The US Navy was ordered to blockade Cuba to prevent additional weapons being brought in, while the US Air Force maintained a twenty-four-hour watch over the island with U-2 reconnaissance aircraft.

At that time, we had an ultra-secret state of alert system of defense conditions, which were called DEFCON (DEFense readiness CONdition), with levels DEFCON 1 to DEFCON 5. DEFCON 1 was the normal state of alert in peacetime and DEFCON 5 meant that we were involved in a nuclear war. In the event of apparent danger, the DEFCON alert would rise with the level of the perceived threat. For example, during the Berlin and Cuban Crises in 1961, the levels were raised to DEFCON 3, which is as high as it had ever been until then. This system was so secret that we were not allowed to even mention the word DEFCON outside of work, even to our families. Ever since the cowardly and horrific air assault on the Twin Towers in New York and the Pentagon in Washington on September 11, 2001, however, the term DEFCON has become public knowledge and entered into common usage.

In October 1962, along with all of North American Air Defense Command, RCAF Station Moisie was placed on DEFCON 3, just short of all-out war. This meant that there was a high level of security and defensive exercises for all personnel, including dependents. The high state of alert continued for two weeks until the Soviet Union backed down, acceding to US demands and withdrawing their rockets; in reciprocity, the American rockets that were pointed at the USSR were withdrawn from Turkey.

Thus, ended the first tense and dangerous period during our deployment at Moisie. A year later, though, we went through another crisis originating in Dallas, Texas.

The following year, in the fall of 1963, we were still very much in the heat of the Cold War with the Soviet Union. I was a Flight Commander at the Crowbar Radar site at Moisie, part of the northernmost chain of Canadian radar sites in the North American Air Defense Command. Our job was to detect any incursions into North American air space by enemy aircraft and to control US and Canadian Fighters against any possible attack from the Soviet Union's Long-Range Bomber Force.

As an officer in the RCAF, you were expected to carry out additional duties along with your normal military duties. One of my extra duties was to serve as the Education Officer for the base. It was my job to help the enlisted ranks enhance their education, so they could qualify for higher and more difficult positions, and then to help them get promoted.

On Friday, November 22, 1963, I was the Duty Officer on the day shift in the Crowbar Radar Station. Together with my eight-man crew, I was the only officer on duty in the Radar Operations Room because it was the beginning of the weekend. At 1:35 p.m., my crew was monitoring the radar and, as Education Officer, I was correcting examination papers when my wife, Catherine, called. Trying to stay calm, she said, "Have you heard that President Kennedy has been shot in Dallas?"

My answer was, "No—are you serious? How do you know?"

It turned out that our daughters, Linda, aged five, and Liza, aged two, had been watching cartoons on the French TV station from Rimouski—the only channel we got—when the program was interrupted by a news flash. Fortunately, Catherine was fluent in French and understood the report about the assassination of the US president.

Here I was, part of the biggest Air Defense System ever devised by man, with instant communication all over North America, and there hadn't been a word from Northern NORAD HQ in North Bay or NORAD Headquarters in Colorado Springs. I immediately picked up the phone and called my Sector Command Post—code name Sword— in St. Margaret, New Brunswick. I identified myself and requested the Duty Sector Commander. When he picked up the phone, I asked him, "Did you hear anything about President Kennedy being shot?" I explained that there was a news report on French TV. The response was negative, so I then requested that he call Northern NORAD Region HQ in North Bay and find out really quickly.

The Duty Sector Commander called me back within a couple of minutes and said that they had not heard anything, nor had NORAD Headquarters in Colorado Springs. My family had provided me with better intelligence than North American Air Defense Command Intelligence. That was unbelievable! I told the Commander, "We are going to DEFCON 3 at Crowbar (our call sign)!"

"You can't do that," he shouted. "If you do, then we have to go to DEFCON 3 and Northern NORAD will have to go too, then

NORAD Headquarters in Colorado Springs will also have to raise the state of alert to DEFCON 3, followed by Strategic Air Command with its nuclear bomber B-52s and missiles!" (He forgot to mention the US and Canadian navies.)

"This could be the start of an attack on North America," I responded, "and I will not make the same mistake that the young US Army Lieutenant on Oahu did in Hawaii on December 7, 1941, when he picked up scores of radar targets headed for Pearl Harbor and took no action. The result was thousands of casualties and the destruction of most of the US Pacific Fleet. Well, not on my watch. I will not go down in the history books as the man who made the same mistake!" In a firm voice, while trying to both stay calm and sound calm for my men, I said, "Sergeant Milks, put Crowbar on DEFCON 3!" The sergeant relayed my command and our Flight started to implement emergency procedures.

All I heard from my Sector Commander was, "Oh, shit!" and immediately, Sector, Region and NORAD itself went to DEFCON 3. This was followed by Strategic Air Command going to DEFCON 3 and launching B-52 bombers for Airborne Alert and the US Navy going to DEFCON 3 and sending some nuclear ships and submarines out to sea for dispersal. The little Czech refugee sure got things moving that day! It wasn't till much later that I realized what I had accomplished.

Under this state of alert, all North American military bases were closed to civilians, all off-duty personnel had to return to duty, armed guards were posted all over the bases to protect critical facilities, and the battle staff had to report for duty, including my Commanding Officer (he didn't complain about me ruining his weekend). I wasn't too popular at the time, but my comrades understood. My action had forced all units of NORAD to increase the threat level to DEFCON 3, including hundreds of fighter and bomber aircraft, dozens of radar stations, thousands of personnel. It had also forced Strategic Air Command to raise their threat level and go to a higher state of alert. Within six hours it was recognized that this was not the beginning of a Soviet sneak attack and we all returned to DEFCON 1.

My wife and young children had provided NORAD with more important information than all the intelligence agencies among the NATO allies just by watching cartoons on our one French-language

TV station. This incident revealed a major breakdown of our intelligence and communication systems. Under the circumstances, all I could think about was how lucky we were that the assassination of President Kennedy had not, in fact, been the prelude to a Soviet nuclear attack.

RCAF Station Moisie soccer team. I'm on the far left in the front row. In the back row: (far left) is the team coach, captain and star, F/O Midge Pennington; second from the left is our forty-two-year-old goalie, F/L Doug French.

17

FLYING AGAIN AND THEN THE FIVE HUNDRED

B y October 1963, our family had spent almost three years at the remote radar site north of Sept-Îles, RCAF Station Moisie, which stood next to the poverty-stricken local fishing village from which the base took its name. It was time to be transferred back to a flying job. I had requested the new All-Weather Fighter, the supersonic and nuclear-armed CF-101, but got my second choice: my old friend the CF-100 that had been reequipped to provide Electronic Warfare Training for NORAD ground radars and fighters.

Despite my disappointment at missing the supersonic fighters, I was quite happy to again fly an aircraft that I knew well and trusted implicitly. The other benefit was that all I needed in the way of training was a one-week Ground School for Aircraft Systems and a couple of familiarization flights. I was to be based with the Electronic Warfare Unit (later 414 Squadron) at RCAF Station St. Hubert on the South Shore of the St. Lawrence across from our hometown of Montreal.

We moved to Ville Lemoyne, about five miles (eight kilometres) from my new base. It was great to be back in the Montreal area, where both Catherine's family and my family lived. An additional benefit was that I could return to Sir George Williams University night school and work towards my university degree, which I finished seven years later. In addition, I was appointed editor of *The Hub*, the station news-paper, where I worked with a squadron mate, F/O Al Alls, a young, bright, hardworking, and pimply-faced recent graduate of the CF-100 Operational Training Unit at Bagotville and a superb Pilot. Al was my advertising manager; he sold advertising to pay for the costs of running *The Hub* since there were no public funds available for this. He was a super salesman and did a great job for two years keeping our newspaper out of debt. Today, he is still a super salesman, working in real estate in Erin, Ontario, and is now also the Mayor of Erin; after his retirement as a Pilot and Director of Air Canada. I am proud to say that we are still good friends today.

I reported to the Electronic Warfare Unit just before Christmas 1963 and within a week I was again checked out on the CF-100; a week later I was promoted to Flight Lieutenant (Captain). Our aircraft were equipped with two chaff (aluminum foil strip) dispensers and one electronic jammer, but the jammers could only be operated by Navigators who had taken a very long and expensive eleven-month course at Hill Air Force Base, a US Air Force base in Utah. Out of thirty Navigators on the squadron, only eleven had taken the extensive and expensive Electronic Warfare course in Utah, which was only open to officers with permanent commissions. Most of us were on Short Service Commissions and the RCAF wouldn't spend the funds to train us. It was a Catch-22. The only way that our squadron could achieve full electronic warfare capability was by training and qualifying all our Navigators on the electronic jammers. Yet, although all our Navigators had the ability to operate the equipment, we weren't permitted to do so.

Upon my promotion to Captain, I was appointed Squadron Operations Officer, a powerful position that permitted me to make all decisions on training, allocation of aircraft, and flying. My appointment ahead of many senior Captains was a promising indication that I would finally be offered a permanent commission the following July. As it turned out I wasn't, and it was one of the lucky non-events in my life.

One of my first actions as Captain was to insist that the CF-100 Navigator Electronic Warfare Leader, Captain Bill Naylor—an old 432 AWF Squadron buddy —check me out on the Electronic Warfare Equipment. Technically, I wasn't permitted to use it because I hadn't done the training course at Hill AFB in Utah. Within a week, though, Bill had checked me out and qualified me on this secret equipment that the RCAF was paying a fortune to the US Air Force for an eleven-month training course on. Since I hadn't had any trouble mastering this exotic equipment, I issued an operational order permitting any Navigator qualified by Captain Bill Naylor to use the Electronic Warfare Jammers and arranged for all the other non-permanent commission Navigators to be trained on their use. Within two months, we had all thirty Navigators qualified to use the Electronic Warfare Equipment. We were now a thoroughly trained and useful Electronic Warfare Squadron for training purposes and combat-ready as well. We'd saved months of training time and saved the Canadian taxpayers a lot of money.

The Commanding Officer of this Electronic Warfare Squadron, which consisted of twenty-eight CF-100s and three very old and slow C-119 Electronic Warfare Transports loaded with electronic warfare jamming equipment, was another RCAF living legend, Wing Commander (Lt. Col.) Joe Lecomte DFC, nicknamed Joe the Group. He was a highly decorated Canadian bomber Pilot and Commander of the famous 425 Alouette Squadron in World War II. This squadron was now a CF-101 supersonic nuclear-armed All Weather Fighter Squadron based at Bagotville—my old base.

By this time, however, W/C Joe Lecomte had lost interest in his career and was waiting out his time to retirement. For the most part, he had his subordinate officers —Deputy Commander S/L Wally Pacholka; Flight Commander S/L Frank Steele; Nav Leader F/L Bill Naylor; Electronic Warfare Officer Wally Gryba; me, the newly promoted Flight Lieutenant and new Operations Officer—run the squadron for him. Joe was a man who had flown and survived dozens of Lancaster bomber missions over Europe during the war and was now just filling in the time until his retirement. He only flew once or twice per month, and never solo; he always had another Pilot with him to make sure that he came back safely.

At the end of every month, the five of us would file our monthly reports, collate them, and bring them to W/C Lecomte for his approval. We had to explain everything that the squadron had done during that past month and why and how we had accomplished our assigned mission. He never remembered our briefings from the previous month and had to be re-briefed every time. Then he would sign the report. He was a good man, but time had passed him by. Looking back, I now wonder if he wasn't in the early stages of Alzheimer's, which was not yet generally recognized or diagnosed at that time.

I learned one thing from Joe Lecomte: he hated air shows because of his strong belief that aircraft crashed and Pilots died participating in them just for public relations. He was right, of course, but the air forces of the world put them on for publicity and to get funds for more new aircraft and to encourage recruitment. Regardless of whether you like them, they are spectacular exhibitions of flying skills by generally young and fearless Pilots with great training, great hand-eye coordination, and supersonic reflexes.

When Joe was approaching retirement in 1965, he accepted an invitation from Jean Lesage, Premier of Quebec, to run for the Quebec legislature for Bagot County, his ancestral home, against Daniel Johnston, leader of the opposition Union National Party. Lecomte and Lesage had been classmates at the University of Montreal in the 1930s. Joe was confident of winning and boasted, "I have more relatives in Bagot County than Danny Johnston has voters!"

Unfortunately, on June 16, 1966, Joe discovered that his relatives all voted for Danny Johnston; he went down to defeat along with his leader and lifelong friend, Premier Jean Lesage. Daniel Johnston and his Union National Party swept the province and Johnston became the new Premier of Quebec. Joe's defeat, along with his retirement, destroyed a good man. He served for a short time as the first Director of the Civilian Flying School at the Cégep (Collège d'enseignement général et professionnel) de Chicoutimi, then he seemingly lost his will to live. He drank more than usual and was killed walking home across the main highway at St. Hubert shortly after the election. Sadly, a true Canadian hero died ignominiously.

The heliport at Canadian Forces Base Valcartier in Quebec City was named in his honour. And it was a great honour—only three Canadian Forces bases have ever been named after an individual; the rest carry only the name of the community where they are located. Joe Lecomte earned that honour.

EVERY MONDAY MORNING, the squadron attended Ground School for the whole morning to learn the latest details about our aircraft, flight safety, tactics, equipment changes and upgrades, planned exercises, air regulations, and any other pertinent information.

In early April 1964, during one of these Monday morning Ground School sessions, we received a telegram from Air Force headquarters in Ottawa advising us that within the next three months, 10 per cent of all Pilots and Navigators would be released from the RCAF. The personnel who would be cut were those in the bottom 10 per cent of the group based on their annual assessments; they would be advised by the end of the week. There were five thousand of us, so five hundred would be fired due to cutbacks in the military budget thanks to Lester Pearson and his pacifist Liberal cronies. The Pearson Liberal government of Canada had decided that since the US had to defend itself from the Soviet Union by defending Canada first because Canada happened to be located between the two superpowers, there was no point in wasting money on the Canadian military. They planned to reduce the size of the Armed Forces and some of us would have to pay the price.

Pierre Elliott Trudeau, who had flirted with communism in his youth and was a long-time pacifist, was the second most influential member in Cabinet. He argued that the government would be better off spending the funds on social welfare to buy votes for the Liberal Party in the next election. They forgot that liberty can only be maintained if a country is strong and willing to defend itself. After all, Canada's liberty was bought with the blood of young Canadians in World War I, World War II, and Korea. Pearson and Trudeau were ably assisted in this policy by Defence Minister Paul Hellyer, who eviscerated the Canadian Armed Forces and reduced our strength by approximately 60 per cent from its postwar peak.

In my view, pride in our nation's ability to defend itself was not as important to Mr. Pearson and the Liberal Party as winning the next election. Lester Pearson—who was a Nobel Peace Prize winner—and Pierre Elliot Trudeau betrayed the Canadian Armed Forces for political gain. This policy direction wasn't changed until another Liberal Prime Minister, Paul Martin, restored our national pride thirty-five years later by funding the new build-up of our military.

I also consider Paul Martin to be the greatest Canadian Finance Minister during my lifetime. While serving in that role, he balanced the federal budget and repaid a large portion of the national debt. He was the first Finance Minister in my lifetime to accomplish this feat. He refused to allow the Big Five Canadian banks to merge so they could compete with the big US and British banks in producing worthless derivative mortgage investments and causing the second biggest equity market crash in history in 2007. By holding firm, Mr. Martin kept the Canadian banks small enough that they didn't have sufficient capital to compete with Wall Street and London in their tailspin spiral into bankruptcy. In doing this, they avoided disaster.

This was very fortunate for Canada. On September 15, 2007, when Bear Stearns and Lehman Brothers went bankrupt and triggered the monstrous crash, most of the big US, British, French, and German banks verged on bankruptcy and had to be rescued by their respective governments. Only the relatively small Canadian and Australian banks escaped the slaughter, thanks to their laws and the strict enforcement of those laws. Canada dodged a bullet. Thank you, Paul Martin! He and Premier Tommy Douglas of Saskatchewan are my Canadian political heroes.

THAT WEEK IN April 1964, when the news came down about the imminent cuts to the armed forces, was unpleasant for all of us; we had no idea who would soon be unemployed. On the Friday night, there was still with no word from Ottawa. Almost all the base officers gathered in the Officers' Mess to have a drink, commiserate, and try to stay calm. Shortly after six o'clock, however, Senior Officers started to circulate among us and ask individual Junior Officers to report to an office upstairs.

This method of termination reminded me of men being led away for execution and I did not like it one bit. Even though I was not in that group being fired, I decided then and there that my Air Force career was over. Future career opportunities would be very limited as Pierre Elliott Trudeau and Paul Hellyer destroyed the proud Canadian Forces to meet their socialist agenda. They certainly achieved their goals: over the coming months, the forces were reduced by 60 per cent to pay for grandiose social programs that almost bankrupted Canada. Canada's defence was left to the US, which was ironic because Trudeau hated the US, but he knew that it was in the Americans' interest to defend us. After all, they needed our oil, water, and land as a buffer against the Soviet hordes.

There is no argument that the RCAF had too many aircrew for the newly reduced mission designated by the Pearson/Trudeau governments, and we got rid of some deadwood in the mass release. However, we also lost some really good officers in this mass reduction. One prime example was F/O Herb Laviolette, an excellent Pilot and officer. He was released and joined Air Canada, where he rose to Captain and then Chief Pilot for the entire Montreal Base of more than six hundred Pilots. The RCAF lost an excellent officer and Air Canada got a good leader. The airline was very happy with this generous gift.

Fortunately, most of the terminated Pilots and some of the Navigators were hired by Canadian and American airlines as the arrival of the jet age and the Pilot needs of the Vietnam war in the US created a North American Pilot shortage.

I WAS STILL attending Sir George Williams University at night to get my university degree, preparing myself for a new career in the future. We were expecting the new Permanent Commission (PC) list to come out on July 1, 1964. I had worked very hard and hoped that the RCAF would recognize my efforts and finally reward me with the coveted Permanent Commission that I felt I had earned. The date came and went, however, without any word at all from Air Force headquarters and the realization dawned on me that after the unprecedented dismissal of five hundred of my fellow officers, and the non-issuance of a PC list on schedule, there was now very little chance of my getting the PC. I would have to settle for more short-term extensions, which was unacceptable to me and unfair to my family.

In addition, I had missed out on my desire to fly the supersonic and nuclear-armed CF-101 All Weather Fighter. This was Canada's best air defense weapon and I wanted to be a part of it. Fortunately, I was able to experience this wonderful aircraft twice at RCAF Station Chatham, New Brunswick, when two old buddies from CF-100 days, F/L Jean Guy Fortin and F/O Roger Cossette took me up on supersonic target missions for their squadron mates to practice on. Both missions were fabulous experiences for me; this was the first time that I had flown faster than the speed of sound.

Just like the earlier experience of my first CF-100 flight, these two CF-101 flights dazzled me. My inability to fly these wonderful aircraft operationally and the "massacre of the five hundred" helped me to decide that, despite my love for the RCAF, my Air Force career was coming to an end. It was time to start looking for a new career.

Flying again in the Electronic Warfare Unit (later 414 Squadron)
at RCAF Station St. Hubert, 1964.

18

BAD NIGHT AT CFB BAGOTVILLE

At the end of June 1964, I was a Flight Lieutenant (Captain), Navigator, Electronic Warfare Officer, and the Squadron Operations Officer for the Electronic Warfare Unit of NORAD. Our job was to provide targets with electronic warfare capability to train the fighter aircraft available to NORAD to protect North America from attack.

Our Squadron consisted of twenty-eight CF-100 former All-Weather Fighters converted to Electronic Warfare Target Aircraft and three C-119 transports converted for the same purpose. As I've said, we were based at Canadian Forces Base St. Hubert, just outside Montreal, Quebec. Our CF-100 crews were mostly older Navigators in their early thirties on their second or third tours of duty, and a bunch of young Pilots in their early twenties just out of the Training Command and the CF-100 Operational Training Unit.

At noon on June 28, 1964, we deployed sixteen CF-100s to Canadian Forces Base Bagotville for a major NORAD exercise that night. Our detachment was commanded by our Flight Commander, Squadron Leader Frank "Stainless" Steele, a model in an RCAF uniform that was always pressed, and boots shined so that you could see your face in them. He was also a good Pilot, but with few leadership skills.

As the Operations Officer of the Squadron, I was one of his three deputies. The others were F/L Wally Gryba, the Chief Electronic Warfare Officer, and F/L Bill Naylor, the Navigator Leader. When we arrived at CFB Bagotville, we were billeted in the bachelor Officers'

Quarters to get some rest as we were going to be up flying most of that night. We got up at midnight, had an early breakfast and proceeded to mission briefing. First, the meteorologist, Barry MacDonald, who had grown up in the Côte-des-Neiges district of Montreal with me, gave us the weather briefing. He explained that the weather was poor over almost all of eastern North America but was acceptable for that night's air defence exercise.

The Wright Patterson US Air Force Base in Ohio was our only available destination and our alternate was Malton Airport, now Lester B. Pearson International Airport in Toronto. Malton was within alternate weather limits, but we would have to cut the mission short to have sufficient fuel to make it there. That was the good news; then there was the bad news:

1. Malton was a civilian airport, with NO facilities for military aircraft—no ladders to leave or return to the aircraft and no power units to get us started when we wanted to leave for home base the next day.
2. Our aircraft were not equipped to do bad weather instrument approaches at Malton, which had a civilian instrument landing system (ILS) but no Air Force Ground Control Approach System.
3. There was NO other alternate airport available within our fuel range that met our required minimum alternate weather criteria.
4. What we were about to do was against both civil and Air Force regulations.

When the time came for the actual mission briefing by Flight Commander Squadron Leader (Major) Steele, Senior Electronic Warfare Officer Wally Gryba, and myself, Gryba and I huddled to discuss aborting the mission due to the poor weather conditions. S/L Steele, however, was all gung-ho. He told me that the exercise would be severely restricted if we didn't fly with our electronic warfare capability and that they had flown in worse weather in World War II. I replied that the war was over and the safety of our crews and aircraft was more important than pleasing assorted Generals in North Bay and Colorado Springs. "Lou," he answered, "start the briefing!"

I briefed the crews on our call signs (APEX 1 to 16), routes, and departure times five minutes apart starting at 3:00 a.m., heading north for two hundred miles (322 kilometres) to get out of ground radar range, then turning onto our individual routes from different initial points (IPs, or turning points), and altitudes. After reaching the initial point, we would turn south and head for our simulated North American targets. After overflying our targets, we would all head for the Wright Patterson USAF Base in Ohio for recovery. The mission would be a little over three hours and we carried only four hours of fuel, just enough to get back to Toronto if we turned back soon enough. I stressed safety and advised our crews to closely monitor the weather reports and fuel, and, in the case of worse weather or any other problem, to divert to Malton Airport immediately. F/L Gryba then briefed us on the radar frequencies we were to jam and when to jam them. F/L Naylor added his briefing on the navigation facilities available to us and radio and radar frequencies, followed by S/L Steele, who basically reiterated that in case of problems, Pilots should head for Toronto.

We went out to pre-flight check our aircraft in a light drizzle with flashes of lightning all around us. The bad weather was approaching Bagotville. We then sat in the briefing room, reviewed our briefing notes, routes, and our only available alternate airport, and waited for our scheduled takeoff times.

APEX 1 was flown by F/O Al Alls, a keen, young, superb Pilot from Ontario; his Navigator was F/L Bill Naylor, the Navigator leader. F/O Alls suggested to S/L Steele that we scrub the exercise because we didn't have a really legal alternate. Our glorious leader brushed him off with "Get to your aircraft now, Alls!" In the military, when you get a command, you carry it out. APEX 1 launched on schedule at 3:00 a.m.

I was flying with a Saskatchewan farm boy and very skilled young Pilot—after all I was thirty years old—F/O (First Lieutenant) Carl Gillis. We were APEX 8 and our takeoff time was 3:35 a.m., so at 3:20 a.m. we headed out to our aircraft. We went through the exit at the Meteorology Section and as we went out the door, the rain got heavier and there were many flashes of lightning all around Bagotville. The meteorologist, my old friend Barry MacDonald, was standing in the doorway and I said, "Barry, that lightning looks awfully close!"

"Don't worry, Lou," he responded, "the thunderstorms are still over Roberval (sixty-two miles, or one hundred kilometres, to the west)." We were using Runway 11, facing east.

Carl and I climbed into our aircraft and strapped in; once we had done that, a ground crew member pulled the safety pins on our ejection seats, climbed down the ladder, and took it away. As soon as Carl fired up the right engine and I started to close the canopy, however, it started to pour. By the time the canopy was closed, it was raining so hard that we couldn't see outside. To our surprise, we got the taxi clearance to Runway 11, but we couldn't move because we couldn't see.

Airport runways are numbered by the first two numbers of the magnetic heading of the runway, so a Pilot can make a last-second check of his magnetic compasses before takeoff. Aircraft take off and land into the wind because it increases the lift for takeoff and, for landing, it reduces the groundspeed allowing the aircraft to touch down at a slower speed.

In the meantime, APEX 7, flown by F/O Dick Lillie and F/L Tom Connolly, was approaching the button of Runway 11 for takeoff. The problem was that APEX 6, flown by F/O George Saunders, a Royal Military College graduate but new Pilot on the CF-100 with limited flying experience, had the same problem we had. He couldn't see the runway, so he held his position, which made F/O Lillie concerned that he would miss his takeoff time. Finally, F/O Saunders advised the Bagotville Tower, "APEX 6 aborting. Request clearance back to the ramp." The tower acknowledged and cleared APEX 6 back to the ramp. This was probably the best decision that young George Saunders had ever made to that point in his life—it saved an aircraft and probably two lives. It showed good judgment and common sense working together for a young Pilot.

As APEX 6 was taxiing back to the ramp, Dick Lillie asked George Saunders if he could pull over a little so that APEX 7 could get into position for takeoff. F/O Saunders acknowledged and moved over to allow APEX 7 to line up on the runway. At that point, unbelievably, APEX 7 was immediately cleared for takeoff!

We were still sitting in our parking position on the ramp when APEX 7 roared by in front of us into the heavy rain from right to left on Runway 11. They got airborne right in front of us. The heavy rain started to ease off for a minute or so later and Carl checked with me whether it was okay to go. I said, "Okay, but with caution!" Bagotville tower then cleared us to Runway 29 for takeoff in the opposite direction. This meant that a cold front had just passed the airport resulting in a sudden 180-degree wind shift.

One thing you learn in flying is that you don't take off during this kind of frontal passage or in a thunderstorm, but unfortunately, APEX 7 had done just that. Even though he wasn't aware of the passage of the cold front at the time, he had made his decision to go and powered up.

As we started to taxi, and the rain poured down even harder, we again discussed the situation and decided to abort. We advised the tower of our decision and got clearance back to the ramp as Carl started to turn the aircraft back 180 degrees to our parking spot. This ended up being the best decision we had ever made. At that instant, CFB Bagotville was hit by a monstrous lightning strike that hit the base power plant supply and all the lights on the base went out. Fortunately, our landing lights guided us back to our parking spot and as we turned into it, the tower advised, "All APEX aircraft on the ground ABORT and return to the ramp. We have lost an aircraft and have five emergencies in progress!" I had dodged yet another bullet!

APEX 7 was going down; the aircraft had lost both engines in the climb and Dick Lillie found himself flying a fourteen-ton glider in the midst of the horrible storm. Fortunately, both he and his Navigator, F/L Tom Connolly, managed to eject safely from their stricken aircraft at 22,000 feet (7,000 metres) but endured a horrible and scary parachute descent through a thunderstorm into the northern bush. The up and down drafts within the storms were severe and travelling at very high speed was like going up and down in a runaway elevator at high speed.

All six CF-100s that got airborne were either down or in emergency situations with very few places to land. Luckily, the five other airborne aircraft only lost one engine each and managed to limp into Ottawa and St. Hubert on one engine under extremely difficult weather conditions. Our Pilots did a great job.

APEX 1 had been in real trouble—climbing through 18,000 feet (approximately 6,000 metres) one engine had exploded. F/O Alls declared an emergency and requested an immediate clearance into Ottawa, the nearest airport available. Approximately eighty miles (128 kilometres) from Ottawa, when his second engine overheated, he throttled back the power and basically glided fourteen tons of steel into the Ottawa airport. Even though he had only minimum power to fly the aircraft, it was enough to keep the radios and navigation equipment working. On touchdown, F/O Alls, shut down his second engine and coasted to a stop; the aircraft had to be towed off the runway to the hangar. The next morning, he was congratulated by the RCAF Director of Flight Safety who took him out to inspect his massively impaired aircraft. Upon inspecting it, the flight safety officer couldn't believe that Alls had managed to bring his aircraft down safely. Pieces of the exploding engine had severely damaged the flying controls on the tail's vertical and horizontal stabilizers.

Thanks to our superlative training and the high-level skill of our crews, no one was killed. These crews reflected the RCAF's superb aircrew selection, discipline, and training. Even the most inexperienced Pilot in our Squadron, F/O George Saunders, demonstrated his good judgment and training by aborting his mission when he recognized the dangerous weather conditions beyond his ability at that time.

In the briefing room, S/L Steele and I called our nearest Search and Rescue Centre in Trenton, Ontario and requested a helicopter to help us find our downed crew. They responded that they didn't have a serviceable helicopter at the moment and that it would take at least twenty-four hours to get one of them to CFB Bagotville just to *start* the search. I asked the idiot on the other end of the phone line if he could imagine what it was like to sit in the northern bush, cold, wet, hungry, and possibly injured, being eaten by mosquitos and black flies. When he said he couldn't, I demanded a helicopter immediately and he recommended that I contact Gerry Tremblay, a former RCAF F-86 Sabre fighter Pilot who flew the Quebec government's helicopter.

He also told me that CFB Bagotville would have to cover the $80 per hour fee for that helicopter. Imagine—we had two men down because they were on duty training for the defence of their country and we would have to pay $80 per hour to find and rescue them. I was embarrassed by our lack of resources and not very proud of my country at that point. Every US Air Force base and US Navy aircraft carrier has at least one helicopter on standby during flying operations. And our budget doesn't have either the aircraft or the funding for a helicopter rescue.

I was even less proud of my superior officer, S/L Steele, when he emphatically stated that he could not authorize an expenditure of that magnitude. That is when I staged my polite version of the Caine Mutiny, suggesting that S/L Steele was obviously very tired and very hungry, and should go to the Officers' Mess for breakfast. Like Colonel Bogey in the Burmese POW camp in *The Bridge on the River Kwai*, he straightened up and said, "You're right, Lou, it's been a rough night and I'm hungry." This pathetic excuse for an officer and alleged leader, who hadn't even gone out to his aircraft in the rain, thought that he'd had a rough night!

Pilots, Navigators, and other aircrew are a brotherhood and Rule #1 is that we do not leave one of our brothers down. We go out and get them, no matter the cost or the conditions; sometimes we even lose lives searching for or rescuing our comrades.

Rule #2 is don't forget Rule #1! If we go down, we expect to be found and rescued; failure is not an option.

Rule #3 is "Do unto others as you would have them do unto you." We were not about to let our pathetic excuse of a leader, who would sacrifice his men in order not to be held accountable for a few hundred dollars, abandon APEX 7 and its crew. We would get Dick and Tom back, no matter the cost. So, I had to take over.

I gathered together all the remaining Pilots and Navigators and told them that I thought that the RCAF would cover the cost but suggested that we guarantee the small sum involved from our squadron fund of approximately $600 (used for our Christmas party) just in case. The response was unanimous: do it.

I called Gerry Tremblay in Quebec City and he was at CFB Bagotville within three hours with his helicopter. Two of our men got on board as spotters and headed out to the area that radar indicated was their last position of Dick and Tom's ejection, while I coordinated the rescue effort.

When a fighter Pilot or Navigator ejects from his or her aircraft seat, the aircraft radar transponder shows a Squawk Four—the seat ejects strips of tinfoil called chaff that fall slowly to the ground, this reflects four lines on the ground radar, making the location easy to track. Thus, we had a relatively good fix on where our mates were exactly located, the accuracy of which was only affected by the prevailing wind conditions and the effects of the thunderstorms at the time of the ejection.

We found both men.

By 10:00 a.m., both Tom and Dick were safe on the ground in Bagotville, wet, cold, and hungry but uninjured. They'd had had a horrible experience coming down in the heavy thunderstorm with the up and down of the high velocity drafts. In that situation, you are cold and wet, with the heavy rain pounding your face, totally disoriented. They estimated that they were in this descent for more than twelve minutes, double the time of a normal parachute jump from 22,000 feet (7,000 metres). Tom had landed on the edge of a cliff, wrapped himself in his wet parachute and waited for daylight; fortunately, he didn't move, or he might have fallen off the cliff. Dick landed at the bottom of the cliff and was eaten alive by mosquitos and black flies. When we found him, his face was swollen to almost double its normal size.

We arranged for air transport back to CFB St. Hubert. Dick got on, but Tom refused—he was apparently suffering from what we would now call post-traumatic stress syndrome (PTSD), although we didn't know what it was in those days. He asked for a train ride back to the base. When he got there, he resigned his commission, took a train to Saskatchewan, and started a new career as a school teacher. To my knowledge he never flew again. Dick Lillie, on the other hand, completed his military service in 1966 and enjoyed a great career as a Captain flying for Air Canada.

The first piece of good news was that both men were safe; the second was that the RCAF paid for the helicopter hours involved in the rescue and our squadron still had its Christmas party fund. Allan Alls completed his military service in 1966 and joined Air Canada as a Pilot as well. He rose through the ranks to Captain, then to a Chief Pilot position, and went on to become an Air Canada Senior Director.

The exercise had turned out to be a disaster and to make things worse, we later found out that Northern NORAD Region had cancelled the exercise before we even launched but had neglected to advise us. S/L Steele was held to account for the fouled-up exercise and retired from the RCAF shortly thereafter. This was another example of poor communications and ill-preparedness; it would have been disastrous in a war. Fortunately, the Cold War never turned hot as the Soviet Union rotted from the inside and disintegrated. I am grateful that they never attacked us. We would have won, but a lot of innocent people would have died, some of them because of our own weaknesses in communication and logistics.

A few days after this debacle at CFB Bagotville, I came home from my night university classes at 11:00 p.m. and Catherine advised me that S/L Steele wanted me to call him regardless of the time. When I called, he very proudly announced that the Permanent Commission List had just come in and I had been awarded a Provisional Three-Year Commission Extension.

"What the hell is a Provisional Three-Year Extension, sir?" I asked.

"If the Air Force needs you, they'll keep you!" he replied.

After eight years of dedicated and loyal service, I was essentially being fired. Now I really had to get serious about another career and immediately started looking for one. I started with the help wanted ads and sent out my résumé, but there weren't too many people interested in Air Navigators or people skilled at fighting air battles. I went for a couple of interviews and found only one interesting position as a management trainee for an electronics firm. My Air Force experience with radar, electronics, and radios provided me with the background for this job and the CEO, who interviewed me personally, was very impressive. He gave me the best job interview that I had ever had. I almost took this job, only deciding against it because it would mean an immediate 33 per cent pay reduction.

In January 1965, F/O Gillis and I were taxiing for takeoff at St. Hubert for a mission with 416 Squadron in Chatham, New Brunswick when one of my circuit breakers popped out. I advised Carl and followed procedure to reset it. A couple of minutes later, as we lined up for takeoff on Runway 06, the circuit breaker popped again and, following procedure, we aborted the takeoff and received clearance to taxi back to the ramp. Unbeknownst to us we were trailing a long cloud of black smoke, but no one in the control tower bothered to advise us.

We pulled into our parking position and Carl set the parking brakes. A member of the ground crew placed a ladder to the cockpit and climbed up to insert the safety pins into our ejection seats. But when I attempted to open the canopy, it didn't open. Removing my oxygen mask, I smelled smoke and yelled, "Fire!" then released the emergency canopy handle and, with all my strength, hurled the three-hundred-pound canopy back along the rails—it was amazingly smooth! I unstrapped myself in seconds, went right over the poor airman trying to insert Carl's safety pin and bolted down the ladder. In my winter flying gear I broke the world record for the one-hundred-metre dash getting away from the aircraft. Carl and the airman also got away and the firefighters put out the fire.

Underneath my seat was our rubber auxiliary fuel tank and underneath this tank was electrical wiring. Two of the wires had shorted, starting a fire. If we hadn't followed procedure and aborted the takeoff, the rushing air flow at takeoff would have fanned the flames, exploding the fumes in that auxiliary fuel tank, and Carl and I would have been toast. Another lesson learned—follow procedures; they were written by smarter people than you.

Another close call; my luck held again!

AIR CANADA AND A NEW CAREER

n the spring of 1965, the Vietnam War was growing out of control and global airlines were expanding rapidly—with the dawn of the jet age, they were converting to new jet aircraft such as the DC-8s and Boeing 707s and needed Pilots with jet experience to fly them. Just as most American airlines needed Pilots in a hurry, American Pilots were needed to supply the US Armed Forces for the Vietnam War. The US Air Force, Navy, and Army would not and could not release their Pilots—they had lost hundreds of them, especially Army helicopter Pilots, and needed everyone available. As a result, the US airlines started to recruit and hire RCAF Pilots by the hundreds. At the same time, Air Canada and Canadian Pacific Air Lines also found themselves short of jet Pilots and Navigators. What a perfect storm! The RCAF had just recently fired five hundred aircrew who found themselves in great demand by North American airlines.

Canadian Pilots were very attractive to American airlines—we spoke the same language, were trained in the same way, and our air regulations were almost identical. We became the golden young men who allowed the American giants like Pan American World Airways, Trans World Airlines (TWA), Eastern Air Lines, and United Airlines to continue their expansion. While most of the five hundred, plus another few hundred from the active ranks of the RCAF and the Royal Canadian Navy (RCN) were hired by the North American airlines, however, the RCAF suddenly found itself short of aircrew. Ironic, to say the least.

Still in my position in the RCAF, I headed to Montreal's Dorval airport on June 25, 1965, for an interview with Peter Powell, Air Canada's Chief Navigator. Peter was a great World War II Navigator and had developed a superb navigation system for Air Canada's DC-8 aircraft using Doppler radar and computer together with Loran and astronavigation. His system was more like CF-100 fighter navigation than the Long-Range navigation used by the RCAF.

After a short interview, Peter told me to get my Ministry of Transport (MOT) civilian Navigator's licence and hired me for a course starting on November 24, 1965. The next day, despite the fact that I would be taking a 60 per cent pay reduction—down from $775 per month to $346—I resigned my commission as an RCAF officer. After all, this was a flying job and the opportunity was just too great to pass up. There was only one problem: for this job I would need to use night astronavigation, using the stars and the planets to navigate like the ancient mariners did, but at 500 mph (800 km/h) instead of eight miles (thirteen kilometres) per hour. I had never done any night astronavigation; I had only done daytime astro in basic training in Winnipeg using the sun and moon. I needed to learn night astro fast since I had to pass six very tough Navigator exams before November 24, 1965.

It turned out that learning night astro was a lot easier than the Long-Range Navigator Flight Cadets had made it out to be back in Winnipeg. My friend F/O Ray English, a brilliant young officer, spent fifteen minutes showing me the difference between day and night astro. Then he took me on a couple of night flights in our C-119 transport electronic warfare aircraft and taught me how to do it in flight at 180 mph. Voila—a new Long-Range Navigator had just graduated from the "Ray English astro academy" with a few hours of training, not the six months that the RCAF took to do it. It was just like the one-week training course for electronic warfare that we had completed at EWU earlier, rather than taking the costly eleven-month training for the same thing with the US Air Force. I still marvel that I was able to qualify as a Long-Range Navigator and Electronic Warfare Officer in less than a total of two weeks, when the RCAF demanded six- and eleven-month courses to acquire the same skill qualifications. All that I could think of was the waste of taxpayer money.

I wrote the six MOT Navigator exams—most of the material was grossly out of date and not applicable to jet aircraft—and passed three on the first try, which was considered to be a good result. I had to wait a month before I could rewrite the failed three, but this time I passed two more. It was a good but not great result since I was running out of time.

By this time, the RCAF was getting desperate for aircrew and begging us to stay in the Air Force. In my case, the Station Commander, Group Captain (Colonel) Johnston, was trying very hard to convince me to withdraw my resignation and keep me in the RCAF. Fearing that I would fail that last exam again and was running out of time for my Air Canada course date, I started to weaken. Luckily my wonderful wife, Catherine, bucked me up, encouraging me to stay the course that I had set and pass that last exam. I succeeded in early October 1965, thanks to Catherine's strong support.

The next hurdle was getting out of a rapidly shrinking RCAF, which was desperately trying to keep flying—hard to do if all the aircrew were joining the airlines. I couldn't get any information about my release date, so on November 17, I requested an interview with G/C Johnston, my Base Commander. I explained to him that the RCAF had rejected me and that I now had a new career, but I desperately needed my release. He explained that he had been fighting Air Force headquarters to get me a Permanent Commission due to my outstanding career, but despite their shortage of aircrew, they were only willing to give me another three-year extension. Unbelievable. I told him that I loved the RCAF, but I had a family and my new career would take care of them.

G/C Johnston was a fine officer and proved it when he replied, "Lou, I really wanted to keep you. You've been a very good officer and the Air Force needs officers like you, but headquarters unfortunately does not agree with me. Because of that, I will have you released on January 2, 1966. Attend your Air Canada course next week and come back on your release date to clear the station. In the meantime, you are on rehabilitation leave to take your course next week. Good luck in your new career!"

This proved to be significant for the rest of my Air Canada career as seniority with an airline is very important for base location, pay, and working conditions for aircrew. Any delay in reporting to Air Canada would have had negative implications for the rest of my career.

On schedule, I started my Air Canada Navigator course at the Ground School at Dorval International Airport on November 24, 1965. We were living in St. Bruno, Quebec, thirty miles from Dorval and only owned one car. Luckily, two of my CF-100 buddies, Rollie Tremblay and Herb Laviolette, were taking the Air Canada Pilot course at the same time and also owned only one car each. The three of us carpooled to Dorval for three weeks so our wives could have transportation two out of three days in the isolated community of St. Bruno.

After finishing Ground School and flying under supervision, I was qualified for flights to the Caribbean at the end of January and on the Atlantic routes in March 1966. Once I was qualified as an Air Canada Long-Range Navigator, I joined the Navigator's Union, the Air Canada Navigator's Association (CALNA). After four months of winter flying to the Caribbean, I was trained to fly across the Atlantic for the summer tourist season. This training consisted of three supervised overseas flights.

By this time, we were all well aware that the US Space Program operated by NASA was inventing new navigation equipment for space travel that would soon make human Navigators obsolete. It was just a matter of time until this equipment was competitive with human Navigators in price and accuracy. There were two types of new equipment that were becoming available, an onboard Inertial Navigation System (INS) based on highly sophisticated gyroscopes and a Global Satellite Positioning System that was transmitted from navigation satellites to the aircraft (today everybody has one in their car or on their cell phone). Most of our Navigators understood that if this new navigation equipment could eventually take men to the moon, it could also guide them to Europe or Asia. The one exception was the president of CALNA, who insisted that the new equipment would never replace a human Navigator. He was a great guy and a great Navigator, but he had this huge blind spot and, of course, within nine years he was proven wrong.

Meanwhile, Air Canada was hiring Pilots every three weeks. I contacted my old CF-100 Pilot, Onil (Lach) Lacharité, who was running a fast food restaurant in Laval, Quebec and told him that Air Canada was hiring Pilots. I mentioned that the airline was especially keen on hiring

French-Canadian RCAF veterans. Without hesitation, he applied for the position.

I decided that it was time for me to prepare for a transition to becoming a Pilot to ensure that I could continue my career with Air Canada after the elimination of human Navigators. To achieve this objective, I needed two things: a commercial Pilot licence and permission from Air Canada to qualify as a Pilot. I requested a meeting with Captain Gath Edwards, director of flight operations, to find out whether he would hire me as a Pilot if I got my commercial Pilot licence. I met with Captain Edwards at Air Canada headquarters at Place Ville Marie in Montreal in April 1966. Our interview went very well, and he told me that as soon as I had my commercial Pilot licence and multi-engine instrument rating, he would put me on a Pilot course the next winter. This was to qualify me for the Pilot seniority list—which was very important—and then I could return to my Navigator duties until that profession was phased out. To say the least, I was ecstatic. We continued with a pleasant chat and I mentioned that Air Canada was getting some great young Pilots.

"Like whom?" Captain Edwards asked.

"Like my old CF-100 Pilot—Onil Lacharité!" I replied.

Captain Edwards asked what was so great about him, saying that he hadn't been impressed by him very much in his interview.

"I flew with him for three years," I said. "He was a great Pilot who learned to fly in English even though his English was very poor, and we were the top crew on our Squadron in 1959-60, one of the nine best in Air Defense Command, and represented 432 Squadron at the 1960 Top Gun Rocket Meet!" Captain Edwards agreed that Lach's English was poor and added that he seemed to have very little personality, which was correct.

"Sir," I responded, "are you hiring a Pilot or a public relations man?"

Instead of answering me, Captain Edwards turned in his chair and called out to his secretary, "Susie, call Lacharité, and tell him that he's on the Pilot course next Monday."

Captain Gath Edwards was a great and honourable man. He had refused to hire his own son Dave, another superb Pilot, to avoid the appearance of nepotism. Dave applied and was hired by Canadian

Pacific Air Lines (our only competitor) and Gath Edward's superior, flight ops VP Captain Lindy Rood, forced him to hire Dave as a result, if he was good enough for Canadian Pacific, he was good enough for Air Canada. Gath was respected and loved by the Pilots he hired, and he loved, trusted, and respected them in turn; they were his family. This was also a great day for me; Lach had a terrific thirty-year career with Air Canada and retired as a Boeing 767 Captain. We even managed to get in a few flights together flying overseas on the DC-8.

Regrettably, Captain Edwards couldn't keep his word to me—our Chief Navigator Peter Powell wouldn't let me go for the Pilot course, fearing that I wouldn't return to the Navigator ranks once I had qualified as a Pilot despite my promises to do so. As a result, I lost more than five years of seniority on the Pilot seniority list. I understood Pete's position, though. He was short of Navigators every summer and had to keep Air Canada's Atlantic Fleet airborne. He was a very nice man who had taken a chance on me by hiring a Fighter Navigator for a Long-Range Navigator's job.

ONE EVENING, WHILE I was operating a Flight 965 from Barbados to Toronto, a passenger with an interest in astronavigation asked permission to visit the flight deck. This gentleman, Dr. Wally Bobechko, was an amateur sailor with some astronavigation experience. He was very pleasant, and I showed him how I managed the astronavigation in the twentieth century at 520 mph (837 km/h). Although, as I've mentioned, astronavigation was the primary method of navigation used to sail around the globe for thousands of years at much, much slower speeds—the same speeds that Wally used as a sailor—it was still very useful for aviation in the latter part of the twentieth century.

I asked Wally if he would like to take a three-star fix and he was thrilled. I pre-calculated the three-star fix for him and showed him how to find the right stars and how to take the two-minute shot of each star. He then took the three-star shots and I transposed them onto my chart. The fix was very good, just a touch short of excellent, and Wally had a lifetime memory to take home. A month later, I got a wonderful full-page letter of thanks, offering to reward my kindness if I ever needed him. I never expected to use his generous offer, but I kept the letter and twenty years later he came through for me when I needed medical help in my new hometown of Toronto.

IN THE MID-1960S, the US space program was advancing rapidly as NASA worked towards fulfilling President John F. Kennedy's promise to put an American on the moon within ten years of the Russian launch of the first orbiting satellite, Sputnik. A lot had to be done to accomplish this high priority mission, including the development of a super-technological navigation system to get there. We could all see an end to the need for human Navigators coming—that is, except for Bill Freeman, president of the Canadian Airline Navigators Association. As I've said, he did a great job representing the Navigators with the company for many years, but simply did not believe and did not want to believe that human Navigators could ever be replaced.

At the next Montreal CALNA Council Meeting, I made a presentation to the council regarding an end to the era of the human Navigator. I stressed that we would have to prepare for the elimination of our jobs and an end of our flying careers. I also suggested that the best way to continue flying was for all Navigators to acquire Pilot licences, as the company was apparently willing to permit this. My presentation was received with general approval, although not from Bill Freeman and a couple of the older Navigators. Bill dismissed outright any talk of Navigators being replaced by navigation devices at any time in the near future.

On January 15, 1970, he was proven very wrong when a Boeing 747-100 flew its first commercial flight for Pan American Airways across the Atlantic Ocean with three Carousel inertial navigation systems derived from the Apollo Space Program, three Pilots and *no* human Navigator! Bill was proven to be even more wrong just seven years and seven months later, when Air Canada Navigators were all replaced by inertial navigation systems, and he lost his job because he didn't have a Pilot licence. Fortunately, he received a generous severance package thanks to Air Canada's generosity and our new negotiating team's skills in winning a fair settlement for all of us.

I started taking flying lessons at Laurentide Aviation at Cartierville Airport in Ville St. Laurent, Quebec on September 21, 1966. My first instructor was John Reid, the son of Senior Air Canada Captain and World War II hero Captain Wendell Reid (RCAF Wing Commander). I had to take a break from my flying lessons between October 13, 1966, and February 13, 1967, when the Air Canada mechanics went on strike for the first time in history. I was laid off for a period and I couldn't afford to pay for my flying lessons. John was a good instructor who taught me well and, on a beautiful cold morning on March 14, 1967, I was able to fly solo in the minimum permissible instruction time of twelve hours.

My first solo was another great day in my life. I took off in a Cessna 150 UGF with John Reid in the right seat on that cold and sunny morning. John told me to do one circuit and land, which was strange since we were supposed to be up for an hour. I did as I was instructed, and he then told me to turn off the runway on landing and come to a full stop on the taxi strip. As soon as the aircraft came to a stop, he opened the door and started to get out.

"Where are you going?" I asked.

As he dropped to the tarmac, John merely said, "Take off, do one circuit, land, and come back here to pick me up." I was stunned and speechless—which doesn't happen very often.

I got Cartierville Tower clearance to taxi to the button of Runway 06, completed my before-takeoff checklist, and roared into the beautiful sky all alone. I climbed to 1,500 feet (457 metres) and turned left to downwind to parallel the active runway. A rush of combined fear, power, and exhilaration swept over me and my brain kept repeating, Don't screw this up or you might kill yourself. There's no one here to help you. After passing the button of Runway 06, I did my pre-landing check and reduced power, selected ten degrees of flap and started my descent. At 1,000 feet (300 metres) to 500 feet (152 metres) per minute at 80 mph (129 km/h), I turned left to base leg, selected twenty degrees of flap, lined up the runway, started another left turn, and continued the descent to touchdown with twenty degrees of flap and idle power. At five feet (1.5 metres) I flared the aircraft—pulled up the nose three degrees to slow the rate of descent—and touched down as smooth as silk. I had done it! I was exhilarated; my feelings were beyond words. I had just soloed, the first step to a Pilot career.

I slowly taxied to where I had left John Reid, picked him up, headed back into the air for another thirty minutes, then landed again and headed back to Laurentide Aviation, where I accepted congratulations from all present. Then they cut off my necktie—a tradition for new Pilots.

The minimum flying time needed to get a commercial Pilot licence in Canada was 150 hours. After a total of 155 hours and fifty-five minutes, I landed the Cessna 150 VQI after completing my commercial check ride test with Mr. Fairservice of the Canadian Ministry of Transport on December 6, 1967. On March 15, 1968, I flew down to Burlington, Vermont on a sunny and very windy day, and passed my US commercial Pilot licence flight test in a Cessna 172 PXO with Check Airman David V. Carr of the FAA. I did this just in case Air Canada didn't hire me and I had to fly for a US airline—it didn't hurt that their pay was much better too.

I spent the whole day in Burlington waiting for my check ride and had to fly home at night. Cross-country night flying is not recommended for new Pilots with only one engine and without any instrument training or qualification. My ten years of flying experience, however, allowed me to fly by visual flight rules (VFR), which basically meant following the main highway from Burlington to Montreal. (My experience of watching my Pilots fly on instruments was a great backup). Since I only had one engine, this was also safer because if it failed, I could land on the highway in an emergency.

Unfortunately, Cartierville Airport was closed at night because they didn't have any runway lights. I had to land at Dorval International Airport, where all the big airlines and jet airliners operated. That was bad enough, but there was an extremely strong right to left crosswind on Landing Runway 24 Right, much stronger than I had ever landed in. My approach was quite good considering the conditions. I touched down with the right wing down to prevent the wind from getting under the wing and flipping me over. I touched down on the right wheel and immediately slammed the nose wheel down and used all my strength to keep it down. It was a very rough landing. Once I got full control, I taxied over to the civil private parking ramp, parked, and checked the aircraft—there was no damage—and had Catherine come and pick me up because we only had one car.

When I got home, there was a Notice to Airmen (NOTAM) from the US Federal Aviation Agency (FAA) in my mail, advising all Pilots of a phenomenon called wheel-barrowing with a description of what had just happened to me. Furthermore, it advised Pilots how to handle a light aircraft landing in very strong crosswinds. It turned out that without training, knowledge, or access to this valuable advice, I had reacted correctly by instinct and reflexes. This confirmed for me that my reaction to unusual situations was good and that flying was in my blood. This was an auspicious start to my career as a Pilot.

20

THE QUEBEC QUIET REVOLUTION AND OTHER CHANGES

While I was taking flying lessons and pursuing my new career, I continued to attend Sir George Williams University three nights a week, participated in CALNA union activities, and became involved with charitable work through Kiwanis International. At the same time, the whole province of Quebec was undergoing massive social change.

Quebec is a wonderful place to live, with Montreal as its crown jewel. French-Canadians are the nicest and friendliest people that anyone would ever want to meet and live with. In my opinion, however, two of their greatest problems stem from their history and the Quebec politicians who used that history to divide and conquer, to prey on the population's susceptibility to the exhortations of these rabble-rousing troublemakers.

After the British conquest of Quebec in 1760, the British very cleverly allowed the French-Canadians to live as a more or less separate society under the control of the Roman Catholic Church. This was done in part to maintain divisions between the French-speaking colony and the new English-speaking settlers, thus preventing the colonials from unifying and throwing the British out like the Americans did. They were successful for a long time. Although it has been a free country since 1867, Canada did not have its own flag for almost one hundred years and did not formally adopt its own national anthem until 1980.

The fate of the uprisings that did occur in Canada demonstrated the effectiveness of the British policy. When the 1837 Upper Canada

(Ontario) Rebellion led by William Lyon Mackenzie and the 1837–38 Lower Canada (Quebec) Rebellion led by Louis-Joseph Papineau were suppressed, most of the insurgents were deported to the British penal colonies in Hobart and Sydney, Australia while the leaders fled to the United States. The same divide-and-conquer technique was used successfully by the British in their colonies in Africa, Asia, Australia, and the Americas. That is how they maintained their profitable control of these rich colonies.

When we arrived in Montreal in 1948, we were shocked by two things:

1. The complete dominance of the French-Canadians by their English compatriots.
2. The separation of English and French, and Protestant and Catholic schooling. My sister and I could not go to French-language schools because we weren't Roman Catholic, although the Protestant (English) school board accepted students of all denominations.

In 1967, a great Canadian, Premier Jean-Jacques Bertrand of the Union Nationale party broke down those barriers. He passed Bill 67, permitting all Quebecers to select the school of their choice for their children. Catherine, who was fluently bilingual, and I wanted our children to also be completely bilingual and sent our daughters to private French kindergarten. In late August, we arranged an appointment with the principal of the French-language school in Beaconsfield to register Linda and Liza. This separatist racist, however, refused to register them because he claimed that they would contaminate his school—not the taxpayers' school, *his* school. If Catherine had not stepped between us, he might have been severely injured.

We filed a complaint with the Lakeshore School Board and they forced him to accept our girls. By this time, though, Linda was nervous about going to French school and stayed in an English-language school, but Liza, with her fluency in French, was accepted. As an adult it proved to be a great career benefit to her in business.

My friend Air Canada Captain Maurice Labine, a French-Canadian from Sudbury, Ontario, had the same problem with the same principal, when he tried to register his children at the same school because his wife was Anglo! He also had to appeal to the school board to gain access for his children that was guaranteed by Quebec law. This principal of the French-language school in Beaconsfield was the worst type of Quebec racist—you had to be French-Canadian from Quebec for generations to be considered "pure laine" (literally, pure wool) Quebecois. No one else mattered to people like him; we were considered to be "maudit anglais" (damn English) and not welcome in our own home.

There was certainly intolerance on both sides, however. I encountered some of it when Catherine and I joined the Summerlea Golf and Country Club in Vaudreuil, Quebec in 1974, sponsored by Captain John Wright for the princely initiation fee of $1,500. Although the club was mostly English-speaking, a year later I was able to sponsor my old friends, French-Canadian CF-100 Pilot Onil Lacharité and his wife, Carmen, to become members. It came as a huge shock when I was soon accosted in the men's locker room by one of the club's directors, Graham Hazelton, and told that we didn't need any more Frenchmen in the club and I shouldn't sponsor any more of them. We got into one fierce argument and came very close to blows. Imagine this nervy jerk, living as a minority in a French-speaking province, wanting to keep French-Canadians out of our golf club! To top it off, he was insulting a man with whom I had shared danger and helped to defend our country during the Cold War.

The good news was that Onil and his spouse were accepted as members. I steered clear of Graham after that because I was afraid that I might hurt him. He typified the warped Quebec Anglo mentality that had allowed them to dominate our French-Canadian brothers for two centuries and triggered the Quebec Quiet Revolution of 1960. Here we were seventeen years later, and this man still didn't understand the changes that were taking place all around him. Not surprisingly, he sold his business a couple of years later and fled to Toronto; he no longer wanted to live in the new reality that he helped to create.

DURING THOSE SAME years, I became very active in the Lake St. Louis Kiwanis Club. My friend and neighbour Air Canada Captain John Crammond had sponsored me for membership in 1967 and the highlight of my time there was being in charge of our largest fundraiser, the Lakeshore Antique Auto Show and Operation Drug Alert.

The Antique Auto Show at the Pointe Claire Arena was an artistic success but a financial disaster; we barely broke even. The weather on the weekend of the show was horrible, with heavy rain and high winds keeping everyone indoors. For the most part, the one hundred-plus beautiful antique cars were admired by their owners and my fellow Kiwanians. Operation Drug Alert (ODA) in 1969, however, was our greatest success. Kiwanis International had decreed that the 1969 theme for all Kiwanis Clubs would be about education and prevention of drug abuse by our children. We all had one thing in common: we knew nothing about drug abuse, but we had to learn fast. Our children were being brainwashed by their heroes in the rock music world that drugs were okay, and they had more influence with our children than we did.

One night, after an evening out with Catherine, while I was driving our babysitter Leanne home, I asked her whether there really was a drug problem in the schools. She said that there certainly was and for the next half hour—most of it sitting in the car in her driveway—she thoroughly covered the seriousness of the problem. She scared the wits out of me as we had two teenagers. Catherine was upset when I got home because I was so late, but I sat her down and repeated what I had learned. She was scared out of her wits too.

"What are you going to do about it?" she demanded after hearing me out. Once again, my spouse was challenging me into action.

"Let's put Kiwanis to work!" I responded.

Kiwanis Clubs are autonomous clubs that belong to Kiwanis International. Committees are set up within the clubs for various projects, which have to report to the president and the rest of the members every week. In this case, the individual who was appointed chairman of the Drug Alert Committee at our club, reported for eight straight weeks "...that he was still investigating the problem." He was a real man of action! Finally, after the eighth week, I got angry and demanded a real report. The ODA chairman immediately resigned, and, thanks to my big mouth, I became the new chairman of Operation Drug Alert at our club.

Our committee worked very hard raising funds to pay for awareness seminars and meetings for parents and their children. We brought in doctors, psychiatrists, police officers, and drug addicts—both current users and reformed survivors of this terrible affliction—to teach and explain. We produced handouts filled with data and articles on and explanations of the root causes of the drug tsunami flooding over us and our children. We continued this work for three years until a bigger and more useful project presented us with an opportunity to make a real difference.

While Operation Drug Alert was very successful in raising awareness among parents about the dangers of drug usage among their children, we had no facilities in the Province of Quebec to assist those who fell victim to this scourge. In 1971, a group of interested and civic-minded Montreal citizens started to explore the possibility of founding a drug rehabilitation facility in the city. As chairman of our club's committee and co-chairman for all the Kiwanis Clubs in Montreal, I was able to participate and assist the J. W. McConnell Foundation in organizing and fundraising for the Portage Drug Rehabilitation Foundation that was established in 1970. I was a member of the Board of Governors for the first three years of its existence, under the chairmanship of Jean Béliveau, the Hall of Fame hockey star of the Montreal Canadiens. In 1971, we opened our first facility on Drummond Street in the heart of downtown Montreal with two counsellors and six residents.

On February 13, 1973, we hired John Devlin, who had run a very successful drug rehab centre in New York City called Daytop Village, as our director and opened our second rehab center in Prévost on Lac Echo, Quebec, just north of Montreal. We were fortunate to have hired the deputy director of Daytop as the new director for Portage Quebec. This man was a rehabilitated drug addict, a graduate of the Daytop Village system, who had prevailed through hard work, abstinence, and perseverance. He was completely rehabilitated and became a great success as our first director. He brought with him the techniques that had helped him to recover and lead a very useful and productive life.

We were fortunate in being able to recruit prominent Quebecers to our Board of Governors. As I've said, the first chairman was Jean Béliveau, and today, Mr. Jean Coutu, the chairman and CEO of the Jean Coutu Pharmacy chain is the co-chairman. This has assisted us in raising funds and getting government cooperation.

The Portage Quebec Prévost facility has been very successful and is still in existence forty years later; thousands of drug addicts and alcoholics have rebuilt their lives there. After a couple of years of very successful operation, we got a contract from the Quebec government to rehabilitate alcoholic and drug-addicted convicts in provincial prisons. Today, Portage is a shining example of successful rehabilitation with an average annual success rate of 75 per cent, one of the best records anywhere. It has since expanded throughout Quebec and even into Ontario, British Columbia, and the Maritimes.

The great success of Portage can be attributed to a careful selection process—candidates must request help, and no one is accepted under duress or threat; the quality of staff, which is 100 per cent made up of rehabilitated graduates of the Portage program; and the hard work and generosity of the fundraisers.

IN 1971, I graduated from Sir George Williams University (now Concordia) with a BA in political science and economics. That same year, a group of other local volunteers and I helped to form the first soccer and hockey leagues for girls in Canada. This was a lot of fun, and I coached both the soccer and hockey teams for two years. Today, Canadian women are world and Olympic champions in hockey and the third best in soccer in the world. It was a real eye-opener for some people that girls could and wanted to play hockey and soccer.

TWO YEARS AFTER my graduation, on Saturday, November 3, 1973, I returned home from an overseas flight at 7:00 p.m., to a phone call from my brother Michael, who told me that Dad had had his third heart attack and was in the hospital in serious condition. I headed straight there, but Dad had passed on by the time I got to the hospital. He was taking a shower and collapsed but was actually gone before he hit the bathtub. Two heroic Montreal police officers tried artificial respiration and mouth-to-mouth resuscitation until the ambulance arrived, without success. My mother was still devastated by his passing forty years later. Our family lost a good father, friend, and advisor, and the kindest, gentlest, bravest, and most honest man I have ever met. I still miss him.

Our whole family was distraught, but my mother was devastated. During the rest of her life, a day did not go by that she did not grieve for her beloved Arnold.

Operation Drug Alert was a project of the Lake St. Louis Kiwanis Club while I was chairman of our local Drug Alert Committee. I'm in the centre and Grant Peterson is on the right. 1970.

Kiwanians aid in rehabilitiation of addict

The Lake St. Louis Kiwanis Club has donated another six pairs of cross-country skis to the Portage Foundation's drug rehabilitation centre at Lac Echo in the Laurentians.

The ski equipment is used by the centre's 50 residents as part of their overall therapeutic treatment.

In three years f operation, the Portage Foundation has seen 46 drug addicts graduate to a meaningful place in society again under the one-year rehabilitation program. The foundation has also helped hundreds of minor drug abusers and their families to solve their problems without resorting to the use of drugs.

The Kiwanis Club of Lake St. Louis has been involved with Portage since the inception of the idea of such a facility six years ago and has supported it as part of Kiwanis' Operation Drug Alert.

Operation Drug Alert

Kiwanian Lou Voticky, on behalf of the Lake St. Louis Kiwanis Club, presents Portage Foundation Director John Devlin (right) with skis and a cheque as part of Operation Drug Alert. The donation is in support of the foundation's treatment of drug addicts who wish to recover from the effects of abuse.

A newspaper clipping about the Lake St. Louis Kiwanis Club donating skis to the Portage Foundation's drug rehabilitation centre at Lac Echo, Quebec. As a member of the Board of Governors, I was very involved in Kiwanis fundraising for the Portage Drug Rehabilitation Foundation and the first rehab facility in 1971. John Devlin (right) was hired as director in 1973.

A thank-you letter for our help in setting up the new wing of the Portage Program facility, 1975.

My graduation from Sir George Williams University (now Concordia) with a BA in political science and economics. Montreal, 1971.

Champions at the Summerlea Golf and Country Club in Vaudreuil, Quebec, 1976. I'm in the middle.

21

THE FIGHT TO BECOME A PILOT AND FLIGHT 965

There were three obstacles to overcome for the Navigator group to become Pilots. First, I would have to convince the majority of the Navigators that a Pilot career was the only way for us to continue flying professionally. Then we would all have to qualify as Pilots and meet the minimum standard for an Air Canada Pilot hire, paying for the whole process ourselves. The final step was to get our union to negotiate the right for us to train and convert to the Pilot ranks with Air Canada and the Canadian Airline Pilots Association and get on the crucial Pilot seniority list.

Job One, clearly, was to get all the Navigators qualified as Pilots to the Air Canada minimum standard. At that time, Air Canada gave preference in hiring to experienced Pilots with at least two thousand hours of Pilot-in-Command time before their twenty-seventh birthday—yes, it was discriminatory—and a multi-engine instrument rating. This posed a major hurdle for Navigators: we were all over twenty-seven and only two of us had a commercial Pilot licence and no instrument rating—Cliff Perry and me.

Since we had no idea when Air Canada would purchase the new navigation systems that would eventually replace us, I decided that I had to take care of my career first and worry about the rest of the group later. My first task was to build up my flying hours to gain more experience at the controls of an aircraft. I flew as much as I could, including working on passing my academic and flying qualifications for my US licence so I could qualify for an American airline if needed. My first choice there was Pan American Air Lines, the leading airline at that time and they required Navigator experience for all their Pilot hires because they used Pilot Navigators in their three-man crews. However, it also became the first major airline to go bankrupt a few years later so it's a good thing that they didn't hire me. I dodged another bullet. My second choice was United Airlines and my third choice was Eastern Airlines. They were both willing to hire me, but fortunately I did not accept their offers—they both also ended in bankruptcy. I dodged two more bullets.

Now came the hard part. Once we had all qualified, we would have to get the power of our union, the Canadian Airline Navigators Association, behind us to be hired as Pilots by our company. I would have to convince the other eighty-four Navigators and especially our president, Bill Freeman, that we needed to negotiate a deal with Air Canada to be allowed onto the Pilot seniority list as soon as we qualified. This wasn't easy—as I've said, our union president had no desire to become a Pilot. As far as he was concerned, being a Second Officer was beneath both his cockpit status and the social status that being a Navigator gave him in his community. There was some truth in this as the Long-Range Navigator was the key man on oceanic flying routes, which endowed us with respect in the Pilot group. It was short-sighted, though; at some point one has to make a choice between social status and earning a living—especially when the basis of that income was about to disappear.

My first recruit among the Navigators was Cliff Perry, who was already a qualified commercial Pilot, and then I started talking to all the younger Navigators and received their strong support. Next, I lobbied Captain Pete Hamilton, president of the Canadian Airline Pilots Association (CALPA). He also supported the idea and promised to bring it up with the governing body of CALPA, the Master Executive Council (MEC) that represented all four Air Canada Pilot bases in Montreal, Toronto, Winnipeg, and Vancouver. Thanks to the great relationship that we had with the Pilots, the CALPA MEC agreed in principle to support our bid to be placed at the bottom of the Pilot seniority list as soon as we qualified as Pilots. This was a great achievement because the Navigators of our main competitor, Canadian Pacific

Airlines, did not receive that kind of assistance from their Pilots. We all owe a great debt to the Air Canada Pilots and especially their leaders, who appreciated our role on the flight deck.

Since the CALNA president refused to cooperate, however, we only had one choice—to get rid of him on the grounds that he no longer represented the views of the majority of the membership and get control of CALNA. By this time, our membership had grown to eighty-six Navigators based in Montreal, Toronto, and Vancouver. We passed a resolution to start the process of bringing the association's constitution up to date. John Caron volunteered to take the lead and executed the mandate brilliantly. He rewrote our constitution—this was the key to our success in gaining control—and reorganized the association membership into three local councils, with two executive representatives from each base joining the CALNA president and secretary on the Master Executive Council. The MEC would be the supreme decision-making body for the association. This was just the opening that we young rebels needed.

We lobbied the young members and managed to get elected and take the control of all three councils as chairmen and secretaries, which gave us control of the CALNA Master Executive Council with six votes against Bill and his secretary, Al Blackwood. The new CALNA MEC consisted of chairmen John Caron in Toronto; Bill Melville, Vancouver; and me in Montreal. Our secretaries were Cal Munroe, Roger Friedel, and Gord Shaver respectively. Later we were joined by Roger Waldman, Terry Still, Don Corker, Cal Munroe, and Ray English.

We next turned our attention to convincing Bill Freeman and the older Navigators that our navigating careers were ending. Al Blackwood surprised us all by telling us that he had already started Pilot training. He joined us even though he was more than ten years older than our rebel faction and was an old friend of Bill's. Now the vote on the CALNA executive was seven to one. We were successful with most of the other older Navigators, but Bill Freeman was determined not to be a Second Officer and fought us at every turn. In labour negotiations, however, the side with the bigger baseball bat wins. We had the votes and the bigger bat because we had the support of the majority of young

Navigators who wanted to maintain a flying career until retirement. The numbers were on our side.

We also received tremendous support from Captain Lindy Rood and Captain Kent Davis, Air Canada's successive vice-presidents of flight operations; Captain Charlie Simpson, who later succeeded Captain Rood and Captain Kent Davis as vice-president of fight operations; and Captain John Wright, and Captain Rollie Cook, both of whom were successor presidents of CALPA.

Every former Air Canada Navigator owes a great debt of gratitude to these splendid men and outstanding leaders.

The MEC tried hard to convince Bill Freeman that the end of the Navigator era was nigh and that we had to start negotiating the conversion of Navigators to other jobs at Air Canada—either as Pilots or, for those unwilling or unable to become Pilots, to ground jobs—as well as severance pay for those wishing to retire. We had to strike while we still had bargaining power, which would disappear as soon as our jobs were phased out by electronic navigation systems. Our President continued to be reluctant and kept delaying a decision; he was very stubborn and assured us that despite the great advances in navigation systems—the Apollo astronauts had gone to the moon without the aid of a human Navigator in 1969—insisted that Air Canada would never replace human Navigators.

John Caron and I approached Roger Waldman, a highly intelligent Navigator who was well respected by senior members of Air Canada management, Captain Rood and Captain Davis, and asked him to join us. We felt that he had the credibility to replace Bill Freeman as president of CALNA. By this time, Roger was also taking flying lessons. He immediately agreed to be our new president and chief negotiator.

Fortunately, under our revised constitution, the MEC had the authority to call for an extraordinary Master Executive Council meeting and elect a new president. At my instigation, the other six council members and I signed the request for the special council meeting, but Bill Freeman refused to attend. We held the meeting anyway and voted to replace him with Roger Waldman as president with the help of Al Blackwood from the older group. This must have been one of the smoothest palace coups in history; no blood was spilled and the only injury was some hurt feelings. We had achieved our first step in winning a fair career continuation with Air Canada.

We made a great team. Roger Waldman was the quiet and persistent negotiator who did most of the talking; John Caron was our quiet cerebral genius who only broke in when the company negotiators didn't understand the finer points and details of our position; and I was the hammer who forcefully and firmly set the company representatives back in their chairs when they got stupid or hard to deal with on anything. As a result, my popularity with Air Canada upper management sank to an all-time low. I didn't care. I did my job and used every weapon at my disposal to represent my brother Navigators to the best of my ability. By the time an agreement was reached two years later, the company negotiators didn't like me at all. Bill Melville from Vancouver was the big quiet man on our side.

The Air Canada negotiating team consisted of Captain Bill Bell, director of flight operations; Charley Eyre, a former Navigator and former chief negotiator for the company; and Norm Radford, the new chief negotiator, a former Tail Gunner in World War II. He didn't like either Pilots or Navigators; he considered us to be overpaid and overrated bus drivers. Everything agreed to had to be approved by Captain Lindy Rood, vice-president of flight operations and, later, his successor, Captain Kent Davis.

Negotiations started in March 1972. Our negotiating position was strong because the company didn't want to hire any more Navigators given that we would be redundant within three years. They needed us to agree to fly between 107 and 115 hours per month in the heavy summer season, instead of our normal eighty-two hours, to cover the time deficiency caused by increased flying requirements during the summer months. In turn, we wanted to be placed on the bottom of the Pilot seniority list in our present seniority order as soon as we had our commercial Pilot licences. We also wanted the company to help us get our multi-engine instrument ratings and further requested that we only take a maximum pay reduction of 25 per cent when we started as Pilots. We were asking that men with up to thirty years of Air Canada service be allowed to start at a rate equivalent to that of a fifth-year Pilot. We thought the pay request was quite reasonable. For those of us who were not interested in becoming Pilots, or were unable to, we requested available ground positions with the same pay terms as the future Pilots. Our last request was for fair severance packages for those who would give up their jobs with the company voluntarily.

Day one of the negotiations was a disaster. Norm Radford dismissed all of our requests out of hand, only offering us first-year Pilot pay of approximately $500 per month. This would have meant a 75 per cent decrease for men with years of service and experience, and families with school-age children. We were not first-year Pilots! We were skilled aviators with anywhere between fifteen and thirty years of flying experience. We had done everything in the cockpit except take off and land the aircraft. We flight-planned, navigated, monitored the weather and the fuel consumption, and we handled the radios, radar, and navigation equipment. We assisted with the safety equipment in emergencies. We had essentially been doing 90 per cent of a Pilot's job for all those years and Mr. Radford wanted to treat us as novices and pay us accordingly. We certainly were not novices and refused to be treated like raw rookies.

At the end of the first day, I told Radford that hell would freeze over before we accepted his offer. This charade continued for twenty-three months—the company negotiators were paid to drag out the negotiations as long as possible in order to weaken our bargaining position. While we Navigators used up our days off from flying to sit through Radford's monotonous blather, he was getting paid. We needed a hammer.

On February 23, 1974, Air Canada gave us one. On a Sunday night when I returned on Flight 871 from Paris and checked my company mailbox, there was a letter advising us that starting April 5, 1974, Air Canada, which had founded, trained and was half owner of Air Jamaica would be assisting that airline on a route from Kingston, Jamaica to London, England by providing aircraft and Navigators who would help Air Jamaica Pilots cross the Atlantic safely. Now the shoe was on the other foot! Air Canada needed our assistance. I had found our negotiating hammer and was ready to use it. No more Mr. Nice Guy—the future of eighty-six Navigators hung in the balance and it might be our last chance to get a fair deal.

I went straight home and called Roger Waldman and John Caron. I told them that we had the company right where we wanted them— we would refuse to fly for Air Jamaica on the grounds that we had no contract with them and didn't know anything about the standards of their aircraft or their Pilots. In addition, I said, we would refuse to fly the voluntary 115 hours that summer, which we had agreed to and been doing for two years in good faith so that we would be treated fairly at the time of redundancy. Roger and John weren't so sure that this was a good strategy, but I assured them that we would crush the company position and we would get our desired contract. I was fully prepared to be the spokesman and the hammer—I didn't care what management thought of me.

The next morning, Roger and I were in Chief Navigator Peter Powell's office at 9:00 a.m. sharp. When I delivered the bad news to Peter, he was stunned. When he recovered his composure, he said, "You can't do this. We have a contract with you and Air Jamaica and their flights are sold out! We don't have time to make other arrangements!"

"That's the point, Peter," I replied. "Right now, we don't have a contract with either Air Canada or Air Jamaica. We've shown good faith by flying up to 115 hours per month without a new contract and we got nothing in return. The company has been dragging out the contract negotiations for twenty-three months. Of course, if you want us to fly for Air Jamaica and do the 115 hours this summer, all that you have to do is meet our very reasonable requests and sign a new contract with us!"

Peter Powell was almost speechless, so Roger and I knew that we had hit a raw nerve. Peter couldn't replace us or fill his requirements for the next two years without our assistance. He even blustered that during World War II he couldn't have refused a command or even a request.

"We respect your wartime service," I answered, "but we are now at peace, with collective bargaining. There are no orders, only requests, and these must be negotiated!"

"We know that you're in a hurry for our approval on these two matters," Roger said, "and you know where to reach us." We took that as our cue to leave.

When Peter called us that afternoon and asked for a meeting the next morning, we responded, "Only to sign a decent contract!"

We brought in our Executive Committee from Toronto and Vancouver overnight, explained the new situation to them at breakfast, got their approval, and went to meet the Air Canada negotiating team at the Dorval base for the last time. We reviewed the contract, which was basically our original two-year-old offer, signed it, and got a bonus. I did not request, I *demanded* that the company pay for the twenty hours of instruction for our multi-engine instrument ratings (cost $50/hour) and they acquiesced. They desperately needed us to sign and agree to fly for Air Jamaica and fly the 115 hours for the next three summers.

After the signing, I told Radford that I had added my late demand for the multi-engine instrument rating cost—which amounted to approximately $10,000 for each of the sixty-two Navigators who became Pilots, a total cost to Air Canada of about $620,000—because he was such a jerk and lousy negotiator. Revenge is best served cold as I learned from *Scaramouche* and the *Count of Monte Cristo*. Radford and I were no longer colleagues; this had become personal and we certainly didn't socialize after that.

The non-Pilot Navigators were provided with equivalent ground jobs or severance packages depending on what they chose to do.

The crowning proof of our success was that six Navigators over fifty years of age acquired their Pilot licences, including the Chief Navigators in Montreal (George Chipman) and Toronto (Bill Henderson) and enjoyed fruitful careers until they retired. Regrettably, George Chipman had a heart attack before he could transition to Pilot and retired medically. Bill Henderson decided that I was not a gentleman because of the way we had ousted his friend Bill Freeman and because of my tough negotiating stand with our employer. He seemed to hold me personally responsible because he continued to treat his long-time close friends John Caron and Roger Waldman with respect. I viewed his reaction as a badge of honour. I had fought for what was right; I had helped save eighty-six careers; and I had done what any good union leader should do: take care of his members. Of course, Bill Henderson also benefitted from our tough stance personally with ten years of flying as a Pilot and another six years as a Simulator Instructor at no cost to him—as a member of management he didn't even pay CALNA union dues! Needless to say, he never thanked me for any of this.

LATER THAT SUMMER, I was flying to build my Pilot-in-Command time in a Piper Tri-Pacer JXT with my thirteen-year-old daughter, Liza, who had been flying with me for approximately four years. I had taught her the basics of flying, including maintaining a scan in and out of the cockpit, and when we were at five hundred feet (152 metres) on a cleared final approach to St. Hubert Airport, she said suddenly, "Dad, there's the shadow of an aircraft over our shadow on the ground!"

I looked out and saw that she was right—there was a shadow right over ours! I immediately broke off the approach and advised the St. Hubert Tower that someone was asleep at the switch there, clearing two aircraft for the approach at the same time with no separation. I was very proud of Liza; by keeping an outside scan, she probably saved our lives. I regret to this day that the airlines didn't hire female Pilots in those days—she would have been a good one.

I COMPLETED MY Air Canada Pilot training at the end of February 1975 with a final checkout and instrument test conducted by Captain Gordie Jones, the calmest and best instructor that I've ever had. I received my Class I instrument rating on the four-engine DC-8 (maximum takeoff weight 355,000 pounds or 161,000 kilograms). This was a giant step up and I was very proud of that accomplishment; the largest aircraft that I had flown up to then was a two-engine propeller-powered aircraft.

Captain Gordie Jones was another one of our living legends at Air Canada. During World War II he flew unarmed twin-engine C-47s— the civilian version was the DC-3—delivering and dropping supplies to Allied troops after the Normandy invasion, among them the trapped British paratroopers at Arnhem, Netherlands. These missions were flown at five-hundred-foot (160-metre) altitudes to ensure the accuracy of the drops while trying to avoid anti-aircraft fire. He also participated in the airlift of Holocaust survivors from the Bergen-Belsen concentration camp to medical facilities in Holland, Belgium, and Great Britain.

In 2014, on the seventieth anniversary of the historic battle there, Gordie and his few surviving mates were flown to Arnhem, Holland to be honoured by the Dutch people and the British Paratroop regiment for their heroic efforts. As a company of British Paratroopers passed the decorated veteran standing on the sidewalk with his son Brian, their Commander rose in his vehicle, saluted Gordie, and issued the "Eyes right!" order to his troops. Like a rifle shot some 160 pairs of eyes snapped to the right. This was a great honour for a very brave, great, and humble man.

"Who are they saluting?" Gordie asked his son.

"You, Dad!" Brian responded.

There is more about Gordie Jones that needs to be told. On March 18, 1976, he was instructing and checking out two Cubana Airlines Pilots on a DC-8-43 leased to Cubana by Air Canada. They had been cleared (in English) by Havana air traffic control (ATC) and were approaching the Havana Beacon at 5,000 feet (1,524 metres). The two Cuban Pilots were flying the aircraft and Gordie was monitoring them from the jump seat behind the Captain.

The two Cuban Pilots followed the ATC instructions, but, at the same time, Havana ATC cleared a Russian Antonov 24B with a Russian instructor and four Cuban student Pilots to the same radio beacon and at the same altitude in Russian. None of the nine Pilots had a complete picture and the Air Traffic Controller had just made a bad mistake. The inevitable happened: the Antonov clipped the DC-8 and took off eleven feet (3.35 metres) of its wing. The Russian aircraft crashed, killing everyone on board. Gordie pulled the First Officer out of his seat, climbed into it, and took control of the DC-8. He brought the aircraft under control and landed it safely, saving 105 passengers and crew.

In communist countries, there was no such thing as accidents—whatever happened was always caused by sabotage or the fault of Westerners. Fidel Castro personally accused Captain Jones, who was not even flying the aircraft at the time of the collision, of causing the accident. From their skewed perspective, the man who took control of a severely damaged aircraft and saved 105 Cuban lives was guilty of causing the accident. Air Canada had to smuggle Gordie out of the country to protect him from a jail term. This man, who taught me how to fly four-engine jets, was a good friend of mine until he passed away.

AS SOON AS I had completed my Air Canada Pilot training, I started flying as a brand-new DC-8 Second Officer immediately. The Second

Officer's primary job was to handle the Flight Engineer duties—monitoring the electrics and hydraulics, the weather, the onboard systems and the fuel—and be a monitor and backup Pilot for the Captain and First Officer.

In the second month in my new position, I flew with a man I'll call Captain Andrew Black and First Officer Steve Crutcher on Flight 960 from our base in Montreal and arrived in Bridgetown, Barbados on the afternoon of April 4, 1975. As was usual in Barbados, it was a beautiful day. We went for a swim in the sunshine, had a quiet dinner, and went to bed at approximately nine o'clock because we had a ten o'clock departure the next morning on Flight 965 to Toronto.

April 5 dawned sunny and hot. We got dressed, had breakfast, and headed for Seawell International Airport. Our flight plan was ready, and we were startled to see that our alternate airport was Minneapolis-St. Paul, two hours from Toronto. This was a definite danger signal—in nine years of flying as a Navigator for Air Canada, we had never used an alternate airport that far from our destination. This meant that there was some really bad weather in eastern North America.

The weather offices in the Caribbean did not have very good communication with the rest of the world at that time; their weather was usually sunny and hot with a few cumulus clouds floating around, and they believed that the rest of the world was the same. The only time that they had to really work was during hurricane season from July to October, and this was April. As a result, all we got for a weather briefing was a shrug of the shoulders and a suggestion to check the North American weather en route—as though we didn't do that all the time! This was sounding very similar to our disastrous night at Bagotville in June 1964.

To ensure a safe flight, an airliner carries flight fuel (the amount of fuel to fly from A to B), alternate fuel (enough fuel to get to another airport if the aircraft was unable to land at its destination), en route fuel (extra fuel to compensate for unexpected head winds or lower altitudes provided by Air Traffic Control), and fuel in tanks (the minimum amount of fuel required to be in the tanks upon landing).

For this flight, we were provided with 92,000 pounds (42,000 kilograms) of flight fuel; 32,000 pounds (14,500 kilograms) of alternate fuel; 7,000 pounds (3,000 kilograms) of en route fuel; and 6,000 pounds (2,700 kilograms) of minimum fuel; for a total of 137,000 pounds (62,000 kilograms) of JP 2, which is basically kerosene. This was sufficient for almost nine hours of flying time as long as we only made one approach and a landing at our destination. If we attempted an approach and landing and missed, and then climbed to cruise altitude and did another approach, our fuel reserve and flying time would be cut by approximately thirty minutes. We needed six hours to get to Toronto and another two hours to get to Minneapolis for a total of eight hours flying time, cutting our safety margin to approximately thirty minutes. An approach and miss at Toronto would therefore cut our reserves to minimum levels for a flight to our alternate. In addition, the DC-8-61 Stretch that we were flying only had a maximum crosswind landing capability of twenty-five knots per hour. This data had to be factored into our projected flight and landing calculations.

Both Captain Black and F/O Steve Crutcher were very experienced Pilots, and even though I was a rookie Pilot, I had eighteen years of flying experience on the flight deck as a Navigator. But I can tell you that by the time this flight landed, we had used all of our knowledge, skills, judgment, experience, and especially luck to bring two hundred passengers and eight Flight Attendants back to Canada safe and sound.

We departed and picked up the first Toronto weather after passing Puerto Rico—it was not good. By the time we contacted New York, it was worse.

The weather in Toronto was very bad—there was a two-hundred-foot ceiling with the wind 30 degrees off the main north-south Runway 33 from the right at forty knots (sixty-five km/h) gusting to sixty-five knots (105 km/h). This was just within legal limits based on angle of wind speed and direction. When we contacted Toronto Flight Dispatch they suggested that we use Cleveland as our new alternate, giving us extra fuel to hold at Toronto if necessary. They had made the same suggestion to our Flight 620 from Los Angeles and that crew had accepted it.

I checked the Cleveland airport charts and discovered that the main runway in use was east-west with a similar wind as in Toronto, making the crosswind illegal for our aircraft. I immediately advised the Captain and then Toronto Dispatch, informing them that Minneapolis was still our alternate. Someone in Toronto Flight Dispatch was asleep at the switch. Upon hearing my call to Toronto dispatch, the next radio transmission was from Air Canada Flight 620 from Los Angeles: "Toronto Dispatch, 620 is diverting to Winnipeg, forget Cleveland!" Their crew had recognized the danger as well.

As I described, we had enough fuel to do one approach at Toronto and still make Minneapolis safely. The Captain decided to attempt a Category II approach at Toronto. In a Cat II approach, the Captain flies on his instruments, the First Officer monitors his instruments and, approaching the decision height, looks for visual cues on the ground—when he sees the ground at that minimum altitude he calls, "Decision height," and describes what if anything he sees. If he sees the ground, he calls it. The Captain looks up and calls, "Landing or Go Around," depending on whether he can see the runway and is able to land. Of course, this procedure is out of date today as airliners do Category III approaches now with almost zero limits and automatic landings.

The Second Officer—in this instance, me—monitors the instruments all the way down and ensures that the Captain does not close the throttles (reducing power) too soon in the strong gusty conditions that we faced that day.

At one hundred feet above decision height, Steve Crutcher called, "One hundred above."

Captain Black responded, "Roger."

At decision height, F/O Steve Crutcher called out, "Strobe light on the left!" indicating that the powerful bright white lights were flashing at the end of a major runway to improve Pilot visual cues.

Black looked up, saw the strobe light, called, "Landing!" and then turned toward the light.

The trouble was that the strobe light we saw flashing was on the left side of the runway and the wind was blowing us right to left. When we saw the runway, we were well to the left and the strong north-northeast gusting wind was blowing us even further to the left. Black made a sharp right turn to make the runway and the landing. I kept my hand behind the throttles to ensure that they stayed in place until Black closed them to flare (reduce the rate of descent of the aircraft). When Black flared and closed the throttles we hit hard on our right undercarriage, straightened out and bounced twice, then stopped very quickly because of the strong headwinds. Wow! That was a close call, and, in gratitude, our passengers burst into applause. Captain Black had done a great job under extremely difficult conditions.

The weather was so bad that it took us forty minutes just to get to our assigned parking spot. All the gates were blocked with drifting snow and we had to park so far away from the terminal building that our passengers and the crew had to be transported to Canada Customs by bus. We were the only flight that made it into Toronto that day; everyone else was smarter than us and diverted to their alternates.

When we finally parked, Captain "Black" turned to Steve and me and said, "You guys weren't scared, were you?" Not much, but our shirts were sure soaking wet! Years later, Catherine told me that she always knew when I had a difficult flight; she could smell the nervous perspiration in my uniform shirts when she washed them.

It took us three more hours to get to our hotel just over a mile away (two kilometres) by taxi. We had dinner—I didn't eat much because I had a pain in my right side—and then went to bed. The next thing we knew we were awakened by crew scheduling at 6:00 a.m. advising us that we were drafted to take a flight to Miami in two hours. By the time we flew to Miami and back to Montreal, I was in a lot of pain and drove straight to the office of our family doctor, Dr. Bill Gossage. He examined me, diagnosed acute appendicitis, and sent me directly to the Lakeshore General Hospital for surgery. Catherine got to the West Island Hospital pretty quickly; our daughters were now teenagers and she was working for Peerless Rugs in downtown Montreal.

After the surgery, I was grounded for thirty days, and Catherine and I took off for our first visit to Hawaii. We spent ten days on Maui and fell in love with that beautiful state. While we were there, unfortunately, I made a big mistake. Catherine urged me to buy a condominium and we should have, but we ended up not buying any real estate there just before the boom. Those condos were selling for $60,000 at that time but sold for $300,000 five years later! Of course, a shortage of money was a major factor in that decision—we had no savings, I had just taken a 35 per cent pay cut to become a Pilot, inflation was in the double digits, and our girls were still in high school.

The contract between Air Canada and the Canadian Airline Navigators Association (CALNA) that would allow Navigators to convert to Pilots took twenty-three months to negotiate. It was finally signed near the end of February 1973. Other leaders in the process include John Caron (back row, third from the right); Roger Waldman (seated in front on the right); and on the left, sitting next to him, is Captain Kent Davis, Vice-President of flight operations. I'm the one standing in the middle with the big grin.

Navigators becoming obsolete

PORT ALBERNI, B.C.: Air Canada is phasing out its navigators as overseas planes are gradually equipped with inertial navitation systems (INS), which don't require navigators. Don Willis, the airlines chief navigation officer, said the 30 navigators affected will transfer to other jobs, mostly as pilots. Willis praised the navigators and said that the airline "has consistently emerged as a top performer in international surveys over the busy North Atlantic route."

There were Navigators who didn't believe that this would ever happen.

Captain Gordie Jones, the calmest and best instructor I ever had, a real World War II hero, and a man who saved 105 lives after a terrible midair collision over Havana, Cuba.

An Irish welcome awaited Flight 807's crew, marking 25 years of Company service to the Emerald Isle.

On hand to greet the flight were Brendan Murray, Manager of Shannon Airport and Ray Joyce, Tourism Division Manager of Shannon Free Airport Development Company.

Shown above, from the left, are: Tom Haughey,

S.F.A.D. Company; Navigating Officer Lou Voticky; Second Officer Hank Ottosen; First Officer Lorne Dyck; Brendan Murray; Captain Gus Cirko; Airport Customer Service Manager Aidan Larkin; Station Agent John Horan; Purser Jacques Grenier; and Ray Joyce.

Champagne and cakes were served to Flight 807 passengers to commemorate the anniversary.

When Irish Eyes Were Smiling. Air Canada Flight 807's crew, marking twenty-five years of company service to the Emerald Isle in 1972. I'm second from the left, Navigating Officer Lou Voticky.

22

MY FIRST FLIGHT AS FIRST OFFICER AND

MY THIRD ESCAPE FROM TYRANNY

On December 21, 1975, I took off on Flight 874 to Munich, Germany along with Captain Bob Lavigne and a First Officer I'll call Ron Smith. We were to spend one night in Munich, take a flight on Austrian Airlines to Vienna, where we would spend one night, then fly home on Flight 879 through Zurich to Montreal.

That evening, the three of us went out for dinner and had a pleasant meal with a couple of good German beers—except for Ron, that is, who had four. Bob and I weren't concerned about it because we had the next day off with a "deadhead"—flying for work as a passenger—on a foreign airline and there was no concern about violating safety regulations. At 10:30 p.m., Bob and I decided to go back to our hotel, but Ron said he would stay a little longer. Since he was an adult and knew the rules, we still weren't concerned and headed back to the Munich Hilton. Our cab pickup for the airport the next day was at 1 p.m.

Bob and I met in the lobby at 12:30 p.m. the next day and the Captain told me that Ron drank all night until he ran out of money. He was paying child support to his ex-wife and neglected to do the same to his ex-girlfriend, an Air Canada Flight Attendant, for a daughter whom he denied fathering; the court disagreed with him. He was three months in arrears for this and she seized his paycheque on December 17. At 1:00 a.m. the previous night—7:00 p.m.in Montreal—he had called his current girlfriend (another Flight Attendant) and she wasn't home. Suspecting that she was cheating, he had called Air Canada crew scheduling in a jealous rage and asked them to track her down, but they had refused. In frustration, he emptied the Captain's bar in his room (twelve shots of hard liquor).

Next, he demanded to speak to the Chief Pilot at the Montreal base, Captain Jack Logan, a truly wonderful man and boss, with whom he argued until he finally screamed that he was quitting. Captain Logan, in an attempt to save Ron from himself, hung up on him. Captain Logan called Bob Lavigne and advised him of the situation, then asked the two us to bring Ron home without letting him anywhere near the flight controls. Great—we were facing eight-and-a-half hours of flying time, with two takeoffs and two landings, not to mention flying the aircraft, while keeping one eye on a mentally disturbed Pilot on the flight deck.

Bob and I decided that we would escort Ron to Vienna and pay for his food since he had spent all his money on alcohol. We picked Ron up in his room took him downstairs to the cab and headed to the Munich airport, boarded Austrian flight to Vienna, then went to the Vienna Hilton. We insisted on no liquor and upon our arrival we asked the Vienna hotel to empty the Captain's bar in his room. We took him out for dinner and for breakfast the next morning, then headed back to the airport. We did our flight planning, boarded our DC-8 aircraft, and sat Ron in what was normally my seat at the flight engineer panel, where there are no flight controls. I removed the fire axe from its normal position beside my usual position and took it with me to the First Officer position to the right of the Captain.

We told Ron that he was not allowed to touch any flight controls or switches without our permission, and I added that if he did, I would bury the pointed end of the fire axe in his skull. Fortunately, by this time he was stone sober and realized that he was in real trouble; he was very placid, and the flight passed without incident.

For my part, I had received a battlefield promotion to First Officer and other than keeping one eye on Ron all day I enjoyed my first chance at the controls. Despite the unfortunate circumstances, it was great to do my first two passenger takeoffs and landings in the Co-Pilot's seat in Zurich and Montreal. After landing at Montreal Mirabel airport, we filed a report with the medical staff for the company and for the union.

Ron was sent off to rehabilitation and recovered successfully after four months; he was able to rebuild his life and career, and eventually retired as a Boeing 727 Captain.

Almost eight years later, on August 28, 1983, I operated an Air Canada Boeing 747 ferry flight from Montreal to Casablanca, Morocco carrying extra crews, maintenance staff, mechanics, and family members, including my wife, Catherine, to do a sixty-day deployment carrying Muslim pilgrims on the annual Hajj pilgrimage from Casablanca to Jeddah, Saudi Arabia. During the flight, almost all of our eighty passengers, including Catherine, came up to visit the flight deck. One of our visitors was a Flight Attendant with her nine-year-old daughter, who was the spitting image of F/O Ron Smith—the man who had denied fatherhood of this little girl and created a very difficult, embarrassing, and stressful flight for Bob Lavigne and me. I'm sure that the judge had not needed a DNA test when he ruled that she was his child. At that instant I wished that we had left "Ron Smith" behind in Munich; only a scumbag would deny his child.

AFTER A YEAR as a DC-8 Second Officer, management requested that I train as a Second Officer on the new three-engine Boeing 727 and become an instructor and Supervisory Pilot for all the newly hired young Second Officers for this aircraft. The B-727 course was great; I fell in love with the Boeing method of teaching and with flying this aircraft. It was a great experience. We had to use checklists for everything; memory items were used only for critical emergencies. I learned that aircraft better than any other that I had ever flown because I had to answer a lot of questions from the new trainees and had to have the right answers. This also helped me greatly when I later transitioned to the Boeing 747, the Queen of the Skies. After a year as a Supervisory Pilot and instructor for all the new hires, on December 4, 1976, I successfully qualified as a B-727 First Officer with Captain Murray Wallace, a great guy and a great instructor.

On my checkout as a First Officer on the Boeing 727, I was flying with my friend and neighbour Captain Dave Edward from Chicago to Vancouver when we had an amazing encounter. I was never a very good dancer, but I loved the twist and could dance it all night. Catherine and

I always did well in twist competitions. The "King of the Twist" was Chubby Checker, and I loved his music and his rhythm. During the trip, one of the Flight Attendants came to the flight deck and told us that none other than Chubby Checker was on board and would like to visit the cockpit!

We were happy to invite him up and chatted with him until just before we started our descent into Vancouver. At that point, Dave suggested that our guest go back to the passenger cabin for the landing. Chubby Checker asked if he could stay up for the landing and we all agreed. Fortunately for my everlasting self-respect and memories, I greased the landing at Vancouver and didn't embarrass myself in front of a man that I admired very much. It was one of my most memorable flights in a thirty-five-year career.

THERE WERE OTHER changes that were happening around me: politics had reared its ugly head again in Quebec with the election of the Parti Quebecois on November 15, 1976, and I knew that I wanted out of the province. Having learned from my family's experiences with Nazis and Communists, I wanted no part of the xenophobic racists who dominated the Parti Quebecois. I love the province of Quebec—I love Montreal and the Laurentian Mountains and the French-Canadian people, who are friendly, kind, and generous. However, I came to detest their politicians, who are and have always been insular and paranoid. They lie to their own people; they encourage them to differentiate themselves from their fellow Canadians and to see themselves as permanent victims—even when French-Canadians have run the Canadian government for half of Confederation, great people such as Laurier, St. Laurent, Trudeau, and Chrétien.

My escape route was bidding into the Air Canada base in Toronto and onto the Boeing 747, so we sold our home in Beaconsfield, Quebec and moved into a rental townhouse. I emptied our safety deposit box and flew its contents to a new one in Toronto. I wasn't crazy about the idea of living in Ontario, but the choice was easy—it was between freedom and living as second-class citizens in Quebec. I chose freedom. After escaping from the Nazis and the Soviets, I had no intention of remaining in a province where 40 per cent of the population detested me because I was not a pure member of their community by birth despite being a good and proud citizen of Quebec.

I made my choice at the right time; I was the last Pilot to get into the Air Canada Toronto base for the next eight years. This decision turned out to mean more than my continued career with Air Canada. Although I didn't know it at the time, it was the beginning of my future business success. Quebec lost an entrepreneur who created forty-two full-time jobs and dozens of supplier jobs in the Toronto area over the next twenty years.

The Quebec separatist movement has hurt the Quebec economy and people more than any other action ever taken by any government in Canada in its entire history. For the past forty years, Quebec politicians have deprived their people of their civil rights and their opportunity to participate in Canada's growth and prosperity. They have lured Quebecers with promises of untold wealth and sovereignty and provided social benefits that they could not pay for. At the same time, they have very cleverly blackmailed the rest of Canada into paying for most of it through equalization payments from the federal government—something established by Quebec politicians and civil servants in Ottawa that now amounts to eight billion dollars annually at the expense of Alberta, Ontario, Saskatchewan, and British Columbia.

As far as I'm concerned, these Quebec separatist politicians only want the titles of Monsieur *le président* and Monsieur *l'ambassadeur,* and a seat at the United Nations. They don't care about the farmer in Lac St. Jean or the factory worker in Montreal. Yet they repeatedly tell them things like "Don't worry. When we become independent, we won't have to repay our debts because Canada owes us" and "Canada will have to continue subsidizing us or we won't let them use the St. Lawrence Seaway or fly over Quebec." They ignore international law and really believe that they can blackmail the rest of Canada (ROC), as they have for the last seventy years.

This was not for me. I learned from my father that sometimes it is better to run than to fight, especially when you are outnumbered, and your fellow victims are giving in without a fight; some of them even making excuses on behalf of their oppressors. Shades of Europe in the 1930s. Quebec's Anglos clearly did not learn a thing from Chamberlain and Daladier. My family and I made the right decision; we fled to Toronto and have had a great thirty-nine years of freedom here.

Fortunately, the people of Quebec finally cast aside the Parti Quebecois (provincial) and the Bloc Quebecois (federal) and elected a good Liberal government, rejecting the politics of anger, hate, jealousy, and victimhood that the separatists peddled. I now again have great hope for the future of Quebec. They even balanced the budget. Their new younger generation has grown up with the Internet and discovering a big, wild world of opportunity beyond Quebec has expanded their horizons (whether that new world speaks French or not).

After I decided that I had not escaped the Holocaust and the Communist conquest of my homeland to live under the boot of a racist regime that wanted to destroy the country I had defended as a member of the Canadian Armed Forces for eleven years, I was lucky to win the bid for a place in the Toronto base of Air Canada and the chance to fly the Queen of the Skies, the Boeing 747.

My course date in Toronto was set for January 4, 1978. I picked up the aircraft manual, packed up Catherine, Linda, and Liza, and we flew to the beautiful green island of Kauai for a three-week Christmas vacation. It turned out to be the last and best vacation that the four of us ever had together. We had the most wonderful vacation of our lives, including a full Hawaiian luau on New Year's Eve, although I don't recommend the poi—it was terrible! Every day when we came back to the cottage, after the beach or golf, I spent two hours studying the B-747 operating manual. By the time we headed home, I had pretty well memorized the aircraft's systems and operating procedures.

I had never been as well prepared for any course in my life as I was for this one. The three weeks of Ground School were followed by a three-hour final exam with a 100 per cent pass mark required. I managed to finish it in two and a half hours and the instructor told me I wouldn't pass because no one who had not used the full three hours had ever passed the exam. I guess no one had ever spent three weeks studying and memorizing the Boeing 747 aircraft manual in Hawaii.

After I successfully passed the exam came eight four-hour sessions in the aircraft simulator, which included an Air Canada and Ministry of Transport check ride, followed by in-flight instruction and checking.

By the end of February 1978, I was fully qualified and started to fly passenger flights. Eight months later, I was awarded the highest-paying block of flights despite being No. 13 on the B-747 seniority list. This was very unusual. In this case, however, it turned out to be because the Captain I would have to fly with for thirty-one days was a Captain I'll call J. T. Brown. Captain Brown was universally considered to be a very unpleasant man and a sub-average Pilot. To my knowledge there wasn't one Pilot who knew him who liked him, trusted his flying, or wanted to fly with him. Thirty-three Pilots on the B-747 actually absolutely refused to fly with him.

The only consolation was that the third Pilot was my good friend Captain Don Tollefson, but regrettably he was on vacation most of that month and would only fly the last cycle to Paris with us at the end of the month. The rest of the time, the poor victim was a junior Pilot on reserve who had no choice.

The Pilots of an aircraft must be a cohesive team. They have to work together—communicate, cooperate, coordinate, monitor, and advise each other—like a well-oiled Rolls-Royce, this is called Cockpit Resource Management (CRM), a philosophy that Captain Brown clearly did not know or understand. There is no room in the cockpit for anyone who believes that he knows it all and who ignores valid input from the other Pilots. The crew must follow the aircraft and airline standard operating procedures (SOPs) and report any incidents that may affect the safety of the aircraft or its passengers by filing an incident report. Filing incident reports protected the Pilot from disciplinary action and, after they were circulated to all the Pilots, helped them to not make the same mistakes.

This, unfortunately, was all foreign to Captain Brown; he marched to his own drummer. He ignored advice from his crew, did not communicate with them except to bark orders at them, followed his own procedures, and topped it off by being obnoxious.

I didn't anticipate any problems working with Captain Brown as I have always prided myself on being able to get along with unfriendly or unpopular people. Besides, I had flown with him on two occasions as a Navigator and managed to work with him reasonably well. Of course, being the only man in the cockpit who could keep a DC-8 on track kept him in line in dealing with the Navigator. However, four very unpleasant flights from Toronto through Montreal to Paris and back, were enough to ensure that I would not be flying with Captain Brown ever again. He was a one-man show and flew the aircraft as if he was flying solo. He ignored our advice and inputs, and he violated Air Canada and Boeing flight procedures as though they did not apply to him.

On October 30, 1978, we arrived in Paris on Flight 870. Don Tollefson and I went out to dinner with Captain Murray Wallace, a great Supervisory Pilot and Instructor who had qualified me on the Boeing 727, and who had brought another B-747 flight in that day. Over dinner that night, Murray told us that he had just received details on the horrendous runway collision in extremely thick fog between a Pan Am B-747, Flight 1736, and a KLM B-747, Flight 4805, at Tenerife in the Canary Islands. Six hundred and forty-four passengers died and only sixty-one passengers and crew on the Pan Am flight had survived the worst accident in aviation history. Since Captain Brown was an unsociable individual and we didn't wish to socialize with him, he didn't have dinner with us and therefore did not hear about the horrible Tenerife accident from Captain Wallace.

Pan Am Flight 1736 was on the Tenerife airport's single runway after landing and had not yet cleared the runway when the very experienced Supervisory Captain of KLM Flight 4805—who was rushing to avoid his crew booking off due to duty time limitations—believed that he had received takeoff clearance from air traffic control and ignored his First Officer's attempt to stop the takeoff because they hadn't received the clearance. The Captain started his takeoff roll and smashed right into the helpless Pan American B-747 that was still on the live runway. In fact, air traffic control had not cleared the KLM flight for takeoff and, in the thick fog, the KLM crew did not see the Pan Am aircraft until seconds before the collision. This accident and the resulting 644 casualties were a direct result of a stubborn, though very experienced, Captain refusing to listen to his very experienced First Officer and violating every concept of Cockpit Resource Management and Crew cooperation. An aircraft crew that doesn't work together has a good chance of not making it to their destination or home for dinner. All those people died because of the pig-headed stubbornness of one man who should have known better and should have listened to his Co-Pilot.

The following morning, on the last flight of the month, Paris was covered in thick fog and we were to operate Air Canada Flight 871 to Montreal and Toronto. Captain Brown and First Officer Tollefson attended to flight planning and weather briefing while I boarded the aircraft to refuel, check the safety equipment, and prepare the aircraft for the flight. We needed almost five hundred feet (150 metres) of runway visibility for a legal takeoff and the current visibility was only about 160 feet (fifty metres). Legally, we could not take off that morning in the current visibility conditions.

When Captain Brown and Don Tollefson arrived in the cockpit, I asked Captain Brown whether we would hold at the gate to save fuel until we had our required takeoff weather limits. It was the sensible thing to do because the weather wasn't scheduled to improve for an hour and there was no point in burning expensive fuel that we might need once we were airborne by sitting on the taxi strip, to say nothing of avoiding air pollution. Not surprisingly, Captain Brown rejected my suggestion even though Don Tollefson backed me up; he too was ignored. I then suggested that we add 1,250 gallons (4,732 liters) of fuel to cover the extra hour of sitting in the fog. Brown curtly dismissed that suggestion too, adding that our Flight Dispatchers knew what they were doing. In a span of two minutes, he dismissed the assistance of both of his fellow Pilots without any consideration or thought. He also obviously forgot that no flight dispatcher had ever run out of fuel and crashed and died because of that lack of fuel, but a few had suckered a Pilot into this fix.

There was only one other stubborn and incompetent Captain at Paris Charles De Gaulle airport that morning, and that was the Captain of Air France Concorde Supersonic Airliner Air France Flight 001 to New York. Every other flight in Paris stayed at their gate to wait out the fog and save fuel. Concorde 001 had higher takeoff limits (820 feet, or 250 metres runway visibility) than our B-747, which meant that they had to wait longer for takeoff clearance as the fog slowly lifted. The Concorde also carried less fuel and had a shorter flight range than we did, so sitting on the ground burning off fuel in thick fog for no good reason was the height of stupidity.

The odds of an accident identical to Tenerife were rising sharply.

Nevertheless, as noted, there were only two stubborn and unprofessional Captains at Charles de Gaulle airport that morning. One was on board Air France 001 and the other was Captain J. T. Brown on our Air Canada 871; they both taxied out on schedule in almost zero visibility, violating all the rules of good airmanship. There were dozens of other flights due to depart Paris and no other Captain departed the gate; unlike the other two, they displayed their good sense, airmanship, and experience. Air France 001 taxied out to the entrance to Runway 27 and, even though we could take off before them, blocked us from being able to get onto the end of the runway—a gross violation of aviation tradition and courtesy.

After we completed our cockpit checks and the doors were closed, we pushed back on schedule. The fog was so thick that the Air Traffic Controllers in the tower could not see the runways, taxiways, or any aircraft. Our visibility from the flight deck was approximately one hundred feet (thirty metres), which meant that, since we sat just over thirty-six feet (eleven metres) above the ground, we could at least see the ground below us. Still, Captain Brown had to taxi very slowly.

We had to park on a taxiway while we waited out Air France 001, and we were therefore also blocking access to the active runway. We sat there for a half hour, burning fuel, adding to the fog, and polluting the atmosphere. Captain Brown started to get restless and called de Gaulle Ground Control: "Ground, Air Canada 871. When we have takeoff limits, can we taxi and backtrack the live runway, do a 180 degree turn, and then take off?"

"Air Canada 871, Ground," came the response. "You will be able to do that when you have takeoff limits." Our problem, however, was that we still did not have takeoff limits or even a taxi clearance onto the live runway. This meant that we had to hold short of the live runway.

Captain Brown said to Don and me, "Give me the before-take-off checklist."

Don and I immediately started the checklist, which required all of our concentration and required us to keep our eyes on our instruments and switches. As a result, we didn't notice that the aircraft had started moving very slowly. When we completed the checklist, we both looked up and realized what was happening—we were taxiing and saw to our horror that we had crossed over the edge of the live Runway 27. Visibility was just as bad as it had been when we boarded the aircraft. Don and I both shouted, "We're not cleared onto the live!" This was similar to what the First Officer on the ill-fated KLM flight yelled in vain at his Captain.

To make matters worse, an Air France Airbus was doing a Category IIIA approach—landing visibility required one hundred feet (thirty metres) so it was basically a blind approach. Captain Brown was replaying Tenerife and about to cause Tenerife Two. To his credit, he stomped on the brakes and stopped the aircraft immediately. Turning to Don he said, "Tell Ground that we are near the Live Runway."

"I can't do that," Don replied. "We're ON the runway!"

Brown repeated the command and again Don refused.

Faced with Don's adamant refusal, Brown called Ground Control himself. "Ground, Air Canada 871. We are near Runway 27."

Ground replied, "Air Canada 871, where exactly are you?"

Brown repeated his last transmission. After a short pause, De Gaulle Ground said, "Air Canada 871, clear the Live Runway 27 immediately. We have an Airbus on final approach doing a Category IIIA approach.

"I can't turn this big B-747 here," Brown responded.

Ground Control was unequivocal. "Air Canada 871 get on Runway 27, head for the first high-speed exit, and clear the runway as fast as you can!"

We rolled onto the runway but couldn't go faster than thirty-three knots (thirty-six mph or fifty-eight kph) because of the poor visibility. When we reached the next exit and turned off, Don and I started to breathe again.

As I've said, Pilots are expected to report all accidents, incidents, and near-misses and there is no punishment if you file an incident report— only your pride suffers. There are, however, serious consequences if you don't file a report and someone else does. Both Don and I said that we would have to file an incident report about what had just occurred, but Captain Brown dismissed it out of hand, saying, "Nothing happened."

Don Tollefson and I were certainly not going to let it go and we both filed incident reports when we returned to Toronto the next day. When I filed my report, Captain Murray Wallace said to me, "The Chief Pilot said that he'd fire Brown the next time he pulled one of these stunts!"

Obviously, Captain Brown had a record of incidents. This time, he escaped punishment by claiming that the ground controller confused him by speaking French on the ground frequency. That was totally untrue; no French was spoken on the Charles de Gaulle Ground Control frequency during this incident. However, Brown's false story fed the paranoia of some senior Air Canada Pilots who were strongly opposed to French being used in Canadian aviation and were fighting a losing battle to prevent it. Brown only had eight months to retirement and the company didn't bother doing anything to stop or even correct him, but Don and I joined thirty-three other Pilots on the B-747 who refused to fly with him after that. We weren't interested in becoming part of the next fatality statistics. In the end, Brown's peers passed judgment on him in the only way that they could. Almost every Pilot on the Boeing 747 was relieved when Captain "Brown" retired when his eight months were up.

AFTER TWO YEARS of commuting, we bought Catherine's small "shack" in Etobicoke—it was all we could afford with Toronto's ridiculously high real estate prices—and moved to Toronto in October 1979. I spent that month on vacation, renovating the shack together with a contractor and breathing in tons of dust. On the last Sunday of October, I was due to fly to Paris on Flight 870 that night. I had my normal two hours of rest, showered, shaved, and put on my uniform, then sat down to watch a Montreal Alouettes football game. I broke out in a sweat and within a few minutes, my uniform was soaked, Catherine took my temperature and said, "You are not flying in this condition!" I had to book off sick at the last minute, which I had never done before. I had no choice; I was very sick.

On Monday morning, I visited a doctor, who examined me and then asked, "How many cigarettes a day do you smoke?" He was amazed when I told him that I had never smoked. My lungs were full, and my chest rattled; this was the beginning of my bronchitis and asthma. I spent the next six months seeing doctors and taking tests of all kinds, but none of them could diagnose what was wrong with me except to say that I had a lung problem. Finally, one doctor sent me to an allergist, his brother-in-law, Dr. Epstein. After an hour with Dr. Epstein and his nurse, we had a diagnosis. I had bronchitis and was allergic to dust and cats; the dust from renovating the house had made me sick and our cat, Spikey, had perpetuated it. It was simple once I knew the cause. Spikey had to go, against the protests of Catherine and our daughters, but since then, I've been very healthy.

We settled in to life in Toronto. Both Linda and Liza reluctantly followed us there, where they both got married to fiancés who followed them from Montreal.

In 1980, Catherine and I joined the Lambton Golf and Country Club, so we could enjoy our passion for golf. We had many great years there and made a lot of good friends. After thirty-seven years, we are still Lambton members.

In the cockpit of an Boeing 747 for Air Canada with Captain Al Johnson (left)
and First Officer Rob Bocock (a former Olympic athlete). 1980.

23

CANADIAN HEROES

During my eleven years of military service and twenty-five years flying with Air Canada, I met and worked with a number of real heroes:

1. Air Canada Flight Attendant Mary Dohey, who convinced a hijacker to release 118 passengers in Great Falls, Montana on November 12, 1972, in exchange for staying with the hijacker as the DC-8 took off again. She kept him calm until the Captain, Vern Ehman, and one of the other Flight Attendants, Johnny Arpin, subdued him. She was awarded Canada's highest civilian decoration, the Cross of Valour, for her bravery in saving those 118 lives. Mary passed away in 2017.

2. Wing Commander John Braham, who shot down thirty German bombers at night and in bad weather and was a prisoner of war. He was the Royal Air Forces No. 1 Night Fighter Ace.

3. Captain Gordie Jones, who flew the heroic missions at Arnhem that I described earlier and saved 105 lives after a midair collision over Havana.

4. Wing Commander Danny Williams, who participated in the dangerous World War II Dambusters bombing raids, codenamed Operation Chastise, to destroy three dams in the German Ruhr valley in 1943.

5. Captain Fletch Taylor, who was shot down during World War II and escaped to and then from Switzerland through occupied

France, unfriendly Spain, and neutral Portugal to Great Britain to fight again.

6. Wing Commander Joe Lecomte (Joe the Group), who served in Bomber Command operations over occupied Europe in World War II. His crew was the only one on his original 425 Alouette Squadron to survive the war.

It was my privilege and honour to work with these great individuals.

DURING MY TOUR at RCAF Station Moisie, I met an amazing man, F/O Pat Brophy, a World War II Lancaster Bomber Tail Gunner who was by then a Fighter Controller. Pat was the key figure in the heroic story of Pilot Officer Andy Mynarski.

On the night of June 12, 1944, one week after the Allied invasion at Normandy, the Lancaster crew took off from Middleton St. George in England for their target, the Cambrai Rail Yards in France, in their new Lancaster KB726. Unfortunately, they were attacked, hit, and severely damaged by a German Junkers 88 Night Fighter. The Captain, Pilot Officer Art deBryne, gave the order to bail out as the Lancaster was engulfed in flames. As Warrant Officer Andy Mynarski, the Mid-Upper Gunner, made his way toward the escape hatch, he saw his buddy Pat Brophy trapped in the tail-gun turret, which was jammed. He went back and tried to free Pat, but it was hopeless; by this time Andy's flying suit and parachute were on fire and Pat waved Andy away so he could save himself.

Andy made his way back to the escape hatch, turned toward his trapped comrade, saluted him, and jumped. When French farmers found him on the ground he was severely burned and died shortly after. If Andy had bailed out without assisting Pat, he probably would have survived; he gave his life to try to save his friend and comrade. No greater sacrifice can a warrior make for his brother-in-arms.

As it turned out, the Lancaster hit some trees, levelled off, and pan-caked into a field, hitting the ground hard enough to break loose the tail-gun turret and throw Pat out of the aircraft. The Lancaster, with its full twenty-bomb load, then exploded. Pat was unhurt, but when he took off his leather helmet, it was full of his hair—he was completely bald. The horrendous fear of certain death had caused all the hair on his body to fall out and, except for one hair on his left eyebrow, it never grew back. Pat's watch had stopped at 2:13 a.m. on Friday, June 13, 1944.

After five nights spent hidden among corpses in a mortuary, the French Resistance—the Maquis—smuggled Pat out through France, Spain, and Portugal to Britain. He testified to Warrant Officer Andy Mynarski's heroism and Andy was awarded the Victoria Cross, the highest military decoration in the British Empire, and posthumously promoted to Pilot Officer (2nd Lieutenant).

Unbelievably, when his hometown of Winnipeg honoured Andy Mynarski and named a school after him in 1950, there were protests that the name was not Canadian enough—meaning it wasn't Anglo-Saxon. Five years after the greatest anti-racist war in history, fought against the evils of racism, Canadian Anglo racists were still sowing their seeds of hatred and discrimination against one of the dead heroes of that conflict, a brave man who had died protecting them and their right to be stupid. These racists were the brothers of the Ottawa bureaucrats who in 1939 had turned away the German passenger ship MS *St. Louis* with 907 Jewish refugees on board, declaring that when it came to admitting Jews, "none is too many." Cuba and the USA had done the same, sending the ship's passengers back to the hell of German captivity, concentration camps, and death.

A NEW CAREER BECKONS

n 1978, I was quite senior on the Boeing 747 and this permitted me to get my monthly flying time in a very compressed time period. The B-747 was the world's largest aircraft, with the longest range of any aircraft, and flew all the long-distance routes. I was able to accumulate a lot of flying time in the fewest possible number of days each month. The maximum monthly flying time allowed was approximately eighty-two hours and, by flying these long routes, I could fly up to eighteen hours in a forty-eight hour period. This meant that I could cover my required flying time in ten to twelve days.

In June 1982, shortly before his retirement, I was flying the Boeing 747 with my good buddy Captain Gordie Jones on a westbound Flight 871 from Paris to Toronto. After we had entered the Oceanic Area at fifteen degrees west latitude with the aircraft on autopilot, Gordie asked me for advice on retirement planning; he was aware of my financial, investment studies and qualifications in this area. After picking my brain for two and a half hours with interruptions every fifteen minutes for position fixes and fuel checks, he suggested that I go into business and advise other Pilots. "Okay," I said, "but only if you become a client."

"You're hired!" he responded. He became my third client after I became a financial planner. Regrettably, he passed away 2014.

Thanks to my wonderful cousin, Eva Kanturek Keith, I contacted ECC Group, a financial planning firm run by two great guys, Chris Snyder and Brian Anderson, two former life insurance salesmen, who were among the first financial planners in Canada. After they interviewed and tested me, they hired me to specialize in financial planning for Air Canada Pilots. I started with them on November 2, 1982.

Another very close friend, Captain Gord McCready, was actually my very first client. He passed away in 2016. My second client was a widow, Mrs. Young, who had no idea what her net worth was and was concerned about her ability to afford vegetables, especially cauliflower, which she considered to be too expensive to buy. It turned out that she was worth approximately $1,500,000—a lot of money in 1983—and she didn't know it. After I had prepared a financial plan for her, I started my review of it with her by saying, "Mrs. Young, I have some very good news for you. You can buy all the cauliflower that your heart desires!" She was a client for many years until she passed away. I had a total of twelve clients in my first year. Gordie Jones was No. 3, the twelfth one was Captain Max Ball, who was a nervous, quiet, and a very conservative investor (he still is). I did a good job for him and he became a one-man advertising agency for me, recommending me to every Pilot he flew with; he got me more clients by word of mouth than anyone else!

In my work as a financial planner, I charged a small fee for advice and did not charge commissions as I was not a registered representative. I arranged with a friend of mine from Lambton Golf and Country Club, Andy Russell, who was an investment advisor at Merrill Lynch Canada, to handle any mutual fund or equity transactions; in return he gave my clients large 67 per cent discounts on all commissions. The two of us were pioneers in discounting brokerage commissions in the Canadian investment industry (we did not win any popularity contests in the industry as a result).

In 1983, Eastern Provincial Airways (EPA) locked out their Pilots in a contract dispute. This caused severe problems for the Pilots and their families. The Canadian Airline Pilots Association (CALPA), asked me to go to Halifax, Nova Scotia, EPA's main base and assist the Pilots with their financial planning. I spent a week interviewing the Pilots who had requested our assistance, provided them with individual financial plans, and made recommendations to the Pilot Association about how they could best help their members. Harry Steele, the CEO of EPA and his management won that fight but lost the war. Shortly thereafter EPA was sold to Canadian Pacific Air Lines and merged into its operations.

After a year of pain and suffering, the Pilots nonetheless won in the end as working conditions and pay were much better at Canadian Pacific.

IN JULY 1984, on the thirty-ninth anniversary of the time my family was being bombed in Shanghai, our first grandson, Nicholas Angle, was born at Mount Sinai Hospital in Toronto to my daughter Liza and her husband, Bob Angle. Three months later, we recognized that Nicholas had a disability: both of his feet were turned inward, and he needed a top-notch orthopedic surgeon in a hurry. After a lot of research, I discovered that the best orthopedic surgeon in Toronto was none other than my old astronavigation friend, Dr. Wally Bobechko, Chief of Orthopedic Surgery at Toronto Sick Kids Hospital.

I called his office on a Thursday and was told that Dr. Bobechko was leaving for volunteer work in Brazil on Saturday and would be gone for two months. This was something he did every year, volunteering to operate and teach surgeons in South America. I identified myself and left my telephone number just in case he remembered me after twenty years. Ten minutes later he called back, and I explained my problem. He told me to bring Nicholas to Sick Kids the next morning at nine o'clock and he would take care of the problem. Catherine, our daughter Liza, and I were there early. Wally examined Nicholas, had him X-rayed, placed casts on his legs pointing his feet 180 degrees apart, and we were done by noon. A small kindness twenty years earlier was repaid one thousand times over by a wonderful doctor. Three months later, the casts came off and Nicholas' foot position had been corrected. He had a normal childhood and became a superb golfer, skier, and hockey player.

Regrettably, Dr. Wally Bobechko, this wonderful, kind, generous, skilled surgeon and humanitarian, passed away prematurely seven years ago, but his legacy lives on.

MY CLIENTELE WAS growing, and it was time for me to establish a more business-like presence, so to achieve this, I formed Admax Financial Consultants in February 1985. I continued to work with ECC, but on a contract basis rather than as an employee.

Canadian Pension legislation limited pensions in Canada to $60,000 annually. The Canadian Airline Pilots Association had negotiated a supplementary pension plan for Air Canada Pilots—the Air Canada Pilot Equity Plan—that was kept separate from the Air Canada Pension Plan and superbly managed for the Pilot Association by Seymour Schulich and Ned Goodman. In 1985, CALPA was advised by their legal counsel that this supplementary pension plan might no longer meet the current federal pension laws. They were presented with two options: they could cash it in and hit all the potential beneficiaries with a large income tax bill or transfer the benefits pro rata directly into the individual beneficiaries' own Registered Retirement Savings Plans (RRSPs) tax-free.

Naturally, the association and its members chose the latter option, which turned out to be a bonanza for my new business because most of the Pilots didn't know enough about investments or RRSPs to make good decisions on their new investments. Pilots trust other Pilots— on the flight deck and outside of it. As someone who had studied the subject and now had three years of experience in the investment business, I was suddenly an "expert" and flooded with requests for assistance. My business grew exponentially; as the old saying goes, among the blind, the one-eyed man is king.

I had a lot of help from Captain Max Ball. He had been my client for three years by this time and I had done a very good job with his investments, so, as I've said, he became my greatest promoter among the Pilots he flew with. This helped my business grow—I never really had to pursue new clients because so many Pilots needed and asked for my help.

My investment philosophy was very simple: I recommended guaranteed investment certificates (GICs) for income and the two top mutual funds in Canada at that time managed by AGF and Mackenzie Financial. I knew nothing about individual equities; I didn't like them or want them in my portfolios, so why would I even consider recommending them to my clients? These became my guiding principles:

1. Never recommend an investment to a client that you wouldn't own yourself.
2. Invest in high-quality income—bonds and guaranteed income certificates.

3. Buy dividend-paying quality equities only.
4. Never gamble on risky equities; instead, hire knowledgeable managers to choose the equities.
5. Always ensure a diversified value portfolio.
6. Hire the very best professional investment managers.

These six tenets became the basis of a very successful thirty-five-year investment advisor career; there have been changes in strategy, tactics, and investments, but never a violation of my basic investing principles.

In June 1985, over lunch, I mentioned the closing of the Air Canada Pilot Equity Pension Plan to my friend Andy Russell of Merrill Lynch, the investment advisor for my clients. He called me an hour later and invited me to a meeting after work with Tony DeWerth, his branch manager; Bill McIntosh, Merrill's chief investment officer; and Kevin Kelly, Merrill's national sales manager, to talk about the dissolution of the Pilot's Plan.

We met at the Merrill office at 200 King Street West and I explained the mechanics of what was about to take place. I could see the Merrill Group salivating at the thought of Merrill getting a large slice of the $156 million in Pilot equity savings. We agreed that I would assist Merrill by doing a road show for my fellow Pilots at our four bases—Montreal, Toronto, Winnipeg and Vancouver—with Merrill Lynch paying the expenses of this trip and providing the speakers to sell their company. In addition, they offered me free office space at Merrill Lynch. I agreed to the office space and parking spot but insisted on paying them rent—I had no intention of being obligated to Merrill Lynch or putting myself and my clients under their control in any way.

The road show was a great success due to Merrill's great reputation at the time and the trust my fellow Pilots had in one of their own—me. Merrill Lynch and I got approximately two-thirds of all the funds transferred out of the Pilot Equity Plan to manage. My reputation was greatly enhanced by being accepted as a partner in this project. The funds were divided between locked-in and not-locked-in RRSPS—the former could only be converted into life annuities, which meant that the annuitant lost control of their assets to the insurance company at time of retirement and conversion to a pension income through an annuity, while the latter could be invested in a self-directed Registered Retirement Income Fund for retirement and the investors maintained control of their own assets even in retirement.

The great majority of the Pilots resented the imposition of government restrictions on their savings. They wanted their locked-in plans freed up, so I started looking for a way to accomplish this.

It was at this time that the Canadian federal Minister of Finance, Michael Wilson, changed Canadian pension law to permit life annuities to be cashed in. This was a huge beneficial change for investors and a blow to the insurance industry, who could no longer hang on to Canadian retirees' pension money forever once they had been converted into pension income. I discussed the problem with my insurance agent, Jim Fraser, and suggested that, if an annuity was purchased and held for a period, and then cashed in and converted to a not-locked-in RRSP, this would accomplish the freeing up of the locked-in accounts. He agreed and promised to look into it.

Jim found the Counsel Life Insurance Corporation, a small insurance company that was looking for growth. After checking with his legal counsel and board of directors, their president, Bruce Hammond, agreed that this procedure was perfectly legal under the new legislation and was willing to proceed. The result was a deluge of new business for Admax Financial Consultants Ltd. from my fellow Pilots. Counsel Life, of course, did even better by charging a fee for the purchase of these annuities and then releasing them back to the client's not-locked-in RRSP at their individual requests.

WE WELCOMED OUR second grandson, David Austerweil, born to our daughter Linda and her husband, Gabe Austerweil, at Mount Sinai Hospital in Toronto in May 1987.

IN JUNE 1987, with all the Pilot Equity Funds transferred out of the Pilot Pension Fund and most of them now safely at Merrill Lynch, Tony Dewerth, the branch manager offered to hire me. I declined but accepted his offer to move into the Merrill Lynch office on King Street West in Toronto as an independent advisor in his branch. To maintain my independence, I insisted on paying rent for the accommodation and facilities.

The stock market at this time was climbing like a rocket into the stratosphere and I became very concerned, not from any particular market knowledge, but I knew that when an aircraft climbs too steeply it will eventually stall and fall out of the sky. We had all done very well in the market as it continued to climb sharply in 1987; it was time for caution and to play defence. In the summer of 1987, I convinced my clients to sell all their equities and buy Canadian government treasury bills paying 9.5 per cent during July and August, and/or GICs for longer periods.

Monday morning, October 19, 1987, will forever be known as Black Monday, the day when the New York Stock Exchange crashed with a big thud. It was awesome to watch from the inside—my entire computer screen was red and most of the Merrill Lynch investment advisors sat in silence watching the financial slaughter, interrupted only by panicky phone calls from their clients. Fortunately, all of my clients were okay; the treasury bills and GICs that they held had not lost any value and were still collecting interest. This was another boost to my investment reputation and business.

Merrill Lynch had just hired a new rookie class of investment advisors and Black Monday was their first day on the job after completing their training. They sat in stunned silence, trying to remember what they had learned on course about cold calling for prospective clients in the midst of a stock market crash. They didn't make too many cold calls that day, but most of them did well over the next thirty years, in part because they started when the market was at a new low—the only way for the market to go was up—and in part because they had seen market dangers first-hand on day one. The most humorous and memorable comment that day was from one of the Merrill Lynch new advisors when a client asked him how he could make a lot of money in the crash. The advisor's response was "Take your money and fly to Las Vegas!"

I spent the next five weeks calling my clients and reassuring them that they were fine, that their assets were safe, and it was time to start reinvesting in the market. I worked the phones five days a week. On Fridays I went home early, got two hours sleep, then flew to Europe that night and back to Toronto on Sunday. On Monday I was back in the office and on the phone. After five weeks of this, I was exhausted, and Catherine insisted that I needed a week off. I had no Air Canada vacation time available, but the Air Canada Mechanics Union (IAM) decided to help us out by going out on their second strike in history.

Catherine and I decided to drive down to Washington, DC and spend a week there. It turned into the most fabulous trip that changed our lives forever. At lunch on the first day of our trip, we stopped at a roadside restaurant just north of Williamsport, Pennsylvania, home of the Little League Baseball World Series. Catherine could see that I was down and when she asked me why, I opened up with a vengeance. "The North American stock markets crashed 26 per cent in the week of October 19 and almost every investment and mutual fund manager in North America went down by the same amount. Haven't these morons ever heard of risk management? Compared to them, I'm an amateur. I get paid a small fee for my advice and I outperformed all of them by using plain common sense! They get paid millions and don't even pay attention to risk or good sense. If I could see danger, why couldn't they?"

"If you're so smart," Catherine replied, "why don't you start your own fund?"

"You have got to be kidding!" I said. "It takes a lot of money to start a mutual fund and we don't have it."

"Can you raise the money?" Catherine asked.

I started coming out of my funk. "You bet I can. My clients, who didn't lose their money in the crash, will happily invest in our company and funds!"

They would, and they did. Catherine had once again challenged me and then given me the answer that I needed to accomplish my third love (after her and flying)—investments! She drove the rest of the way to Washington while I sat in the passenger seat preparing a business plan, calculating how much it would cost to launch a fund company and survive for three years with no profit. I estimated the actual cost and then added 50 per cent, coming up with a sum of $350,000 for a successful launch. I knew that I could raise that amount easily. The next step was to plan how to accomplish that at minimum after-tax cost to my future partners in a limited partnership in case we weren't successful. Then I had to structure a plan for our new organization, then figure how to achieve credibility. The last component was to figure out an exit strategy for my partners and ourselves if that became necessary.

Our time in Washington was great. We visited all the main attractions, such as the Smithsonian Institution and the Arlington National Cemetery, the US Capitol Building, the monuments and memorials on the National Mall, and, finally, the White House. We were there during Soviet President Gorbachev's visit to meet President Reagan and when we arrived at the White House, I was cornered by a man with a microphone, a camera, and a Russian accent. He was from Radio Moscow TV and asked my opinion about his president's visit to President Reagan. I explained that I was Canadian, not American, and he should try asking an American as there were certainly enough of them around. He insisted that he would appreciate my perspective and opinion. Being one who has never hesitated to give an opinion, I told him and his viewers in Moscow what a great occasion President Gorbachev's visit was and that it was time for the US and the Soviet Union to become friends. This was delicious irony that the citizens of the Soviet Union, whose brutal dictatorship had forced our family to flee forty years earlier and in 1968 crushed a democratic uprising in my former homeland, wanted my comments about their president's visit on a peace mission!

ON MY RETURN to Toronto, the first item on my new agenda was to hire a reputable law firm and a reputable accounting firm for immediate credibility. I hired Tom Baldwin of Stikeman Elliott, a good lawyer in commercial law and in maximizing billing of our small company, and Paul Schroeder of Smith Nixon, a superb accountant whose auditing and advice was worth every penny that we paid him; in fact, I'd say that he was underpaid for the great work he did for us. (I have tried hard to make that up.) I always followed the legal and accounting advice that I was given. When Paul went into private business, I allowed a banker from CIBC to convince me to ignore Paul's advice with regard to one item, which almost ended up getting us into regulatory trouble for insufficient regulatory capital.

The best advice that Paul gave us right at the beginning for the future of the company and the investors was to increase our capital base by 50 per cent through callable capital. This meant that each partner had to agree to provide up to 50 per cent more capital to his investment commitment if the company needed the funds; it also provided greater tax shelters for the partners. Just before we became profitable in the thirty-sixth month, we did have to exercise the "callable capital provision" in the agreement, although we didn't actually request the funds involved. Paul is still a good friend and I certainly don't ignore his advice whenever it is offered.

Paul, Tom, and I prepared an Offering Memorandum for a Limited Partnership (LP) for Admax International Investments Limited Partnership and scheduled a cocktail party just before Christmas 1987 to make a presentation to fifty of my Pilot friends and two other close friends, David and Catrien Goldsworthy. Unfortunately, the LP could only have twenty-five partners and the only fair way to allot the partnerships units was to offer them to the first twenty-five people to sign up. My presentation was quite simple: I outlined our success in the crash on Black Monday and our success in beating almost every money manager in North America and explained that we hoped to form a new and different mutual fund company that would outperform the others in the future by being defensive—sell in down markets—as well as offensive—buy in up markets.

To accomplish this, I told those gathered, we needed to raise $350,000 to cover operating costs for three years. Their investments—including the callable capital—were 100 per cent income tax deductible; in the event of failure, they would only lose less than half of their investment. We needed to break even in three years or the company would go under, losing half the invested capital after tax. If we did break even at the three-year mark, we would have a successful and valuable company and their partnerships would be converted tax-free into shares and they would become shareholders. All proceeds from selling the company shares would be tax-free income as we were eligible for the small company capital gains deduction of $500,000 per investor. I also advised them that they were all my friends, but the only way that we could allocate the partnership units was on a first-come first-served basis. By 9:00 a.m. the next day, we had our maximum of twenty-five partners, including both Goldsworthys. Shortly thereafter, my oldest friend, Walt Niemy became a partner by buying the shares of an original partner who, for personal reasons, had to cash in.

Thus Admax International Investments Ltd. was born. The next step was to build a top-notch team to manage the new corporation. My first requirement was a second-in-command to handle my weaknesses— that's all the back office needs in the administration of a financial corporation. In addition, that person had to be organized and trustworthy, have industry connections, and, most important, have common sense.

My first choice was Debra Pickfield, who worked for my friend Andy Russell. I had watched her working for Andy and was impressed by her hard work, skills, and dedication to her career. I explained my plans and offered her the job and part ownership in the company. It was a great move; she built the organization, set up the back office and handled all its requirements, and provided me with a lot of good advice. She also held down the fort when I was out of town either flying or travelling to sell our mutual funds.

I had planned to make her vice-president of administration, but the Ontario Securities Commission would not permit me to serve as president because I had another job—flying for Air Canada—despite the fact that I was in the office at least forty hours per week. They called that my part-time job. As a result, I became chairman of the board and chief executive officer, and Debra became president. Catherine gave up her career in real estate sales and joined us as our accountant. In January 1990, we hired our second employee, Mona Chong, another alumni of the Andy Russell training academy and a jewel in our crown. She became an important part of the Admax team, so important that thirty years later she is still my executive assistant and partner.

I was determined to manage mutual funds that would outperform the current crop of approximately sixty funds available in Canada. We launched our first two no-load (no commission) mutual funds—named the Captains Equity and Captains Bond Funds—and hired Merrill Lynch Asset Management to manage them. We only raised three million dollars for them, not enough to pay the rent on our small office. To make matters worse, the fund performance was poor.

By the end of 1989, we realized that we had to change strategy. We needed to differentiate our products to a full fund family that would allow investors to switch inside the group and we needed top managers. We also needed to charge commissions, so we could pay investment advisers and give them an incentive to sell our funds. The first step was differentiation, which we accomplished by bringing out the first performance funds in Canada. The managers got a bonus for outperforming their relevant index.

For step two, we hired the top Canadian management at Canada Life to manage our new Canadian Performance Fund, and Fred Moran Investments to manage our US Performance Fund. Moran was a specialist in telecom, cable TV, and the dawning era of the cell telephone, and had been the No. 1 US manager for three straight years. He was a man years ahead of his time—he saw the great future in cable TV and cellular telephony before the rest of the investment community.

Step three was the most difficult. We needed to pay commissions but had no money to pay them. We didn't want to borrow the funds from a bank; it was unlikely that any bank would have lent it to us in any case. Our solution was to launch a Limited Partnership Tax Shelter to pay these commissions. We hired Research Capital to be our underwriter and I instructed our counsel, Tom Baldwin, to copy the prospectus of Mackenzie Financial, a pioneer in this field, and change the names and dates. We did this to keep costs down. Tom did as instructed and then arranged a meeting with the counsel for Research Capital to finalize and approve the wording for our new CANAM Partnership.

On the day of the meeting, they met at noon and asked me to appear at 3:00 p.m. to finalize the prospectus. Naively, I agreed, thinking that this was a foolproof prospectus prepared by top-notch lawyers for Mackenzie Financial, the biggest mutual fund company in our field. I arrived at the appointed hour and the following is what occurred. The Research Capital counsel began by saying, "We have a serious problem. We cannot agree on one item. You have the income from the sale of these funds flowing from the funds to Admax to the CANAM Partnership. Why is that?"

Trying to stay calm, I responded, "Because that is the way the Mackenzie Financial Partnership is written, and we are trying to reduce costs and avoid reinventing the wheel."

To that the Research Capital counsel replied very sarcastically, "You are not Mackenzie Financial!" No kidding, I thought, this clown wasted four years in law school learning to state the obvious.

With my temperature rising, I said, "We never claimed to be. What do you want?"

"We want the income to flow directly from the mutual funds to the partnership," answered the attorney for Research Capital.

By this time, I was ready to explode. "I have no problem with that. Do it! But tell me why you two have been sitting here arguing over a non-issue for three hours at my expense of more than $300 an hour each and having lunch on my bill instead of calling me and asking me about this matter?" They had no response to that and just sat in stunned silence. Talk about unfairness to a client! I walked out feeling that my partners and I had been robbed of more than $1,800 by two unscrupulous lawyers. That was an expensive lesson in law. I monitored my lawyers carefully after that!

Admax mutual funds performed moderately well, but they were not world beaters. I spent a lot of my time researching investment sectors that regularly outperformed the market averages and investment managers who achieve outperformance.

25

CELLULAR PHONES, CABLE TV, AND SPORTFUND

I n December 1989, as the once-mighty Soviet Union collapsed, Czechoslovakia broke away from its financial and military dependence on the USSR. The Czechs staged a Velvet Revolution in December 1989 and cut their ties with their former masters.

Czechoslovakia had an antiquated telecommunications system that did not meet the country's needs. A week after the momentous events in the country, I got a call from Fred Moran, our US portfolio manager, asking me if I had any contacts in the Czech government in Prague. I replied that I didn't, but was sure that my uncle Vilda Kanturek, a prominent divorce lawyer there, probably did.

Fred said that he was forming a large consortium to provide Czechoslovakia with a modern cellular telephone and cable TV system and offered me a partnership in return for my providing access to the Czech government. I accepted and called Uncle Vilda. When he heard what I was calling about, he responded, "Are you crazy? We're in the midst of a revolution here!"

"I know you can do it!" I said, appealing to his ego. "Didn't you tell me that you knew everybody in power?"

"Of course, I do," he retorted, "but this is a revolution, not handling their divorces!"

Despite his initial reaction, he called me the next day, January 3, to tell me that we had a meeting the following day with the Minister of Transportation and Communications. He seemed to have forgotten that travelling from northeastern North America to Prague required an overnight flight, so I convinced him to delay the meeting for one week to Thursday, January 11.

I met Richard Bernstein, Moran's deputy, in Frankfurt on Thursday, January 11, and we took a Lufthansa flight to Prague. We were met at the aircraft by the Deputy Minister of Communications and his aide, rushed through customs, and drove straight to the Communications Ministry in an ancient, beat-up, ratty white Russian Skoda, the Czech version of a limousine. Despite our exhaustion, as soon as we had been introduced to Transportation and Communications Minister Frantisek Podlena and his senior staff, the negotiations started. The discussions went on for two straight days and by nightfall Friday, we had a signed a twenty-five-year agreement giving us the cellular telephone and cable TV rights for Czechoslovakia in return for building a telephone and cable infrastructure for the entire country.

Three weeks later, Richard and I flew to Bratislava, Slovakia and got their provincial government's approval to include them in our deal. We then flew back to Prague to meet our new international consortium partners, which included industry giant British Telecom, and requested an audience with the US Ambassador, Shirley Temple Black, since our managing partner, Fred Moran, was an American. The old movie star totally ignored us and did not even let us meet with her commercial attaché.

At the same time, Bell Atlantic, an all-American company, arrived in Prague and received the red carpet treatment from Ambassador Shirley Temple Black, who held a cocktail party at the embassy for our Czech partners and high-ranking government officials. Bell Atlantic used the festivities to offer the Czechs all the infrastructure plus twelve million US dollars—not to mention future contributions to President George H. Bush's next campaign or library. Our contract and all our hard work to achieve it had been totally ignored by the US Ambassador.

Now the Czech government had a dilemma. They didn't want to break our contract, which was owned by Moran and Admax, so they approached our strongest partner, British Telecom, and asked them to beat the Bell Atlantic offer. The British arrogantly told them that they already had a twenty-five-year contract—which they did not; we did—and they expected the Czech government to honour it.

The Czechs asked them to check with Fred Moran and me, but again, in the best British arrogant manner, they told the Czech government representatives that that wasn't necessary because we were no longer interested in pursuing our rights and were out of the consortium (an outright bald-faced lie)! That was all the Czech government needed to hear; they broke our contract without even talking to us. We only found out about this betrayal after I contacted the Czech Deputy Minister of Transportation and Communications to arrange another meeting. Another lesson learned about a lack of honour among politicians and big company senior executives.

The irony of all this was that Bell Atlantic got only a five-year contract, which they used to establish themselves for the future. They really had no interest in starting a cellular network in a poor country that couldn't afford the cost (the average income was $100 per month in Czechoslovakia at that time). In five years, they built three cellular towers in downtown Prague and had a total of approximately 567 subscribers—mostly diplomats and Western businessmen—and the coverage was only for the downtown core. At the end of their five-year contract, the Czech government turned the contract over to Siemens of Germany, who built an actual network throughout the Czech Republic. We would have accomplished that in three months.

We had been burned by two telecom giants, British Telecom and Bell Atlantic, but neither of them benefited from depriving us of a great business opportunity. They blew their chance by not fulfilling their obligations. The next contract went to AT&T in the US, and the one after that went back to Siemens of Germany.

IN 1992, WE were approached by a very bright and charming young man named Joel Albin, who was seeking to launch a labour-sponsored mutual fund—a tax shelter—that would be involved in financing sports enterprises. He was asking Admax to be a partner and sponsor because we had the securities licences, knowledge, back office, and distribution network to sell the product and to operate it. Labour-sponsored mutual funds were permitted by the Canadian government to encourage job creation and maintenance. They were designed to provide investors with

100 per cent income tax write-offs in return for investors leaving their investments with the fund for seven years.

Joel was very intelligent, knowledgeable, and aggressive in his determination to succeed. He had an excellent business plan that included bringing famous athletic personalities into the project. He had a magnetic personality and could charm the brass off a door handle.

We liked the plan but doubted that Joel would be able to recruit the star athletes that he was seeking. He really fooled us on that one! He recruited Canadian Hockey Hall of Famers Darryl Sittler and Brad Park, Canadian Football Hall of Famer and president of the CFL Player's Association, Dan Ferrone, whose organization sponsored the fund. Dan became a board member and later chairman of the board of directors, a great guy and very hard worker. He brought in National Football League Hall of Famer Franco Harris and Canadian Olympic skier and medal winner Laurie Graham. Then he went on to recruit David Mirvish, the son of legendary Toronto theatre icon Ed Mirvish and now the chief executive officer of the Mirvish Group of companies to the board of directors.

After much consultation with our board of directors, legal counsel and auditors, we decided not to join in the partnership, but we offered to handle the back-office duties and distribution for a fee. In addition, I demanded a seat on the board for myself in order to keep an eye on the operation. Joel accepted our terms and Sportfund was launched. The fund sold reasonably well and Joel started to fund various sport-related businesses.

Hockey is not just Canada's national sport, it is a national passion and a national virus. Joel pulled off a real public relations coup by funding a junior hockey team based in the Toronto suburb of Mississauga in partnership with Canada's No. 1 TV personality, ex-NHL coach Don Cherry. With the loquacious Don Cherry, former coach of the Boston Bruins, as its part-owner, coach, and spokesman, the Mississauga Ice Dogs were a public relations success, but the team did not do well on the ice or at the box office. They were finally sold and moved to Niagara Falls.

Some of the funds' investments turned out well, but others did not, which inhibited growth and forced the board to make a crucial decision that the fund would have to either close down or merge with a stronger partner. The Sportfund board of directors decided to sell the fund to another labour fund, Retrocom. Joel resigned, and Dan Ferrone became the chairman and chief executive officer until the completion of the sale and merger.

26

HONG KONG, SHENZHEN, AND QUEBEC CITY

(A TALE OF THREE CITIES)

n early 1992, I was approached by a wonderful lady, Bernice Wade representing Regent Pacific of Hong Kong, about my interest in exploring a merger with their small group of Regent International Funds based in Kitchener-Waterloo. The Regent funds had five Asian, one European, and one world income fund with a total of approximately about $47 million in assets. At that point, Admax International had seven North American funds with just under $100 million in assets. A merger made sense because it would provide us with a complete family of fourteen mutual funds covering North America, Europe, and Asia. However, since the Regent Funds were only entitled to 33 per cent of the new partnership and Regent Pacific wanted a 51–49 per cent partnership, Regent Pacific agreed to buy in for the difference. All of these funds were reinvested in the new partnership to assist in the marketing and growth of the new larger group of funds. The result was Admax Regent Mutual Funds, with Regent's president, Grant Rush, joining us as vice-president of sales. Grant's specialty was dealing with mutual fund dealers and was therefore a very useful addition to the team.

We also acquired two superb Asian money managers and super salesmen in the merger, Peter Everington and Jim Mellon, who were principals at Regent Pacific in Hong Kong. These two men drew huge crowds to our presentations because of their record, ability, knowledge, and showmanship. All the negotiations were carried out by Bernice

Wade and myself, and finalized at her home in Bradenton, Florida. She was an excellent but fair negotiator.

When we inherited Grant Rush, the president of Regent Canada and appointed him VP of sales, his arrival took a large load off my shoulders; up to that point I had been the CEO and the chief salesman and marketer. Grant took over the sales to the mutual fund dealers and I continued to deal with the fully licensed investment advisors at the big brokers. Our assets under management (AUM) were now approximately $150 million and we had to grow Admax Regent. To succeed we needed more volume in order to spread our expenses over a larger base and reduce costs.

We were successful in selling our mutual funds from coast to coast, but we were spread thin and had some big gaps in our success. Our biggest weakness was in Quebec, specifically in Quebec City. I had focused my salesmanship on a six-man CIBC Wood Gundy branch in Quebec City, managed by a dynamic manager, Michel Bourbeault and his sidekick, Michel Blais. For five years, I flew up to Quebec City, made presentations in my poor French, wined them and dined them, with no sales or even any acknowledgement of my efforts.

In 1983 I had met a very bright, hardworking, and charming Air Canada Flight Attendant, Marie-Andrée Deschênes, who was a French-Canadian from Quebec City. She became a client and we became friends. In 1993 she had thoughts of retiring as a Flight Attendant due to minor medical problems caused from flying and was ready for a career change. I thought she'd be the ideal candidate to charm the two Michels and their band of four and offered her a job as our Quebec regional manager. She was hesitant at first, but I explained that the most important qualities she needed for the job was a willingness to learn and common sense. She would have to pass the mutual fund dealers' course and we would train her after that. When she heard that, she agreed to give it a try and spent the summer of 1993 studying for the mutual fund course

Marie-Andrée took a leave of absence from Air Canada and we started a training process that took us to Montreal, Trois Rivières, and Quebec City so she could meet the representatives who were selling our funds, watch our presentations, and learn the intricacies of the fund business. With her French-Canadian background, her common sense, her ability to deal with people, her charming personality, and her acceptance of the quite different and hard-partying Wood Gundy branch, I then turned her loose on the two Michels and their group. Marie-Andrée did a great job. Whenever she had a problem, she called the office and we helped her resolve it via long distance. Marie-Andrée proved to be one of our best hires; she was the perfect fit for our business in Quebec and also helped in covering the Maritime provinces. Without her presence, I don't believe that we would have penetrated Quebec as well as we did.

ON APRIL 22, 1993, our third grandson, Dylan Hughes, was born to our daughter Liza and George Hughes, again at Mount Sinai Hospital in Toronto.

IN EARLY NOVEMBER 1993, I was invited to the CIBC Wood Gundy chairman's council in Hong Kong by my good friend, supporter, and later partner, Tony DeWerth, chairman of Wood Gundy Private Clients. Other mutual fund companies were also invited, but they had to pay $50,000 for the privilege of co-sponsoring the event. Tony knew that our small company could not afford to pay, so we got a free ride. This President's Council meeting was a chance to make presentations about our mutual funds to the top 190 investment advisors at Wood Gundy, all in one place. I knew a large number of these advisors, but the majority did their best to avoid me and the other mutual fund representatives because they preferred not to deal in mutual funds for their clients.

I arranged for our ace Asian portfolio manager, Peter Everington, to do our presentation and as usual he was the star of the show. He was not only a knowledgeable manager, with an excellent track record, but he was also a super salesman. The good news was that Peter outshone all the other presenters and gave us much needed exposure to some of the top investment advisors in Canada.

Wood Gundy had arranged a trip to the neighbouring first Chinese Special Economic Zone of Shenzhen in Guangdong Province the day after the presentations and they invited me along. Four buses carrying 160 Wood Gundy employees and guests headed out of Hong

Kong and into Communist China. At the border crossing, we were all counted, identified, and vetted at the Immigration and Customs House. We visited Safari Park—a very poor copy of Disney World—and the Chinese Folk Culture Village, a large bazaar.

We were to meet at the bus stop at 12:30 p.m. sharp to be driven to lunch followed by a visit to the local museum, which featured the world-famous Qin Dynasty Terracotta Warriors. After a short shopping delay at the Culture Village, I arrived at the designated bus stop at exactly 12:30 p.m. to discover that all four buses had already left! The guide leader on each bus was supposed to account for all the passengers on the bus before any of the buses moved; this was, after all, paranoid Communist China and all hell would break loose if a foreigner was found to be running loose in China without a guide. Our guide had not done his job.

There I stood in the hot sun with no idea where lunch was being served or where the museum with the Terracotta Warriors was. I was alone in China, unable to speak the local Chinese dialect, with my passport, two credit cards, and some Hong Kong and US dollars. My Air Force survival training kicked in. I added up my aforementioned assets and reviewed what I would need to stay out of a Chinese jail, then to get out of China, and return to the safety of Hong Kong. I calculated that I needed to find someone who could speak English, I needed a supply of water—the first key to any survival—and I needed to get to the museum where the Wood Gundy group would be at 2:00 p.m. I also needed an escape plan in case I could not achieve the latter.

Step one was to find a large international hotel where someone was sure to speak English. I hailed a taxi and kept repeating "hotel" and demonstrating "large" with my hands. The driver did in fact drive me to a large hotel and I paid him off generously. Unfortunately, there was only one person at the hotel who allegedly spoke English, but when they brought her to me, although she was a very beautiful china doll of about eighteen whom any father would be proud of, she didn't speak a word of English.

It was time for part two of my plan. I grabbed another cab and with sign language asked him to bring me to a food market, where I bought two large bottles of water. I got back in my cab and with more sign language, I described horses. When he finally seemed to understand what I was asking for, he drove me to the local race track! Finally, he understood museum and took me to one; regrettably it was not the one that contained either the Wood Gundy people or the Terracotta Warriors.

Back into the taxi I went and kept repeating "Hong Kong." My driver took me to one of the four border crossing stations, where I paid him off generously and with great trepidation entered the Customs House. I tried to cross over to the British side as nonchalantly as possible, but no dice; they had no record of me entering Shenzhen and were not about to let this round-eye—the Chinese term for Caucasians—leave.

I left the Customs House and got into another cab, again waving my arms and repeating "Hong Kong," and was driven to another transit point. Again—no luck. Luckily, though, I ran into a wonderful British couple in the Customs House who were heading back to Hong Kong. I explained my problem to them, gave them my business card and Tony DeWerth's phone number, and asked them to call Tony and let him know that I was in trouble and stuck in Shenzhen.

While I was waiting at this crossing point, I reconnoitered the Customs House and discovered that the border guards no longer carried guns as they had when I had visited there in 1986 with Catherine. This was very important in case I had to make a run for the border, which was usually less than one hundred metres (three hundred feet) from the Customs House. I then grabbed another taxi and after I did my best imitation of a train, the driver delivered me to the Shenzhen railway station, where I continued to enrich the cab drivers of Shenzhen with another generous donation.

I marched into the railway station like Alex Guinness as Colonel Bogey in *The Bridge on the River Kwai*, with not a hint of fear or trepidation, and headed for the first immigration officer I saw. He took one look at my passport and promptly took off like a scalded cat, still clutching my passport. I suddenly realized that the Chinese authorities must be looking for me and took off after him; without my passport, I was either going to spend years in China at best or in a Chinese prison at worst. I chased him halfway around the station and when I caught him, wrested the passport away from him. He was glad to give it back to me—the fear in his eyes showed that he thought this crazy Canadian might do him serious harm!

I walked out of the station fast, but not fast enough to draw unwanted attention, got into a crowd and quickly got lost in it. I headed for a taxi stand to find my last driver waiting for me with a big smile on his face; he knew when he had a sucker on the line. Again, I yelled "Hong Kong" and he drove me to yet another customs crossing. Miracle of miracles, it was the one that we had come through that morning. I do not take rejection lightly and after being turned back three times by Chinese customs, I decided that it was time for some Royal Canadian Air Force escape and evasion. It was time for the execution of my escape plan. I again paid off my driver generously and proceeded toward freedom.

I walked around the Customs House and as I turned the last corner, I saw the border crossing fifty metres (165 feet) ahead of me with an opening big enough for a bus to drive through. However, there was also an unarmed customs officer standing five metres (fifteen feet) from me. Pretending that I was supposed to be there, I smiled at him and waved; he looked at me in amazement and I walked right by him without a backward glance. Ten metres (thirty feet) from the fence and no gun- shots. I took off as fast as my fifty-nine-year-old legs would carry me. I didn't slow down until I had turned a corner in the road.

I stopped and gathered my thoughts. I was alive, unhurt, had my passport, and had just used my military training to escape from Communist China. I was probably the only white man to successfully escape from China in many years. I found it ironic that the people who had saved my life and that of my family in World War II had made it very difficult for me to return peacefully to my hotel in Hong Kong. After all, the only thing that I'd done wrong was to miss my bus.

Suddenly, I heard the sound of an engine and took off again, but looking back I saw that it was a Hong Kong bus. I took out a red $100HK bill (thirteen dollars US) and waved it at the driver. Naturally he stopped, I boarded, gave the bill to the driver, and before I could sit down, we turned another corner and stopped right in front of the British Customs House. I went inside to hear a big roar from thirty- nine Wood Gundy employees, whom the British would not allow back into Hong Kong without me. I smiled and said, "I know that you don't want to buy my mutual funds, but you didn't have to leave me in China to get rid of me!"

We all boarded the bus in relief. I was exhausted and slept for the one-hour trip back to our hotel. When we got there, I headed for the shower and then to the big Wood Gundy cocktail party that night. I was welcomed like a returning conquering hero, all the investment advisors who had done their best to avoid me for three days—that is, to avoid a sales pitch—wanted to hear my story. I was happy to pass it on along with my usual sales pitch.

The nice British couple whom I met in the Customs House in Shenzhen, had contacted Tony and told him of my predicament, as had the guide leader. Tony's only comment was, "That's good. Other than me, Lou is the only other person in this group that has the ability to escape from China!" This turned out to be the best unintentional publicity stunt in the history of our company—every top producer at Wood Gundy (including the two Michels) knew me and the Admax Regent Funds after that.

The combination of Marie-Andrée Deschênes and my escape from China proved to be a bonanza for us in Quebec City a month later. Marie-Andrée gave me a call and asked me to get there as soon as possible because the gang of six wanted to see me. We had an excellent Canadian performance fund and the Quebec City branch wanted to transfer all their Canadian funds over to our group from a competitor's Canadian fund that hadn't had any performance for the past five years. The advisors in the branch wanted to serve their clients by switching to a better fund without cost to their clients. The problem was that these mutual funds had large redemption fees attached to them and the band of six was wondering whether we would agree to compensate their clients from the commissions that were due to the investment advisors when they bought our funds for these clients at the expense of their sales representatives.

I had no idea if this was legal and called our legal counsel, Lorie Haber. He checked the law, rules, and regulations and called me back with the green light—it was perfectly legal as long as the clients were fully compensated. I agreed to the Wood Gundy request, hoping for some later return for our hard work. In the next two months we got $56 million in new business from the Quebec City branch of CIBC Wood Gundy, increasing our total assets under management and the Quebec City Wood Gundy clients were switched from a terrible investment to a very good one at no cost to them. Marie-Andrée was worth her weight in gold.

27

SUPERIOR FUND PERFORMANCES

After the exciting trip to Hong Kong and China, it was time to concentrate on some new and innovative funds in our fund family. The first one was the brainchild of a brilliant value investor and avid student of Benjamin Graham, Picton Davies, who invented the Polymetric method of investing. Picton wrote the monthly *Polymetric Report* for more than four thousand loyal and avid subscribers who faithfully invested in the generally small capitalization companies that he analyzed and recommended. He was recognized as an expert investor and widely admired across Canada. His companies' stocks were generally small capitalization stocks that traded in small daily volumes—which was to cause problems for us later on.

My friend, Tony DeWerth, introduced me to Picton Davies, and we worked very hard to recruit him as the portfolio manager for a new Canadian Polymetric Fund. The fund was a marketing success—we raised over $100 million in the first year—but the fund was a poor performer, only breaking even over three years of its existence. Due to the nature of the low-volume small-capitalization stocks that Picton recommended, we couldn't get enough stock at a reasonable price to duplicate his success without seriously affecting both the Toronto and Vancouver stock exchanges. With our large Polymetric Mutual Fund, we would have ended up owning a lot of small companies, which is a no-no for anyone other than Warren Buffett (no mutual fund should own more than 3 per cent of any company). As a result, the fund performance was poor and we had to merge the fund into our very successful Canadian Performance Fund.

In 1994, our Regent Korea Fund was the No. 1 mutual fund performer in Canada with a return of 34.6 per cent, a great achievement for a small mutual fund company and earned us a lot of attention and publicity. The credit for this great achievement went to Peter Everington and Jim Mellon in Hong Kong as their faith in the Korean economy was richly rewarded.

At that time, I was busy doing research on the type of mutual funds that were successful in the US but were not available in Canada. I found that the sector that was totally ignored in the Canadian fund industry was healthcare, which had had years of great performance in the US and, despite being a sector fund, had a greater capitalization than the entire Toronto Stock Exchange. I then discovered that the No. 1 healthcare fund in the US was managed by Oppenheimer Investments in Denver, Colorado and the No. 3 fund was managed by Invesco, also in Denver.

We were planning a family skiing vacation at Snowmass, Colorado in February 1994, which would give me a perfect opportunity to visit the two top health sector managers in Denver. I hoped to interview both companies about managing a healthcare fund for Admax Regent. I arranged to meet the Oppenheimer Management team in the morning of February 23, and the Invesco management team at 3:00 p.m. on the same day.

The meeting with Oppenheimer was very cordial; they were very keen to work with us, however they needed approval from their head office in New Jersey. The meeting with Invesco was even better; they were keen to go, their head office was in Denver. We agreed to the terms of a letter of understanding and Invesco head office approved it before 5:00 p.m. the same day. After calling our legal counsel and outlining the terms for the contract, I caught the 8:00 p.m. flight back to the Aspen airport and Snowmass to finish our family ski vacation. On the way home a week later, we spent a night in Denver and I signed the management contract before flying back to Toronto. We launched Admax Health Sciences Fund managed by Invesco within two months and it was very successful. This mutual fund got the attention of the media and the investment community because it was very different and performed so well.

In January 1995, I was doing a two-week Western Canada swing to promote our mutual funds and timed it to break on Friday afternoon in Calgary, Alberta, so I could get in a weekend of skiing with my oldest friend, Walt Niemy. Walt had just retired for the second time, first from the RCAF as a Brigadier General after thirty years of service to his country, and then as president of Canadair's military division after eight years. Walt and Donna Niemy had just bought a beautiful townhouse in Canmore, just outside Banff National Park and very close to the Lake Louise Ski Resort.

It was an extremely cold weekend, with temperatures averaging -16 to -20°C (-3 to -4°F) and a wind chill factor hovering in the -30 to -35°C (-22 to -31°F). Two tough old warriors were not going to let that stop us, however. Not very many intelligent people ventured onto the Rocky Mountains that surround Lake Louise under those conditions, so we pretty well had the hills to ourselves. We enjoyed two days of hard skiing—like two dumb eighteen-year-olds with no brains and no fear— we bombed the hills. The highlight was the Olympic ladies' downhill course, where we hit sixty miles an hour (100 km/h). Neither of us fell even once; we escaped with nothing more than cold feet and faces.

Exactly fifty-three weeks later, disaster struck. Walt was in Vail, Colorado, skiing with some of his old RCAF and USAF buddies on an annual ski trip. On the Sunday night, I got a terrible phone call from Donna. Walt had accidentally run into a woman on top of Vail Mountain travelling at less than five miles an hour (8 km/h) and shattered his C3 and C4 vertebrae. He was now paralyzed from the neck down and awaiting surgery in the excellent Vail Hospital attended by two of the best orthopedic surgeons in the US. The irony of the two skiing trips and their different results have haunted me for years. This horrible accident convinced me to give up skiing, one of my great loves. Surgery was scheduled for Monday at noon. I made immediate arrangements to fly to Vail on Tuesday; Walt was my oldest and best friend, and he was in serious trouble.

Monday night, after seven hours of surgery, Donna called to tell me that the surgery had been successful, but Walt would be evacuated by

Medevac to Calgary Foothills Hospital on Tuesday. I couldn't believe that they would move him so soon after such a devastating injury and complex surgery, but his Canadian insurance company insisted, and his doctors approved of the move. I cancelled my flight to Vail and booked a flight to Calgary for Catherine and myself. We flew to Calgary on a brand-new Air Canada Boeing 767 commanded by an old friend, Captain Jacques Ledoux on one of his last flights before retirement. Landing in Calgary, Jacques greased the landing onto the runway and Catherine still says it was her best landing ever. That, unfortunately, was the highlight of the trip.

It was difficult arriving at the Calgary's Foothills Hospital knowing that instead of a big, vibrant, strong, and active man we would see a helpless quadriplegic and a shattered spouse. Although he was immobile, however, he greeted us with a big smile and Donna, though obviously devastated, held up courageously. Aware of Walt's courage and determination, we firmly believed that he would recover, and we tried very hard to make him believe that. We talked about playing golf again next year and about our long-planned parachute jump in Arizona on January 1, 2000, to welcome in the new century.

A horrible accident changes your perspective and makes you re-evaluate your values and outlook; you quickly learn what is really important. Health, friendship, love, and loyalty become more important and having fun goes to the back of the line. Despite our brave faces, we knew that there would be no welcoming of the twenty-first century with a parachute jump. The Niemys' life had suddenly been turned upside down and we had to start planning for any eventuality. The next day, Walt, Donna, and I started on a new financial plan in case he did not recover, or he passed away. He could no longer invest as he had in the past; he needed to remove all the risk from his portfolio and he needed income. We were able to complete the transition within four months. Since Walt couldn't turn the pages of a book, we kept him supplied with audio books to keep his mind active.

Both Walt and Donna held up very well—their courage and determination were an inspiration to all of us and our families. We provided as much support as we could both from Toronto and on a number of trips to Calgary, but the situation was bleak. Walt could not return to his home in Canmore, which had two long sets of stairs and insufficient medical support. He was forced to live in rehab in Calgary.

On a Tuesday evening in May, I got a call from Walt telling me that he would be in Toronto on that Thursday evening. I offered to meet him at the airport, but he asked me to meet him at the Lyndhurst Rehabilitation Hospital instead. It was great to see him again and to have him close by where I could be of more assistance. Lyndhurst is a wonderful rehab centre and, in the months that Walt was there, we witnessed many miraculous recoveries, especially among the younger patients. Walt also improved markedly, but his progress was stymied by aging bone and muscle.

I had made it a habit to visit Walt at Lyndhurst at least three or four times a week after work and on weekends. One evening in October, at approximately 6:00 p.m., I arrived at his room to find it empty, his bed was stripped, and the mattress folded over. I was shocked and assumed the worst. I found a nurse who told me that Walt had been taken to Sunnybrook Hospital emergency by ambulance and that he was in very bad shape. I drove straight over to Sunnybrook and found him in Emergency in a terrible condition. I stayed with him for the next eight hours, giving him any help that I could, and made sure that the nurses and attendants didn't forget him. I communicated with Donna in Canmore, where she was busy selling their home and preparing to move east to Toronto.

At approximately 10:00 p.m., Walt's conditioned seriously worsened; we both thought that this could be the end. I made sure that the medical personnel were giving him needed medication, and I kept him talking by asking him about his life and experiences. I had no intention of letting him slip away. I kept him talking about his military flying and close calls, including a "Broken Arrow" nuclear incident in which there was no damage, just a scare when he commanded an RCAF Nuclear Strike CF-104 Squadron in Germany and a close call on a CF-5 test flight in Nevada, when he was a test Pilot.

After about an hour, he started to improve and by two a.m., he was almost back to normal and I was able to head home. Donna arrived the next day by air to care for him. The staff at Lyndhurst were terrific; they did all they could for Walt and then released him to the Niemys' new wheelchair-accessible home in Toronto. Walt found the cold winters in Toronto that kept him a virtual prisoner in his own home for five months each year very difficult. After a couple of years, the Niemys moved to the warmer climate of Sidney on Vancouver Island, where he was less restricted and able to enjoy life. I flew out to see him at least once or twice a year, and we would spend the day together just like old times, solving the world's problems and sipping good Scotch.

Walt was a man who combined high intelligence, great determination, and amazing courage. His career featured positions as Commander of an RCAF Nuclear CF-104 Squadron, Commander of the RCAF Flight Test Establishment, Commandant of the Royal Military College, Director of Flight Operations for the RCAF, and president of the military division of Canadair. My life has been enriched by having him as a friend.

Donna Niemy took care of Walt for almost eighteen years, until July 2014 when she had a terrible accident. She slipped and fell backwards in a friend's kitchen, hit a kitchen island and broke her neck. She was totally paralyzed and passed away four days later. Her courage, love, and caring for Walt is an example for all of us. Her three children, Peter, Carole, and Eric, and their families, as well as our family and all of the Niemys' friends in Victoria mourned her passing.

Admax International Investments is named the best performing mutual fund in Canada for two years running, 1994 and 1995.

My friend and business partner Tony DeWerth and me in 2000.

28

ADMAX REGENT

M ark Bonham, the founder and CEO of BPI Mutual Funds called me one day in 1995 to ask me to join him and his second-in-command at a lunch to discuss a possible merger. At this point, we had approximately $250 million of assets under management (AUM) and BPI had approximately $180 million AUM. Debra Pickfield and I joined them for lunch and let them talk; it turned out that they weren't actually thinking merger—they wanted to take over Admax Regent and my reward would be running the foreign mutual funds. Talk about chutzpah—these guys had more than enough of it for a salesman selling ice in the Arctic.

I thanked them for their generosity in offering me a job that I already had and politely explained that if anyone would be taking over anyone it would be us taking them over as we were much larger, more diversified, and had better financial backing. This really spoiled lunch and we parted, never to discuss the matter again. Years later, I learned again that the some of the best deals are the ones that you don't make: when Mark got into regulatory problems with the Ontario Securities Commission, I was happy that I wasn't his partner. The life lesson from this incident was that one should never be so anxious to make a deal that you lose sight of the values involved.

That same year, 1995, Admax Health Sciences Fund was the No. 1 mutual fund in Canada with returns of 87.6 per cent. The fund manager was fired by Invesco in the first week of 1996 due to unauthorized personal trading, but he was replaced by his very capable assistant manager, who also did an excellent job for the health fund. Unfortunately, exactly one year later, the new manager quit to start his own hedge fund and—as he said to me—to become a millionaire. He didn't.

On October 4, 1996, American Barrick (ABX) cancelled their agreement to buy into Bre-X (BRX), the company that had allegedly discovered the biggest gold mine in the world in Indonesia. This was bad news for us because our Canadian Performance Fund manager, Kevin from Laketon Investment Management, held quite a bit of the stock in our Canadian Performance fund. I called him as soon as I got to the office and asked Kevin to sell the entire position, but he argued with me and refused. In early January 1997, the stock price was down again, and I ordered him to sell half, which he did at twenty-four dollars per share.

On March 19, 1997, Michael de Guzman, the No. 2 geologist at Bre-X was thrown out of a helicopter in Indonesia (reported as suicide). I immediately called Kevin and this time I ordered him to sell the rest of BRX; again, he refused and, when I threatened to fire him, he sold out the rest of our position at eighteen dollars. Overall, the fund got an average of twenty-one dollars per share; two weeks later the shares were worth zero. I fired Kevin for insubordination, sold all the crap in the fund, including YMG (a Philadelphia-organized scam of a Russian crime syndicate) at twenty-four dollars. In September it was discovered that YMG was a scam and their shares were also then worth nothing. I bought the five big Canadian banks with the cash available; they had their best five months ever and so did the Admax Canadian Performance Fund. Another lesson learned—common sense, good luck, and quality baffles brains and believing analysts (especially the gold analyst at Nesbitt Burns—boy, was he wrong but luckily for him, he couldn't be fired because that would be admitting liability)—every time.

IN JUNE 1996, my vice-president, Grant Rush, came to me with a proposal. My partners in Regent Pacific were apparently either short of cash or just wanted to get out of Canada because they had offered to sell him their 49 per cent share of Admax Regent. Grant is a great guy and a hard worker, but he didn't have the funds to buy the shares and had therefore brought in a group of his mutual fund dealer friends to put up the money. Together, they made an offer for those shares.

I was not about to accept a bunch of mutual fund dealers and Grant as my partners. I called Hong Kong and requested a copy of the offer from Jim Mellon and Peter Everington; they faxed it to me immediately. I suspected that they needed cash because the offer was below the value of Admax Regent at the time. I then called Jim and Peter back and told them that I would exercise my rights and match the mutual fund dealers' offer as per our partnership agreement—a little item that had clearly slipped their minds.

My next move was to meet with Bernice Wade, Pacific Regent's North American representative in Bradenton, Florida. We finalized an agreement to complete my repurchase of their shares at a bargain price and Admax Regent became Admax International Investments again. Working through this with Bernice was a great pleasure; she was a fair and straightforward negotiator. The result was a great deal for my own partners and myself and freed me to find a buyer for Admax. In the meantime, our Regent Pacific–managed funds were doing poorly, so I took this opportunity to turn over the management of our international funds to Invesco.

We'd had a terrific eight-year run; we'd grown Admax from three million dollars in assets under management to more than $360 million and had the No. 1 mutual fund in Canada two years running. I have always felt that the time to sell is when you are on top because there is only one way to go from there—down. I started to look for a buyer for our beloved Admax. I selected Invesco as the preferred buyer because they were a global giant and had done a great job managing some of our funds, especially the Global Health Fund. After months of negotiations, we agreed to terms and on December 31, 1996, we sold Admax to Invesco International and became Invesco Canada.

On January 1, 1997, I became chairman and chief executive officer of Invesco Canada. We were now part of a huge global international financial services company and even though I oversaw the Canadian operation, we were only a small part of a global giant and I had to report to my superiors in Atlanta.

After Invesco, a large no-commission company, bought Admax, they purchased AIM Funds in Houston, Texas, a large and very successful commission fund company. I travelled to Houston to learn all I could about their marketing and back-office operations. I came back very impressed and advised our head office in Atlanta that we should be a part of AIM to assist us in growing. INVESCO was not happy but agreed with my reasoning.

The management of AIM was great, and they provided us with good ideas and advice; they also sent a senior executive to Toronto to assist us. That was the beginning of the end for me at Invesco; slowly but surely, this executive took over our operations and I was shunted aside. They were very nice to me, promised to fulfill my contract, but asked me to stay out of the way. This is called constructive dismissal. I advised them that I was a Triple Type A personality and could not sit around collecting a paycheque for just being an observer. I said that I was willing to leave if they honoured my contract.

On May 18, 1998, I had retired from Invesco Canada, closing another chapter of my life. Three days later, I started another career as an investment advisor with BMO Nesbitt Burns; twenty years later, I continue this career full-time with another prestigious investment firm.

ON APRIL 6, 1999, Max Janousek was born to Ivan Janousek and my daughter Linda, completing our poker hand of four jacks (grandsons).

29

THE DREAMERS

The inscription on the Statue of Liberty says:

> Give me your tired, your poor,
> Your huddled masses yearning to breathe free,
> The wretched refuse of your teeming shore.
> Send these, the homeless, tempest-tossed to me,
> I lift my lamp beside the golden door!

The "Star Spangled Banner" refers to the United States of America as "Land of the Free, and home of the Brave."

THE 1.8 MILLION Dreamers certainly qualify, but unfortunately their fate has become a political football. I hope that the members of the US Congress, the nine justices of the US Supreme Court, and the Executive Branch remember this.

As a two-time refugee from oppression and death, I can understand the Dreamers' fear of being sent to a country and culture that they don't know or understand, where the language is one they do not speak, where they have no family or friends. To a country where crime and violence are endemic, where their very safety may be at risk and their ability to earn a living is very low.

The Dreamers are a major asset to America. They are young in a country with an aging population; they speak English; they study and work; they are educated in American schools where they started every day with the Pledge of Allegiance; and they salute the American flag. They are as American as apple pie.

I have loved America since September 3, 1945, when American Forces liberated us in Shanghai and I majored in the US Constitution in university. I have faith in the American system of checks and balances, and, therefore, I believe that the politicians and judges will come to their senses, that America and the Dreamers will eventually win.

Plan A: Keep fighting for your rights and do not leave the United States until you have received your documentation for your US permanent residence because you may not get back in even if you are granted US residence. Immigrants are responsible for their own legal fees (CAD$15,000–$20,000 or USD$11,500–$15,500).

Plan B: Prepare for the worst by exploring opportunities for immigration to Canada and/or Australia. Search online for immigration lawyers in those two countries and find out if there are any opportunities for access there.

Plan C: If Plans A and B are not working and you are not granted US permanent residence, and you don't want to end up in Mexico, El Salvador, Guatemala, or Honduras, your final option is to travel to Canada, Finland, or Sweden, three refugee-friendly countries, and claim refugee status protection. Dreamers from El Salvador, Honduras, and Guatemala have the best chance of achieving this objective because of the high crime rates in those countries and probably have more gang members than police officers. Legal fees for refugee claimants to Canada, Finland, and Sweden are paid by the government.

With regard to immigration application, a claim can be made under the Federal Skilled Worker designation for individuals with difficult-to-fill or impossible-to-fill jobs in Canada. For example, in Canada a claim can be made under Section 97, which states that "a person in Canada whose removal to their country of origin or countries of citizenship… would subject them personally (b) to a risk to their life or to a risk of cruel and unusual treatment or punishment." This claim can be made successfully by minors, women, and natives, or citizens of Honduras, El Salvador, and Guatemala, who are generally the potential victims of crime in those countries. It is more difficult for adult males and citizens of Mexico, Costa Rica, and Nicaragua.

Furthermore, a claim can also be made under Section 96, which states that "someone who fears return to their home country by reason of a well-founded fear of persecution for reasons of race, religion, nationality, membership in a particular social group or political opinion."

Anyone who has spent a year working or studying in Canada has a better chance of being accepted.

The immigration process for refugees is slow—the Immigration Refugee Board is now processing requests from January 2014 (!) and applicants cannot go through the process on their own. You must have an immigration lawyer to guide you through the jungle.

Canada uses a points system for immigrants. To make a successful application, you must obtain 67 per cent out of 100. In assessing the suitability of an immigrant or refugee applicant, the following are considered:

1. Age
2. Education
3. Language Proficiency in English or French
4. Canadian education or work experience
5. Being a skilled worker
6. Already being hired for a job in Canada

Do not bring guns, Mace, or pepper spray to Canada—they are illegal and definitely not welcome!

Canada's acceptance rate for refugees was 44 per cent in 2013; in 2017 this rate was approximately 70 per cent. The best provinces to apply are New Brunswick, Nova Scotia, and Quebec (especially if you speak French). During the past two years, Canada has experienced an influx of approximately 20,000 illegal refugees (mostly Haitians and Nigerians through Quebec), who are not in any danger, as are the American Dreamers.

The Canadian Immigration Service has not been able to deal with this flood of humanity and it is estimated that approximately 90 per cent are still in Canada awaiting adjudication.

In the meantime, on November 7, 2018, the Liberal government of Prime Minister Justin Trudeau delivered an apology to the 907

Jewish refugees aboard the MS *St. Louis* who were fleeing from Nazi death camps and were turned away by the Liberal government of Prime Minister Mackenzie King on June 7, 1939, because Canada did not want any Jews. As I've mentioned earlier, one deputy minister in Ottawa, when asked how many Jewish refugees Canada should accept, wrote in a memo to the prime minister that "none is too many." Many of those refugees did end up in Nazi death camps; 254 of them died in the camps; and, since almost all the survivors are now dead, they never heard this apology.

Phony Liberal government apologies have become monthly events, as Prime Minister Trudeau apologizes again and again for the evils of the Canadian people toward various minorities (to enhance his image as a humanitarian). It was not the Canadian people who committed the human rights crimes against Canadian Indigenous people—they were committed by Liberal governments and Roman Catholic and Protestant residential schools—or against the Jewish, Chinese (subject to the Head Tax), and Indian (denied access when fleeing oppression like the Jews) peoples. Those Liberal governments violated human rights not the Canadian people, who played no part in any of these crimes against humanity. They were committed by arrogant and racist Liberal governments. Make your apologies in the name of the Liberal Party, not the innocent Canadian people. Hypocrisy, crocodile tears, and phony apologies don't cut it, Prime Minister. Do something positive: invite the American Dreamers to Canada!

Becoming a Canadian resident can be a lengthy process and can be expensive for immigrants. But success is rewarding; the Canadian people are friendly to newcomers and almost all of them speak English.

EPILOGUE

On June 16, 2014, my mother, the author of *Knocking on Every Door* and the driving force in saving all fourteen of our family's lives, passed away three weeks short of her 101st birthday. She was a tough, highly intelligent, and hard-working woman. She was not always a lady—after all, she'd spent most of her life fighting for her family—but she was a great human being. She helped senior citizens for twenty-five years and Czech refugees after the Soviet rape of Czechoslovakia in 1968. On top of all that, she was a master bridge player.

This autobiography was written at the urging of my editor, Andrea Knight, who was aware of my varied history, from my youth, escaping the Holocaust and the Communist seizure of my native country, to fulfilling my dreams of having a lengthy career as a Navigator and Pilot for thirty-five years; and on to great success as a Bay Street executive for another thirty-five years (with a nine-year overlap of working seven days a week).

My life has been exciting—sometimes too exciting—but it has been rewarding and very educational. I have travelled the globe mostly voluntarily, but sometimes on the run. This book, however, is about more than that—it is about confidence, determination, hard work, overcoming hurdles, and, finally, the great amount of luck that resulted from the first three. Most importantly, it is about my refusal to be a victim.

I was lucky to escape from the Nazis and Communists due to the wisdom, determination, and courage of my parents, Arnold and Anka Voticky. They had the courage and intelligence to escape oppression twice in our lives. We were persecuted and victimized, and many members of our family were murdered. Nonetheless, we survived, and the family grew again. Today, Arnold and Egon Voticky's families thrive in Canada, the USA, Mexico, and Chile because the brothers had the courage and foresight to plan ahead and escape from their native land.

When I was forced to go to work full-time to support my family at age sixteen, my luck continued when I was able to attend night school at Sir George Williams High School and, later Sir George Williams University. I owe a lot to Sir George Williams, now Concordia University, in Montreal.

Then I really got lucky when I met the love of my life, my best friend, spouse, and partner of sixty years, Catherine Shapcott, a beautiful pony-tailed blond with blue eyes and a big smile. I fell in love with her the day I met her, and she has put up with all our ups and downs. She has supported me for sixty years through crises and triumphs, and produced two wonderful healthy daughters, Linda and Liza, who have produced four big beautiful and healthy grandsons—Nicholas, David, Dylan, and Max. They are now followed by great-grandson Benjamin, who arrived in 2017 at St. Joseph's Health Centre in Toronto. He has the honour and privilege of being the first of the sixth generation of Votickys in Canada.

Our terrific family and all the members of my extended family, as well as some of my friends, are alive today thanks to my parents, Arnold and Anka Voticky.

I HAVE LEARNED a lot through all my experiences and have been fortunate in having met and enjoyed the friendship of many fine individuals in flying, business, golf, skiing, team sports, and my personal life; they have enriched my life with their knowledge, advice, humour and assistance, and enriched the life of my family and myself. At the top of the list are:

My RCAF Pilot Onil Lacharité on CF-100 All Weather Fighters. We were two young inexperienced kids who grew together into the best and deadliest crew out of twenty-eight crews on 432 All Weather Fighter Squadron during the Cold War in 1960 when the threat of a Soviet attack on North America was at its peak. Our twenty-one RCAF

Canadian Fighter Squadrons helped the NATO Alliance deter a Soviet attack by protecting North America and Western Europe, while US air power was diverted to the Vietnam effort. We did an excellent job and 90 per cent of us were only high school graduates. Today we would not even be accepted for Air Crew training—everyone must have a college or university degree now.

Brigadier General Walter Niemy, with whom I served two tours in the RCAF, a lifelong best friend, golf and skiing buddy, whose bravery in the face of personal pain and suffering were those of a warrior, and whose trust and friendship were a big part of my life.

A portrait of courage, Captain Gordie Jones, a true World War II hero, who never fired a shot. He flew unarmed C-47 transports to supply trapped British Paratroopers at Arnhem, at five hundred feet (152 metres), through withering anti-aircraft fire. Later, as an Air Canada Captain instructing Cubana Airlines Pilots over Havana, he took over after a midair collision with a Russian transport and landed a DC-8 with eleven feet (3.35 metres) missing from one wing, saving at least 106 lives. He also launched my Pilot career by teaching me to fly the DC-8 at Air Canada and my business career by encouraging me to go into the investment business.

Mona Chong, my trusted assistant for thirty years, has been an important and integral part of my success in business.

Tony DeWerth, a good friend and trusted business partner, whose knowledge of the investment industry and trust were invaluable.

The almost three hundred Air Canada Pilots and Flight Attendants who trusted me to successfully care for their retirement funds, including the twenty-five of them who became business partners.

IT IS MY hope that this book will encourage readers who have had setbacks in life to realize that they have opportunities that are only limited by their imaginations. All you must do is dream, plan, and work hard to reach your objective. If I could do it, everyone can! Here's just one example:

Date: September 3, 1945, eighteen days after Japan's surrender in World War II.

Location: Shanghai, China

Principal: Eleven-year-old stateless refugee—ME!

Event: Arrival of American liberators, heralded by the roar of sixteen fighter aircraft of the famous US Army Air Corps Flying Tigers flying very low over our home in the Shanghai Ghetto.

My mother asked me, "Why are you watching the airplanes?"

"Because some day I will be flying them!" I responded.

"Don't be ridiculous," my mother retorted, "you will get killed!" That was the only time in my mother's life that she was wrong.

Result: I quit school at sixteen to support my family, worked full-time, and attended night school. I worked hard and got my Navigator Wings at Stevenson Field, Winnipeg on October 27, 1957, and my Air Canada Pilot Wings on January 30, 1974.

I retired from flying on the Boeing 747 on February 24, 1991, after thirty-five years of flying with more than 20,000 flying hours.

I retired from Air Canada in February 1991, because I was working seven days per week in my two careers as a Pilot and CEO of a major mutual fund company. Today, I still work full-time as an investment advisor. I have been very fortunate in my life and rewarded with a wonderful healthy family.

If I could do it, anyone can. That is why I refuse to be a victim. Everyone can fight their way back to a good life. They just must try hard enough. As General George Custer said, "What counts is not how many times you are knocked down, it's how many times you get up."

The sun rises in the east every morning.
Life goes on.
Live it to the fullest and refuse to be a victim!

Milan "Lou" Voticky
2018

My brother, Michael, (left) and me with my mother, Anka Voticky,
on her 100th birthday. Montreal, 2013.

Egon Voticky, my father's brother who had escaped to Chile with his wife, Inka, and my parents in 1937. Left to right: Uncle Egon; Aunt Inka; my father, Arnold, and my mother, Anka. Chile, 1970.

My extended family who now live in Chile and Mexico. Pictured here are my cousin Tommy Voticky's daughter Alicia and her family in 2013.

More extended family. This photo shows Tommy's daughter Andrea and her family, also in 2013.